Creative Learnin
and Virtual Envi

Originally published as a special issue of the *Creativity Research Journal*, this volume gives a balanced and reflective account of the challenges and opportunities of technology-enabled creative learning in contemporary societies.

Providing a current and updated account of the challenges posed by the Coronavirus to online education, chapters more broadly offer conceptual reflections and empirically informed insights into the impact of technology on individual and collective creativity and learning. These thoughts are explored in relation to school achievement, the development of digital educational resources, online collaboration, and virtual working. Further, the book also considers how the creative use of technology poses risks to learning through the accidental or deliberate dissemination of misinformation, and online manipulation of common societal values in the era of COVID-19.

Creative Learning in Digital and Virtual Environments looks at the connection between creativity, learning, and school achievement, and analyses the impact of virtual environments on creative expression. It will appeal to postgraduate students in the fields of creativity and learning, as well as to students and academics involved with broader research in areas such as the role of technology in education, e-Learning and distance education.

Vlad P. Glăveanu is Associate Professor and Head of the Department of Psychology and Counselling at Webster University Geneva, Switzerland, as well as Associate Professor II at the University of Bergen, Norway.

Ingunn Johanne Ness is a Senior Researcher at the Centre for the Science of Learning & Technology, University of Bergen, Norway.

Constance de Saint Laurent is a Postdoctoral Researcher at the University of Bologna, Italy.

Routledge Research in Education

This series aims to present the latest research from right across the field of education. It is not confined to any particular area or school of thought and seeks to provide coverage of a broad range of topics, theories and issues from around the world.

Recent titles in the series include:

Pedagogy in the Novels of J.M. Coetzee
The Affect of Literature
Aparna Mishra Tarc

Integrative and Interdisciplinary Curriculum in the Middle School
Integrated Approaches in Teacher Preparation and Practice.
Edited by Lisa M Harrison, Ellis Hurd, and Kathleen Brinegar

The Generation of Utopia
Decolonizing Critical Curriculum Theory
João M. Paraskeva

Sport, Physical Education, and Social Justice
Religious, Sociological, Psychological, and Capability Perspectives
Edited by Nick J. Watson, Grant Jarvie and Andrew Parker

Quality and Equity in Education
Revisiting Theory and Research on Educational Effectiveness and Improvement
Leonidas Kyriakides, Bert P.M. Creemers, Anastasia Panayiotou, & Evi Charalambous

Creative Learning in Digital and Virtual Environments
Opportunities and Challenges of Technology-enabled Learning and Creativity
Edited by Vlad P. Glăveanu, Ingunn Johanne Ness and Constance de Saint Laurent

For a complete list of titles in this series, please visit www.routledge.com/Routledge-Research-in-Education/book-series/SE0393

Creative Learning in Digital and Virtual Environments

Opportunities and Challenges of Technology-enabled Learning and Creativity

Edited by Vlad P. Glăveanu, Ingunn Johanne Ness and Constance de Saint Laurent

Routledge
Taylor & Francis Group
NEW YORK AND LONDON

First published 2021
by Routledge
605 Third Avenue, New York, NY 10017

and by Routledge
2 Park Square, Milton Park, Abingdon, Oxon, OX14 4RN

First issued in paperback 2022

Routledge is an imprint of the Taylor & Francis Group, an informa business

Publisher's Note
The publisher has gone to great lengths to ensure the quality of this reprint but points out that some imperfections in the original copies may be apparent.

Library of Congress Cataloging-in-Publication Data
Names: Glăveanu, Vlad Petre, editor. | Ness, Ingunn Johanne, editor. | Saint Laurent, Constance de, editor.
Title: Creative learning in digital and virtual environments : opportunities and challenges of technology-enabled learning and creativity / Vlad P. Glăveanu, Ingunn Johanne Ness, Constance de Saint Laurent. Other titles: Creativity research journal.
Description: New York, NY : Routledge, 2021. | Series: Routledge research in education | Originally published as a special issue of the Creativity research journal. | Includes bibliographical references and index.
Identifiers: LCCN 2020025116 | ISBN 9780367556754 (hardback) | ISBN 9781003094630 (ebook)
Subjects: LCSH: Virtual reality in education. | Education—Effect of technological innovations on. | Creative ability.
Classification: LCC LB1044.87 .C7535 2021 | DDC 371.33—dc23
LC record available at https://lccn.loc.gov/2020025116

ISBN: 978-0-367-55678-5 (pbk)
ISBN: 978-0-367-55675-4 (hbk)
ISBN: 978-1-003-09463-0 (ebk)

DOI: 10.4324/9781003094630

Typeset in Bembo
by Apex CoVantage, LLC

Contents

Acknowledgements

The editors are grateful to the Webster Center for Creativity and Innovation (WCCI) at Webster University Geneva and the Centre for the Science of Learning and Technology (SLATE) at the University of Bergen for supporting the international symposium that led first to a special issue and now to this volume. We are also grateful to Mark Runco, the editor of the *Creativity Research Journal*, for supporting us and permitting the special issue to be turned into a book. Constance de Saint Laurent would like to acknowledge the support received from the Swiss National Science Foundation (grant P400PS_180686). Last but not least, we thank all the contributors for their time, energy, and ideas.

Contributors

Ronald A. Beghetto, Arizona State University, USA.

Martina Benvenuti, Italian Institute for Didactic Technology (ITD) & the National Research Council (CNR), Italy.

Samira Bourgeois-Bougrine, Université de Paris, France.

Antonio Bova, Catholic University of the Sacread Heart, Italy.

Eleonora Brivio, Catholic University of the Sacread Heart, Italy.

Arkadiusz Brzeski, The Maria Grzegorzewska University, Poland.

Jean-Marie Burkhardt, Gustave Eiffel University, France.

Claude Chaudet, Webster University Geneva, Switzerland.

Alice Chirico, Catholic University of the Sacred Heart, Italy.

Pietro Cipresso, Catholic University of the Sacred Heart, Italy.

Giovanni Emanuele Corazza, University of Bologna, Italy and University of Paris, France.

Marta Czerwonka, The Maria Grzegorzewska University, Poland.

Constance de Saint Laurent, University of Bologna, Italy and London School of Economics, UK.

Olga Dysthe, University of Bergen, Norway.

Nataly Essonnier, Claude Bernard University, France.

Benjamin Frantz, Université de Paris, France.

Andrea Gaggioli, Catholic University of the Sacred Heart, Italy.

Aleksandra Gajda, The Maria Grzegorzewska University, Poland.

Carlo Galimberti, Catholic University of the Sacred Heart, Italy.

Vlad P. Glăveanu, Webster University Geneva, Switzerland and University of Bergen, Norway.

Dorota M. Jankowska, The Maria Grzegorzewska University, Poland.

Maciej Karwowski, University of Wroclaw, Poland.

Chronis Kynigos, The National and Kapodistrian University of Athens, Greece.

Izabela Lebuda, University of Wroclaw, Poland.

Todd Lubart, Université de Paris, France.

Elvis Mazzoni, University of Bologna, Italy.

Ingunn Johanne Ness, University of Bergen, Norway.

Peter Richard, Université de Paris, France.

Giuseppe Riva, Catholic University of the Sacred Heart, Italy.

Jana Trgalová, Claude Bernard University, France.

Introduction

Creativity, Learning, and Technology in the Age of the Pandemic

Vlad P. Glăveanu, Ingunn Johanne Ness, and Constance de Saint Laurent

At the moment of writing, almost half of the world population has been either in full lockdown or a version of it for about two months because of COVID-19. Besides the tragic loss of life, all aspects of society have been affected by the pandemic. Key among them is education and the fact that most of it turned into home-schooling for younger students, or remote or online classes for older ones. Depending on technology for teaching and learning is certainly not new, but a growing trend since at least the start of the century. And yet, the scale, intensity, and length of technology-mediated education are certainly unprecedented. And they make us acutely aware of the numerous possibilities as well as the formidable challenges and constraints involved by the use of technology in the "classrooms" of today and those of the future. The question of what technology "does" to our learning and creativity is perhaps one of the biggest questions we will have to tackle in a transformed, post-pandemic world.

This big question underlines, one way or another, all the chapters included in this book prepared at a time when COVID-19 did not even exist. What brought the different contributors to this timely topic was the basic observation that creativity, learning, and technology are buzz words in education, organisations, and society at large, and have been for a long while. As the process meant to bring about original and effective outcomes (Runco & Jaeger, 2012), creativity is called upon to deal with the pressing challenges of today, from solving everyday problems to tackling the alarming effects of climate change. The success of creative processes depends, however, on learning and, in particular, on our ability to make use of what we know and to learn from new experience, especially from the experience of failure (Kapur, 2008). Creativity and learning are more than two facets of the same coin – they depend on each other and, in their inter-relation, help individuals develop a sense of agency about themselves and their social and material environment (Karwowski & Beghetto, 2018).

This environment is constantly changing. One of the major transformations, accelerated in recent decades, is represented by the emergence of digital technologies that enable us to explore virtual worlds and to be more interconnected with each other than ever before. This interconnection gives creativity and learning researchers hope, especially those working within a sociocultural tradition (see Glăveanu, Ness, Wasson, & Lubart, 2019). According to this theoretical position, interactions with others are the cradle of learning and the source of our creativity. But reality proves to be much more complex. We learn when using technology, but what we learn ranges from important life skills to conspiracy theories. We could be at our most creative in online environments, yet this creativity can be used for either prosocial or antisocial purposes, sometimes both at the same time. And, as we teach and learn remotely, we can explore new affordances that enable a more creative approach or, equally, feel disempowered by the use of technology and the lack of direct, unmediated human contact.

In this volume we aim to unpack some of the complexities surrounding the creativity–learning–technology relationship. The included chapters aim to shed light on at least two and sometimes all three of these themes and range from broad conceptual reflections to concrete empirical examples. They are expanded presentations given initially at an international symposium co-organised by the Webster Center for Creativity and Innovation (WCCI) and the Centre for the Science of Learning and Technology (SLATE) at Webster University Geneva on 7 December 2017. This symposium marked the start of a continuous collaboration between these centres leading to a second symposium on interdisciplinary collaboration (in Bergen in 2018) and a third one on the real-world impact of creativity (in Geneva in 2019). The scope of the first edition, jointly organised by the three authors, was to discuss topics related to the use of technology in education, art, and design; creativity and learning in education; creativity and virtual reality; technology-driven innovation in organisations and society, among others.

First, the connection between creativity and learning. Views on this relationship vary, from considering the two as largely distinct phenomena to largely synonymous (see, for instance, Piaget's view that to understand is to invent; Piaget, 1973). More recently, work on the concept of "creative learning" (Beghetto, 2016) provides a tempting theoretical proposition, but one that also opens new questions about what "non-creative learning" might be. Another important debate in this area has to do with the contribution both learning and creativity make to school achievement. It has long been debated whether schools "kill" creativity or, in other words, if creativity does at all contribute to and is required by school achievement – there is evidence that the latter is the case (Karwowski, 2018). In this volume, Karwowski, Jankowska, Brzeski, Czerwonka, Gajda, Lebuda, and Beghetto go further and present their work on the Creativity and Learning in School Achievement Test (CLISAT) in order to capture the interplay between creativity and learning and study its contribution to achievement in specific domains. The authors discuss a large, cross-sequential study using CLISAT, report the validity and reliability of this new measure, and discuss its relationship with intelligence and divergent thinking.

The connection between creativity and learning in the context of school becomes increasingly mediated by the use of technology, for both students and teachers. A good example of how math teachers, teacher educators, and researchers collaborate in order to design educational digital resources is offered by Kynigos, Essonnier, and Trgalova. The research reported was part of a wider European project (MC2) that aimed at developing socio-technical environments in order to foster creative thinking in mathematics. In their chapter, the authors focus not only on the empirical part of the project, but also on developing the notion of "social creativity", a concept that has attracted interest for decades (see Montuori & Purser, 1997; Lebuda & Glăveanu, 2019). Practical lessons about interdisciplinary collaborations are derived, particularly on the use of complementary knowledge and skills.

The theme of collaboration is explored in depth in Ness and Dysthe's chapter on the topic of "Polyphonic Imagination". In this chapter, the authors analyse idea generation processes in multidisciplinary groups within an organisational context. Besides offering empirical evidence of different stages in a group's creative activity, they theorise the value of multidisciplinarity as a multi-voiced/polyphonic stimulation of fantasy. By drawing on cultural-historical and dialogical ideas, the two develop a new vocabulary to capture the relational co-construction of knowledge as a specific form of imagination. While this study is grounded in using a mix of qualitative methods, a more quantitative approach to the same topic is proposed in this volume by Gaggioli, Mazzoni, Benvenuti, Galimberti, Bova, Brivio, Cipresso, Riva, and Chirico. They use the model of Networked Flow (NF) to map the factors that underpin optimal creative collaboration. In addition, Gaggioli and colleagues explore with this model both physical and digital spaces, adding a technological element to groupwork. There are several similarities between the frameworks of collaboration developed in these two chapters. Most importantly, they both consider the role of culture and social interactions for creativity. Whether in the form of a socially infused type of imagination or as a network of material and symbolic resources, collaborations cut across the intra- and the inter-group levels. Second, they consider the role of time in creative production, either in the form of stages or in the study of evolving networks. Third, they suggest important features of group creativity in online and offline spaces: the existence of multiple "voices" and the temporal dynamic of flow.

A question remains, however, as to the impact of working in virtual environments on individual and collective types of creativity. This comparison has been made by Bourgeois-Bougrine, Richard, Burkhardt, Frantz, and Lubart in their chapter on the impact of Multi-User Virtual Environments (MUVEs) on the expression of creative potential. Importantly, the authors propose an exploratory study of brainstorming sessions in real and virtual environments, the latter recreating the environment of the former. The participants engaged with a practical problem related to transport and improving mobility in Paris. The findings revealed a favourable effect of working in

MUVEs on fluency and originality, but also showed that they don't favour everyone equally – those with a higher risk-taking propensity were significantly more creative than others. Therefore, there is more to explore at the intersection between individual differences and social psychology studies of creativity and technology.

Any such explorations of the links between creativity, learning, and technology shouldn't romanticise the role of digital or virtual environments as a key enabler of creative learning. Members of online communities learn considerably from each other, but what they learn might be misinformation. They can and do create, but part of this creativity, at least on social media, is malevolent (Cropley, Cropley, Kaufman, & Runco, 2010), leading to the generation of new and "catchy" slurs and conspiracy theories. These phenomena are analysed in the chapter by de Saint Laurent, Glăveanu, and Chaudet, focused on the role played by linguistic creativity in building anti-immigration communities on Twitter. This research reminds us that learning and creativity are much more than cognitive processes. They are infused with affect and deeply social in their origins and dynamic, and it is these affective and social elements that point us to the importance of issues such as identity, in- and out-groups, and societal values in analysing technologically mediated interactions.

At the same time, one of the main take-aways from this volume is that such interactions are highly complex, and they shouldn't be either demonised or romanticised. No, the use of technology doesn't automatically make us more creative even if it shapes to a great extent the ways in which we engage in creativity (Literat & Glăveanu, 2016). Equally, they don't squash creativity or hamper authentic dialogues, online and offline. Similar to the invention of writing millennia before and of the printing press centuries ago, digital technologies and social media will radically transform society – we see these effects all around us. We need, however, to develop more balanced and thoughtful accounts of these effects. The post-truth era some claim we are living through has been partially ushered with the help of technology, and yet, it is equally true that social media underpins social movements and protests around the globe (Kelly Garrett, 2006).

Creative potential, the topic of the chapter by Corazza and Glăveanu, is multifaceted, and its many dimensions – individual, social, and material – all interact in a complex manner with technology. The dynamic and integrative framework of creative potential proposed by the two authors can guide future explorations of information and communication technologies (ICT) on creativity and, for this matter, learning as well. Both these phenomena have, at their core, the mission of expanding human possibility, and in the 21st century, possibility is intimately related to ICT, whether we like it or not. Above and beyond the "virtual world potential" identified by Corazza and Glăveanu, the world of today is open to new, technology-enabled forms of creative learning, collaboration, and Polyphonic Imagination. This volume invites us to be open, in turn, to a reflective and constructive exploration of these phenomena.

We end with a collective reflection on the opportunities and challenges of teaching online during these past months. Instead of offering a single narrative about this rapid change, however, we opted for the format of a conversation between contributors as we believe it captures best the dialogical, fragmented, and heterogeneous nature of current debates about the positive and negative consequences of technology and its impact on education on the long term. Authors were invited to consider the implications of research presented here or elsewhere as well as their practical experience in addressing this "hot" issue. We can only hope that readers will resonate with these reflections and, perhaps, find something useful in them that could guide their educational thinking and practice now and in the future.

References

Beghetto, R. A. (2016). Creative learning: A fresh look. *Journal of Cognitive Education and Psychology, 15*(1), 6–23.

Bourgeois-Bougrine, S., Richard, P., Burkhardt, J.-M., Frantz, B., & Lubart, T. (this volume). The expression of users' creative potential in virtual and real environments: An exploratory study. *Creativity Research Journal.*

Corazza, G. E., & Glăveanu, V. P. (this volume). Potential in creativity: Individual, social, material perspectives, and a dynamic integrative framework. *Creativity Research Journal.*

Cropley, D. H., Cropley, A. J., Kaufman, J. C., & Runco, M. A. (Eds.). (2010). *The dark side of creativity*. New York: Cambridge University Press.

de Saint Laurent, C., Glăveanu, V. P., & Chaudet, C. (this volume). Malevolent creativity and social media: Creating anti-immigration communities on Twitter. *Creativity Research Journal.*

Gaggioli, A., Mazzoni, E., Benvenuti, M., Galimberti, C., Bova, A., Brivio, E., . . . Chirico, A. (this volume). Networked flow in creative collaboration: A mixed method study. *Creativity Research Journal.*

Glăveanu, V. P., Johanne Ness, I., Wasson, B., & Lubart, T. (2019). Sociocultural perspectives on creativity, learning, and technology. In C. A. Mullen (Ed.), *Creativity under duress in education? Resistive theories, practices, and actions* (pp. 63–82). New York: Springer.

Johanne Ness, I., & Dysthe, O. (this volume). Polyphonic imagination: Understanding idea generation in multidisciplinary groups as a multivoiced stimulation of fantasy. *Creativity Research Journal.*

Kapur, M. (2008). Productive failure. *Cognition and instruction, 26*(3), 379–424.

Karwowski, M. (2018). The flow of learning. *Europe's Journal of Psychology, 14*(2), 291–295.

Karwowski, M., & Beghetto, R. A. (2018). Creative behavior as agentic action. *Psychology of Aesthetics, Creativity, and the Arts, 13*(4), 402–415.

Karwowski, M., Jankowska, D. M., Brzeski, A., Czerwonka, M., Gajda, A., Lebuda, I., & Beghetto, R. A. (this volume). Delving into creativity and learning. *Creativity Research Journal.*

Kelly Garrett, R. (2006). Protest in an information society: A review of literature on social movements and new ICTs. *Information, Communication & Society, 9*(2), 202–224.

Kynigos, C., Essonnier, N., & Trgalova, J. (this volume). Social creativity in the education sector: The case of collaborative design of digital resources in mathematics. *Creativity Research Journal.*

Lebuda, I., & Glăveanu, V. P. (Eds.). (2019). *The Palgrave handbook of social creativity research*. London: Palgrave.

Literat, I., & Glăveanu, V. P. (2016). Same but different? Distributed creativity in the Internet age. *Creativity: Theories – Research – Applications*, *3*(2), 330–342.

Montuori, A., & Purser, R. (1997). Social creativity: The challenge of complexity. *Pluriverso*, *1*(2), 78–88.

Piaget, J. (1973). *To understand is to invent*. New York: Grossman.

Runco, M. A., & Jaeger, G. J. (2012). The standard definition of creativity. *Creativity Research Journal*, *24*(1), 92–96.

1 Delving Into Creativity and Learning

Maciej Karwowski, Dorota M. Jankowska, Arkadiusz Brzeski, Marta Czerwonka, Aleksandra Gajda, Izabela Lebuda, and Ronald A. Beghetto

Creativity researchers tend to view creativity and learning as related phenomena (Beghetto, 2016; Guilford, 1967), but there are different ways to conceptualise the nature of this relationship. A case can be made that creativity enhances learning through the use of imagination (Leopold, Mayer, & Dutke, 2018; Mayer & Gallini, 1990; Vygotsky, 2004), remote associations (Lee, Huggins, & Therriault, 2014), and originality (Dollinger, 2011). A case can also be made for learning serving as a necessary condition for creativity (Anderson & Krathwohl, 2001). Indeed, researchers have long recognised that prior knowledge and experiences serve as a basis for creative thinking (Guilford, 1950). It is also possible, however, to make a case that too great a focus on formal learning can hinder creativity (e.g., Simonton, 2017), and alternatively, placing too much emphasis on creative expression may hinder learning by making it less goal-oriented and unfocused (Baird, et al., 2012; Mooneyham & Schooler, 2013).

Empirical work examining this relationship has also provided somewhat variable findings. A recent meta-analysis (Gajda, Karwowski, & Beghetto, 2017) has offered a bit more clarity, indicating a positive, albeit modest correlation (r = .22) between creativity and academic achievement. Although there is both theoretical and empirical work suggesting a relationship between creativity and learning, many questions remain, including: What is the nature of the relationship between creativity and academic learning? Does this relationship differ across academic domains? Is academic learning a necessary condition for creative expression in a given academic domain? How might researchers more effectively measure both creativity and learning in an academic context?

In this chapter, we explore these questions by way of examining the links between creativity and learning. We open by briefly introducing a continuum that researchers may find helpful in conceptualising and assessing the relationship between creativity and learning. We then describe the Creativity and Learning in School Achievement Test (CLISAT), a new instrument developed with the goal of assessing creativity and learning in academic domains. Next we report on a study that had three goals: (1) examine the psychometric properties of the CLISAT (i.e., factor structure, reliability, and validity), (2) explore the relationship between CLISAT scores and measures of intelligence and divergent thinking, and (3) examine the conditional relationship between creativity and learning in math and language. We close with a brief discussion of implications for theory and research.

Conceptualising the Assessment of Creativity and Learning

There are an ever expanding array of methods and measures that researchers can use to examine potential links between creativity and academic learning (Freund & Holling, 2008; Gralewski & Karwowski, 2012). With respect to creativity, this includes approaches that range from self-report measures to the more objective creativity tests, including recent large-scale efforts aimed at measuring creative problem solving in large scale assessments (e.g., Programme for International Student Assessment 2021 measurement, but see Beghetto, in press).

Given these numerous options, there is little consensus in the field as to how to best measure creativity (see Kaufman, Plucker, & Baer, 2008). Similar ambiguity exists in the case of school achievement tests. Attempts to improve measurement of these constructs have been undertaken by several scholars (Alexander, Singer, Jablansky, & Hattan, 2016; Dumas & Alexander, 2016; Greiff, et al., 2013; McNeish & Dumas, 2017; Wüstenberg, Greiff, & Funke, 2012). With growing array of options available, how might researchers assess creativity and learning?

One way to address this question is to take a step back and recognise that all measures include assumptions about the nature of the constructs being assessed. Sometimes these assumptions are made explicit, other times they are not. Moreover, sometimes researchers inadvertently use measures that are based on assumptions about creativity that are not aligned with the goals of the study. As mentioned, creativity scholars typically conceptualise learning and creativity as related constructs. The assumptions about how to assess this relationship, however, can range on a continuum from viewing creativity and learning as separate constructs to mutually dependent or combined phenomena.

Figure 1.1 depicts this continuum of conceptualisations. Prior to discussing the various points on the continuum, it is important to note that the points are not meant to represent discrete categories, but rather highlight the variability in how creativity and learning can be assessed – ranging from approaches that attempt to assess the constructs separately to those that attempt to measure them simultaneously.

The continuum in Figure 1.1 spans conceptions that tend to use more general and separate measures of creativity (left side of the continuum) to those that use more situationally specific and blended approaches (right side of the continuum). The far left side of the continuum represents approaches that attempt to assess creativity and learning separately, using domain general assessments (e.g., domain general divergent thinking tests for creativity,

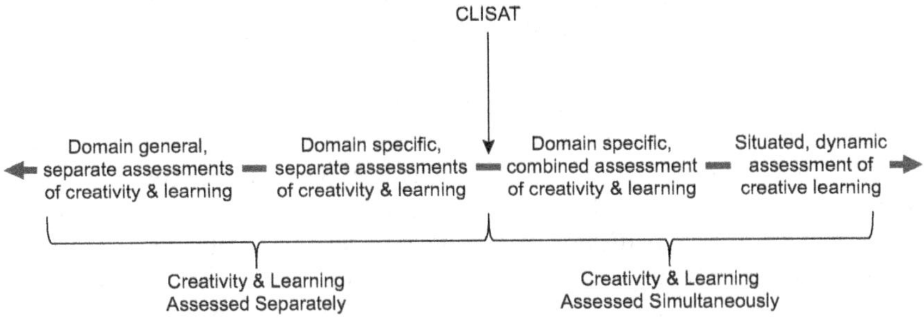

Figure 1.1 Continuum of conceptualising the assessment of creativity and learning

Note: CLISAT = Creativity and Learning in School Achievement Test

grade point average for learning). Historically speaking, this is one of the most common ways that researchers have examined the relationship (see Gajda, Karwowski, & Beghetto, 2017).

In more recent years, however, scholars have emphasised the role that domain plays in both creativity and learning (Alexander, Schallert, & Reynolds, 2009; Baer, 2014). Consequently, there has been an effort to develop more domain or subject matter specific measures of both creativity and learning (e.g., Skiba, Tan, Sternberg, & Grigorenko, 2016). Given that academic domain seems to play an important role in both creativity and learning, approaches assessing creativity and learning using domain specific tasks form an important step toward improving the measurement of these constructs.

When scholars assess creativity and learning as separate constructs, they tend to focus on questions such as: What is the nature of the relationship between these two separate constructs? As they tailor those assessments to specific domains, they can also examine questions such as: What role does domain play in the relationship? and To what extent does prior learning serve as a necessary condition for creativity in specific domains (e.g., Anderson & Krathwohl, 2001; Krathwohl, 2002)?

Moving along the continuum, when scholars view creativity and learning as mutually dependent constructs, they tend to focus on how creativity and learning work more closely together in specific domains, contexts, and situations (Beghetto, 2016; Guilford, 1967; Vygotsky, 2004/1967). This perspective represents a long theoretical tradition in the field of creativity studies, which includes positing learning as a special case of a creative process (see also Guilford, 1950; Rubenstein, Callan, & Ridgley, 2018; Treffinger, Isaksen, & Firestien, 1983), creativity as a special case of learning (Rubenstein, et al., 2018), and even some combination of both, typically referred to as *creative learning* (see Beghetto, 2016). These perspectives resemble a classic Piagetian perspective (Piaget, 1973) that posits that students can memorise material but such memorisation is not sufficient to call it learning. Consequently, to really learn, personal understanding is required and this understanding is inherently associated with the transformation of the knowledge by the individual, so a creative act (Runco & Jaeger, 2007).

Creativity researchers who attempt to assess the mutually dependent relationship between creativity and learning focus on examining questions such as the following: How does prior experience convert into creative outcomes? How do creative insights lead to new understanding? What kinds of socio-situational factors influence creative learning of individuals? How do individual creative insights contribute to the learning of others?

There is limited but growing theoretical and empirical work along these lines. Such work focuses on clarifying the design logic needed for simultaneously assessing creativity and learning (Beghetto, in press) as well as demonstrating how more dynamic, blended, and situated methodologies can be used to conceptualise and study creative learning (Anderson, Haney, Pitts, Porter, & Bousselot, 2019; Gajda, Beghetto, & Karwowski, 2017; Jankowska, Czerwonka, Lebuda, & Karwowski, 2018; Karwowski, 2018).

The Creativity and Learning in School Achievement Test (CLISAT) falls somewhere between the separate and mutually dependent ends of the continuum (as illustrated in Figure 1.1). As we discuss in the next section, the CLISAT represents a step in the direction toward assessing creativity and learning in the same test, using domain specific tasks.

Introducing CLISAT

The CLISAT measures academic achievement and creative-learning relevant processes. As illustrated in Figure 1.2 (see Panel 1), it covers a broad range of subject-relevant content, while tasks capture different skills. Importantly, a number of tasks are devoted to measuring creativity-related operations, including the ability to associate, combine, modify, or transform ideas. Both parts of CLISAT – i.e., math and language – follow a similar structure (Panel 2). They are organised in separate, yet associated blocks or testlets.

Each block starts with one or more closed-ended, knowledge-based tasks, which are then followed by open-ended tasks where participants are asked to provide creative solutions. Examples of tasks are presented in Panel 3. In the version of CLISAT used in this study there are 24 tasks in total – 12 in language and 12 in math. In the language part, seven tasks have a closed-ended character, while five tasks are aimed at measuring creativity-relevant processes. All five language tasks were scored for fluency (i.e., number of appropriate ideas generated); two of them were also scored for originality (i.e., rated uniqueness of response), and three were scored for flexibility (i.e., number of different categories that a response could be assigned to). In the math portion of the test, eight tasks are closed-ended, and four tasks measure aspects of creative thinking in math. All open-ended tasks were scored for fluency; two of them were additionally scored for originality, and two were scored for flexibility.

The team members who developed the criteria for scoring the CLISAT creativity tasks decided to score all items for fluency and approximately half

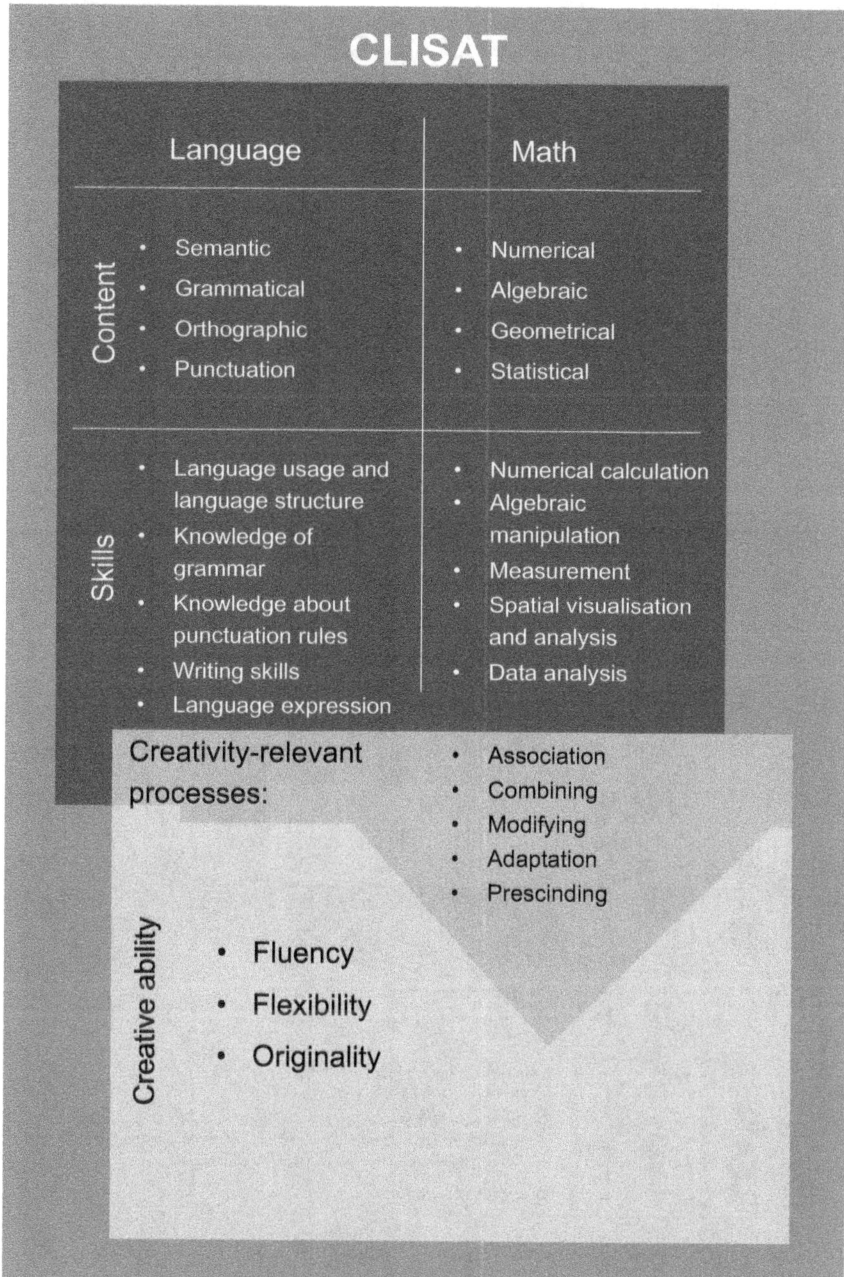

Panel 1: Overall philosophy of CLISAT

Figure 1.2a Overview of CLISAT: Panel 1 illustrates overall philosophy of CLISAT, while Panel 2 shows the structure of tasks within both subtests; Panel 3 provides example tasks

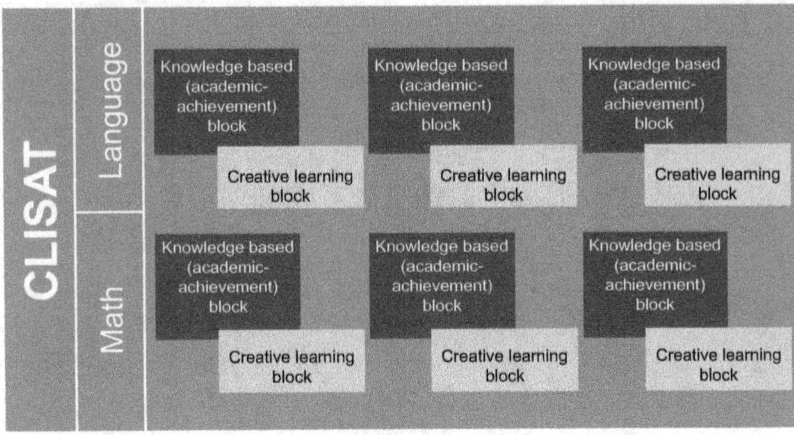

Panel 2: Testlet-like structure of tasks within both parts of CLISAT

Figure 1.2b (Continued)

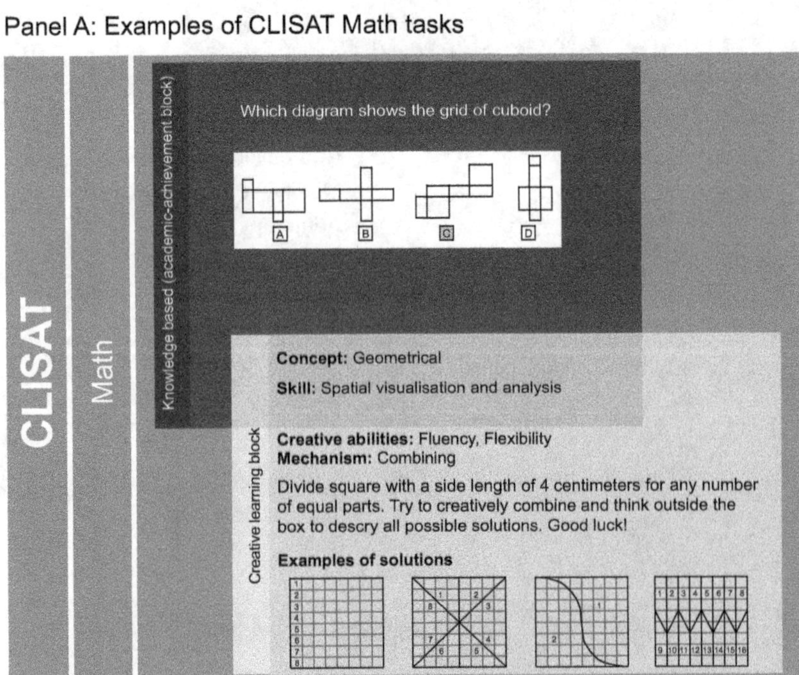

Panel 3: Example math and language tasks from both parts of CLISAT

Figure 1.2c (Continued)

Panel B: Examples of CLISAT Language tasks

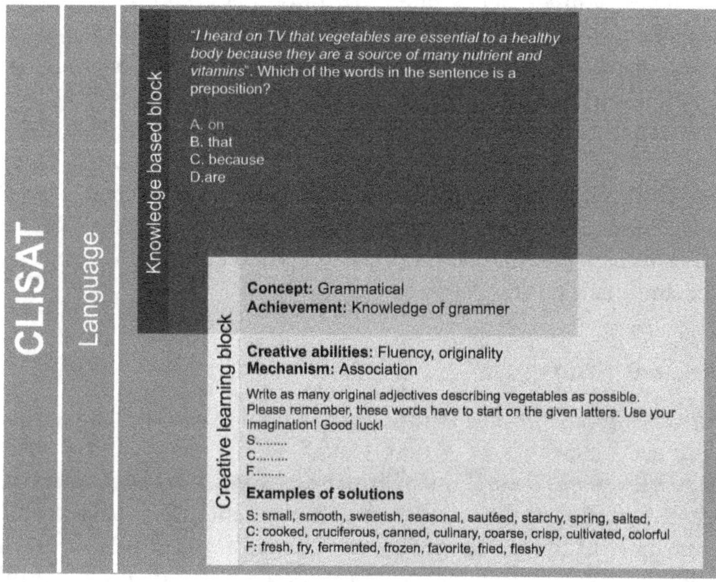

Panel 3: (Continued)

Figure 1.2c (Continued)

for flexibility and the other half for originality. This decision was based on the nature of each task as well as the pragmatic constraint of having such a large number of items to score in a large-sample study. Given that fluency scores are the most straightforward and efficient type of creativity-relevant process to score (i.e., count the number of appropriate responses), all responses were given a fluency score. As far as flexibility and originality, the scoring team attempted to provide some balance when determining which items seemed the most appropriate to score for flexibility versus originality.

One task from the language test, for instance, required participants to create as many sentences as possible starting with letters "**L** . . . **D** . . . **R** . . . [+ sentence completion]". A possible example might look like "**L**ena's **D**og **R**uns [faster than she does]". The number of sentences proposed served as the *fluency* score; *flexibility* was determined by having judges use an a priori developed coding schedule to determine the number of different categories to which the second and third word from the sentence could be assigned.

Similarly, one of the tasks in the math part required participants to provide as many different mathematical operations using the numbers [3, 4, 20, 24, 72] and symbols [+, −, x, :, =] provided. A number of proposed operations served as an index of *fluency*, while *flexibility* was determined based on the number of different categories of proposed operations assessed against the a priori developed answer key. In all cases where flexibility was assessed, the theoretical scope of scores ranged from minimum = 1 (one category, lack of flexibility) to maximum = X, where X could be equal to fluency (in the situation where a judge determined that responses could be assigned to different categories).

In items that judges assessed for originality, they used a 5-point rating of the uniqueness of the responses where *1 = all typical (unoriginal) responses, 2 = mostly typical, only a few original responses, 3 = equally typical and original responses, 4 = many original responses, 5 = all or mostly all original responses.* Creative CLISAT scores for language and math were calculated separately by standardising (z-scoring) fluency, flexibility, and originality scores in language and in math and then averaging those standardised scores into separate language and math creative scores.

The Present Study

We had three goals for this study. First, we endeavoured to examine the psychometric properties of a new test: The Creativity and Learning in School Achievement Test (CLISAT). As discussed, CLISAT contextualises creativity by putting it into academic achievement tasks (in this case, math and language). Our second goal was to examine CLISAT's correlations with relevant cognitive predictors (i.e., intelligence, divergent thinking). Finally, we attempted to go beyond simple correlations between academic achievement and creativity and focused on examining the pattern of these relationships. More specifically, we are interested in exploring the question of possible reciprocal relations between creativity and academic achievement and more generally in the role creativity plays in academic achievement.

Given the data we used in this study comes from the first wave of a two-cohort longitudinal study (or cross-sequential study), we can only provide a somewhat tentative examination of the directionality of the links between our two constructs of interest. Still, we are able to provide some new insights into the nature of the links between creativity-related processes and academic achievement.

Method

Participants

Participants in the study included 2,372 sixth-grade elementary school students (n = 1,227; 52%) and first-year middle school students (n = 1,145; 48%) from Warsaw, the capital of Poland. The sample was composed of 1,243 girls (52%) and 1,129 boys (48%). The students participated in a longitudinal study, and the following data come from its first wave. Students of 61 schools (30 middle schools and 31 elementary schools), attending 174 classes, participated in the study. After exclusion of incomplete data, the group of students who solved CLISAT was smaller, yet still allowing for complex statistical analyses ($n = 1{,}912$ in the case of math and $n = 1{,}682$ in the case of language).

Measures

Creativity and Learning in School Achievement Test (CLISAT)

The CLISAT used in the first wave of this study consisted of 24 tasks – 12 math and 12 language. Both parts of the test were created in the form of testlets (see, e.g., Wainer, Bradlow, & Wang, 2007), i.e., groups of tasks that included closed-ended, knowledge-based tasks developed on the basis of the curriculum (eight tasks in math and seven tasks in language, scored *0 = incorrect, 1 = correct*), as well as open-ended tasks that were developed to capture processes relevant for creativity and academic learning (four tasks in math and five tasks in language).

The reliability of academic achievement tasks was appropriate given the short length (Cronbach's αs based on tetrachoric correlation matrix were estimated at $\alpha = .78$ in the case of math and $\alpha = .68$ in the case of language). We discuss the reliability of the creative part of the CLISAT in the results section, together with data on CLISAT's validity. As the CLISAT is currently used in subsequent waves of the cross-sequential study (with anchor tasks and new tasks developed), at this point we are unable to provide more detailed examples of each item because the test is still in use. Once the cross-sequential study is finished, however, a detailed description of all CLISAT's items along with scoring guidelines will be published and made available upon request.

Divergent Thinking

We used three tasks to measure divergent thinking. The first was about providing ideas for an unconventional use of toothpaste. The second, to come up with unconventional consequences of a situation where there would be no cell phones or the Internet. The third, to list similarities between a chocolate bar and a computer. Responses to each of the tasks were rated by the "snapshot method" (Silvia, Martin, & Nusbaum, 2009), i.e., fluency (the number of ideas) and originality of all responses of the given respondent in each task. In the first step, two judges (third and fourth author) rated the works of 200 students together. The judges used an ordinal scale, where *0 = unoriginal or largely unoriginal responses, 2 = original responses*, and *1 = all intermediate situations*. Reliability for the initial coding of the 200 tests, estimated on the matrix of polychoric correlations, was high ($\alpha = .80$) and increased after discussing discrepancies and coding a further 100 tests ($\alpha = .85$). Therefore, consecutive tests were coded by one of the two judges. Divergent thinking tests were completed by 1,348 participants.

Intelligence

To measure intelligence, we used a set of 26 tasks created in the International Cognitive Ability Resource (ICAR) project (Condon & Revelle, 2014) – available in the public domain – and a scaled set of items of various types that have already been used in Polish studies (McKay, Karwowski, & Kaufman, 2017). Participants completed ten tasks that required reasoning, ten that were based on matrices that resembled those of Raven's test, and six tasks that required mental rotations. Confirmatory analysis of the hierarchical model (with three latent factors loading on a general factor of *g*) was conducted in the *lavaan* package within the R program (Rosseel, 2012), with the Weighted Least Square Mean and Variance Adjusted (WLSMV) estimator (Beauducel & Herzberg, 2006). The model showed a good fit as assessed by typically applied criteria and recommendations (Hu & Bentler, 1999): comparative fit index (*CFI*) and Tucker Lewis Index (*TLI*) above .90, root mean square error of approximation (*RMSEA*) and root mean squared residual (*SRMR*) below .08. The fit parameters of the hierarchical model were as follows: *CFI* = .941, *TLI* = .936, *RMSEA* = .024, 90% *PU*: .021–.026, *SRMR* = .027. Reliability estimated on the matrix of tetrachoric correlations was high (α = .84).

Procedure

This study was conducted during three classes (lessons). During the first class, students solved CLISAT. The second class was devoted to completing intelligence and divergent thinking tests. During the third class, students completed a number of self-report scales that included measures of personality, academic self-concept, and basic demographic variables. We obtained informed consent from all students, their parents, and school principals. Due to the longitudinal character of the study, parents and students were informed about data confidentiality, but also about the necessity to identify the respondents in consecutive waves – consent to process personal data was provided by the parents.

Results

Given the goals of our study, we report results in three steps. First, we discuss the factor structure of CLISAT and its reliability and validity. Next, we focus on the relationship between CLISAT scores and intelligence and divergent thinking. Finally, we explore the more nuanced relationship between creativity-relevant processes and academic achievement as measured by the CLISAT. To this end, we used two relatively new statistical methods. First, we applied Necessary Condition Analysis (Dul, 2016), which is a formal test of whether one variable can be considered a necessary condition of the other. Next, we used quantile regression (Dumas, 2018; Koenker & Hallock, 2001) to explore whether academic achievement predicts creativity-related processes at different levels of the distribution of the CLISAT creativity scores, and we also examined whether CLISAT creativity scores predict academic achievement in language and math differently, at varying levels of academic achievement's distributions.

CLISAT's Validity and Reliability

The CLISAT used in this study consisted of nine creative tasks (four math and five language based) that were included as part of a broader booklet and were preceded by more typical, closed-ended academic achievement tasks. Thus, each creative task represents a specific testlet – initial tasks are based on school knowledge and skills, while creativity-related tasks invite students to go beyond simple memorisation and to develop and elaborate their ideas. As all creative tasks are by definition open-ended, they were scored by a group of six coders: the first to sixth authors of this study.

In the initial coding, each task was independently scored by two coders according to pre-specified criteria. The scoring criteria included fluency (scored for each task), flexibility, or originality of proposed solutions. Inter-judge reliability was acceptable (originality, task 3) to very high (fluency and flexibility) (see Table 1.1). Consequently, the remaining tests were coded by one coder only.

Confirmatory factor analysis (CFA) was conducted to examine the assumed, domain-specific, two-factor solution of the creative part of CLISAT. The CFA model was estimated with maximum likelihood estimator with a robust standard error (MLR) in the laavan package for R (see Figure 1.3). The two-factor model was characterised by a good fit: CFI = .972, TLI = .965, $RMSEA$ = .043, 90% CI: .000–.071, $SRMR$ = .084.

Table 1.1 Inter-rater reliabilities for the initial coding of CLISAT

	Fluency	*Flexibility*	*Originality*
Math			
Task 1	.96	.86	—
Task 2	.92	—	.76
Task 3	.98	—	.73
Task 4	.96	.96	—
Language			
Task 5	.99	—	.92
Task 6	.92	—	.79
Task 7	.99	.87	—
Task 8	1	.93	—
Task 9	.90	.86	—

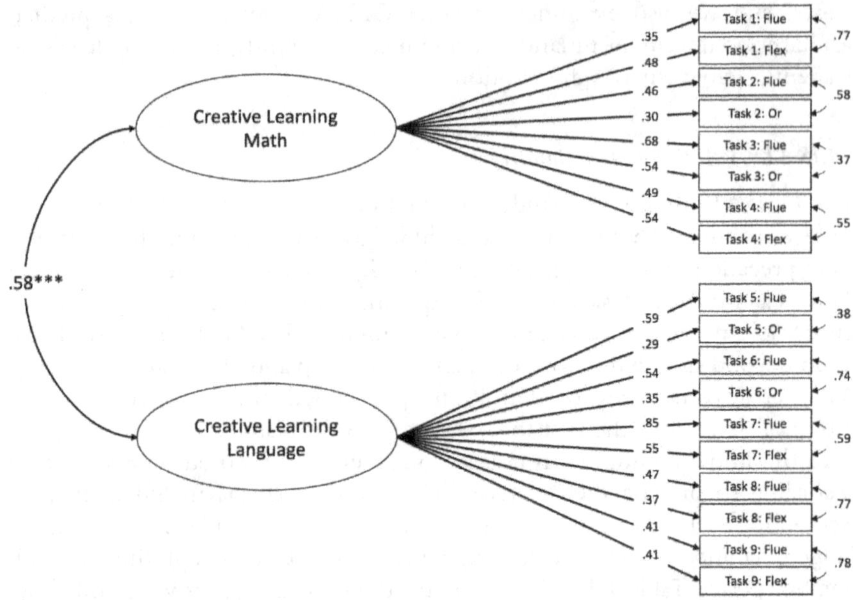

Figure 1.3 Confirmatory factor analysis of the creative part of CLISAT

All factor loadings were statistically significant and resulted in acceptable composite reliability in the case of creativity and learning in math (H = .74) and high in the case of language (H = .84). The latent correlation between variables was statistically significant and robust (r = .58), yet still indicating a sufficient level of discriminant validity of the items (see Figure 1.3).

To examine whether the pattern of predictors of academic achievement in math and language and CLISAT creativity scores in these subjects differed, we conducted four separate regression models (with academic achievement in math and language and creativity and learning in math and language serving as dependent variables). Each model followed the same two-step procedure.

In the first step, we included intelligence as a predictor into the model. In the second step, we added divergent thinking indices (fluency and originality). We hypothesised that intelligence will serve as a more robust predictor of academic achievement while divergent thinking would rather explain the variability in the creative portion of the CLISAT than in the academic achievement part. These expectations were largely confirmed (see Table 1.2).

The models explained between 13% and 24% of the variance of dependent variables. While intelligence explained a substantial portion of variability in academic achievement, especially in math (β = .48), but also in language (β = .37), the role of divergent thinking was stronger in the case of creative processes than in academic achievement. As illustrated by the R^2 change, although divergent thinking added only 1.3% or 1.6% of the

Table 1.2 Regression models with academic and creative scores regressed on intelligence and divergent thinking

Predictors	*Academic Scores*		*Creative Scores*	
	Math	*Language*	*Math*	*Language*
Step 1: Intelligence				
IQ	.48***	.37***	.38***	.20***
R^2	22.6%	13.4%	14.6%	4.2%
Step 2: Intelligence and Divergent Thinking				
IQ	.45***	.34***	.35***	.15***
Fluency	.07*	.07*	.08**	.23***
Originality	.07*	.05	.11**	.12**
R^2	23.9%	15%	17.7%	12.8%
ΔR^2	1.3%	1.6%	3.1%	8.7%

Note: Standardised coefficient (β) is presented.

*$p < .05$; **$p < .01$; ***$p < .001$

variance in academic achievement in math and language, respectively, it was associated with 3% of creativity and learning in math and almost 9% (twice more than intelligence) in the case of creativity and learning in language. Thus, although the role of intelligence was visible in all tasks, the overall pattern obtained was consistent with our predictions.

Pattern of Relationships Between CLISAT Academic Scores and Creative Scores

Our final analysis focused on shedding light on the more nuanced patterns of relationship between CLISAT creative and academic scores. Specifically, we were interested in examining the conditional relationship between creativity and academic achievement and whether different levels of CLISAT academic scores relate to different levels of creative scores (and vice versa).

A recently developed statistical technique – the necessary condition analysis (NCA) (Dul, 2016) – allows for testing whether one variable serves as the necessary condition of the other. The NCA quantifies the pattern of the relationship between variables. Rather than relying on average-based links, like typical correlation or regression analyses do, the NCA assesses the pattern presented on the scatterplot. If indeed X is a necessary condition of Y, then a low score in X makes Y impossible: there is no Y without X. However, a high level of X does not guarantee Y. Hence, even if X is necessary, it is not sufficient to cause Y. The NCA was used in creativity literature to show that intelligence may be considered a necessary yet not sufficient condition of creative ability (Karwowski, et al.,

2016) or creative achievement (Karwowski, Kaufman, Lebuda, Szumski, & Firkowska-Mankiewicz, 2017).

Dul (2016) proposed an effect size (*d*) for the NCA as well as some cut-offs to decide whether necessary condition occurs in the dataset. Specifically, Dul suggested two types of effect size: ceiling envelopment with a free disposal hull (CE-FDH) and ceiling regression with a free disposal hull (CR-FDH). CE-FDH is a piecewise linear function along the upper left of observations in the scatterplot. This effect size measure is recommended for nominal or ordinal NCA analyses. CR-FDH estimates a regression line through the upper-left edges of the CE-FDH function and is recommended if the variables are measured on interval or ratio scales. Theoretically, both CE-FDH and CR-FDH can range between 0 and 1. Based on NCA analyses from different fields, Dul (2016) proposed the following thresholds while interpreting the effect size: below .10 – "small effect", between .10 and .30 – "medium effect", between .30 and .50 – "large effect", and above .50 – "very large effect". For a dichotomous decision, i.e., claiming whether one variable serves as a necessary condition of another or not, Dul (2016) offered a cut-off $d = .10$. Recent developments in the NCA methodology (Dul, van der Laan, & Kuik, 2018) include a permutation-based significance test that should be used together with effect size.

We examined the simple, bivariate correlations between the results in academic achievement-oriented and creativity-oriented parts of the CLISAT and found a robust relationship in each subject area (math, $r = .38$, $p < .001$; language, $r = .31$, $p < .001$). A relationship across subject areas and constructs was also found: academic achievement in math was correlated with creativity and learning in language ($r = .22$, $p < .001$), and academic achievement in language was related to creativity in math ($r = .27$, $p < .001$).

We were, however, interested in going beyond simple correlations to examine whether there is evidence for academic achievement serving as a necessary condition for creativity-related processes. Using NCA we found evidence for this conditional relationship in math, but less so in the case of language. Specifically, the NCA for math (see Figure 1.4, left panel) demonstrated a significant ($p < .001$) and moderate-to-strong effect size (CR-FDH $d = .25$). Indeed, high scores in the creative part of the math test were hardly possible when the results in closed-ended, school-based part were low. In the case of language, however, the effect size was not only weaker, $d = .10$, but also non-significant ($p = .17$). The right panel of Figure 1.4 shows that the empty upper-left corner is smaller, and high scores in the creativity-related language tasks were possible even when academic achievement in language was quite low.

Our final step extended the NCA by applying quantile regression analysis. We followed the argumentation presented by Dumas (2018) that in order to accurately estimate the links between more reasoning-based and creativity-based phenomena in educational settings, scholars should not only examine whether academic achievement predicts creativity, but also whether

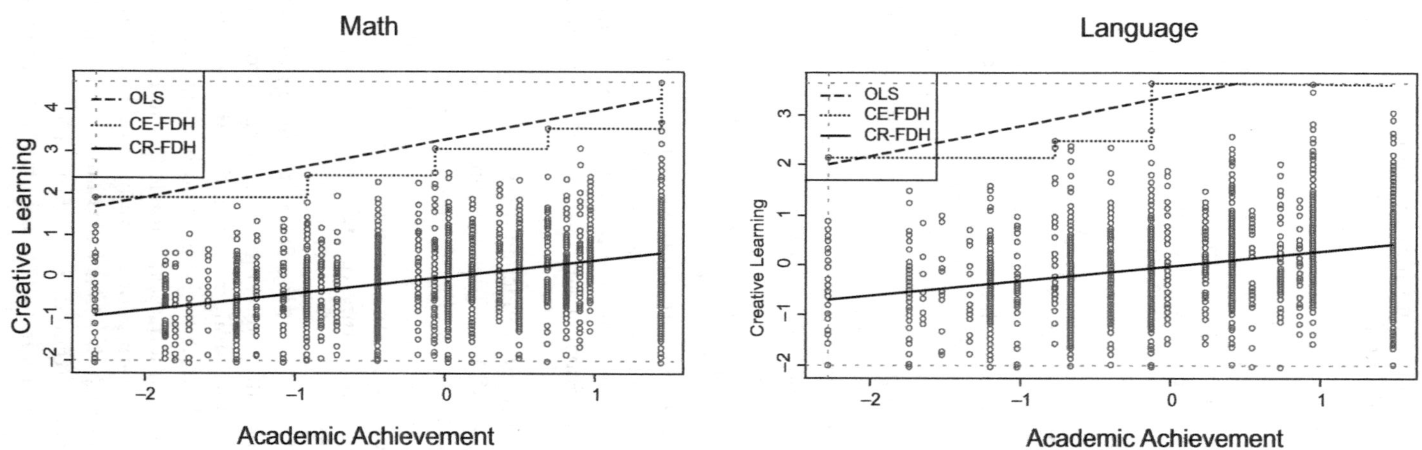

Figure 1.4 The relationship between academic achievement and creativity and learning in math and language

Note: All variables were standardised to facilitate comparability.

creativity can predict academic achievement. Although data collected at the same point in time prevents us from making strong causal claims, quantile regression models can shed initial light on the more nuanced relationship between creativity and academic achievement.

Quantile regression allows researchers to model the relationship between two variables at different points on the distribution of the variable of interest. This approach is particularly useful when there are reasons to expect that the predictor variable is related more strongly with the dependent variable only up to a certain point (e.g., as the threshold hypothesis assumes; Jauk, Benedek, Dunst, & Neubauer, 2013; Karwowski & Gralewski, 2013), or that its role in explaining top scores is greater than average (as the typical ordinary least squares regression assumes) or low results.

Unlike segmented regression (Jauk, et al., 2013), which identifies a specific breakpoint in the predictor's distribution – i.e., a point (or several points) where slopes of regression lines differ – quantile regression estimates the intercept and slope for many researcher-specified moments of the distribution of dependent variable. In other words, researchers can use this technique to examine whether the results in the 10th percentile of CLISAT creative scores are predicted by academic scores to the same extent as the results in the 50th or 90th percentile. Comparing these patterns can illustrate how a predictor variable differs in explaining very low or very high scores in the dependent variable.

We used the *quantreg* package for R (Koenker, 2018) and estimated quantile regression for nine prespecified percentiles of dependent variables distribution, namely: .10, .20, .30, .40, .50 (median), .60, .70, .80, and .90. As our academic achievement tests for language and math had only 23 (math) or 19 (language) levels, we were unable to properly model the estimates at the 90th percentile of the distribution, and so in these cases the 80th percentile was used.

As mentioned previously, we modelled the links in both directions, e.g., we examined whether CLISAT academic scores predict CLISAT creative scores (separately for language and math), and vice versa. While the former (academic predicting creative) may be considered as an extension of the earlier-presented NCA analyses, the latter serves more as a way for exploring the mutually dependent nature of creativity and learning (Beghetto, 2016; Karwowski, 2018).

As illustrated in Table 1.3, academic competencies in math robustly predicted creativity in math with quite a similar effect size across the distribution of creativity scores – βs ranged from $\beta = .36$ at the 10th percentile to $\beta = .43$ at the 60th. In other words, despite the previously identified necessary condition-like pattern, basic mathematical knowledge and competencies were equally as important in explaining low, medium, and high scores in creativity in math. On the other hand, when we examined whether CLISAT creativity in mathematics is able to predict academic achievement, the observed pattern was different: creativity in math more effectively predicted academic

Table 1.3 Quantile regression analyses: CLISAT academic and creative predictions across quantiles

Quantile of Dependent Variable	*Academic → Creative*		*Creative → Academic*	
	Math	*Language*	*Math*	*Language*
10th	.36	.29	.45	.35
20th	.40	.28	.46	.41
30th	.42	.29	.47	.40
40th	.42	.28	.45	.37
50th	.42	.30	.42	.40
60th	.43	.30	.38	.38
70th	.39	.33	.35	.33
80th	.42	.35	.32	.25
90th	.41	.35	—	—

Note: All variables are standardised (M = 0, SD = 1) for this analysis. All reported coefficients are statistically significant (p < .001).

achievement in math at lower quantiles of these achievements (up to the 40th, with βs between .45 and .47), while its role for predicting very high academic achievement (above the 70th percentile), although still substantial, was lower (βs between .32 and .35). These results suggest that dealing creatively with mathematical tasks on the CLISAT is predictive of math achievement, particularly at the lower quantiles of achievement.

In the case of language, the obtained patterns were less systematic. Academic achievement predicted creativity in language across the tested quantiles, with effects ranging from β = .28 to β = .35. Hence, no curvilinear trends were observed. In the case of the opposite direction, creativity in language on the CLISAT predicted academic achievement equally effectively at low and high parts of the distribution, except for the highest estimated quantile (80th), where the effect declined to β = .25.

Discussion

Creative students usually manage to do well at school (Gajda, Beghetto, & Karwowski, 2017), but the links between creativity and academic achievement, even if positive, leave much room for exceptions – including underachievement of highly creative kids (Kim, 2008). While these findings tend to be interpreted in light of possible teachers' biases toward creative students (Westby & Dawson, 1995), or their incomplete understanding of what creativity is (Andiliou & Murphy, 2010; Gralewski & Karwowski, 2013), we think that the reasons are more complex.

One potential reason for mediocre correlations between academic achievement and creativity may stem from more psychometric than substantial problems. As was recently emphasised (Gajda, Beghetto, & Karwowski, 2017), while academic achievement tests by definition focus on correctness (appropriateness) of the proposed solutions, creativity tests tend to focus more on originality than appropriateness (despite standard definitions of creativity recognising both novelty and task appropriateness; e.g., Runco & Jaeger, 2012). Thus, there are reasons to assume that better measurement of both constructs would make these links stronger, and using more sophisticated analytic techniques may help provide more nuanced insights into the relationship between creativity and academic achievement.

In this chapter, we took an initial step in this direction by introducing a continuum for how creativity and achievement can be conceptualised and then describing the CLISAT – a new measure that assesses creativity-related processes and school achievement in mathematics and language. As discussed, CLISAT consists of a number of tasks that are subject-specific (math and language), but also focused on knowledge-base and creative mental operations. Importantly, however, these operations in the context of CLISAT are fulfilled on very specific, school-based material – unlike in typical divergent thinking tasks. While we are currently changing a large portion of tasks between subsequent waves of our study, the core philosophy of CLISAT remains unchanged – all the time the tasks are organised in the form of testlets, where closed-ended, knowledge-based tasks are followed by creative tasks based on very similar content.

The results of this study provided initial evidence for the CLISAT's reliability and validity. The assumed two-factor structure was confirmed, serving for both theoretical and discriminant validity (relatively modest latent correlation between factors, r = .58). As predicted, intelligence explained a larger portion of the variability in closed-ended, knowledge-based tasks than it did in CLISAT creative tasks, even when its role was still substantial. However, divergent thinking ability was more closely related to CLISAT creative than academic tasks – again, consistently with our expectations.

It goes without saying that the links between creativity and learning are complex. Given the correlational design of this study, we were unable to fully untangle it. Still, our NCA and quantile regression analyses shed new light on more complex patterns of interrelations. Specifically, the results highlight that having academic knowledge in a domain seems to be important for creative expression on task in that domain. This may be particularly the case in math, which aligns with previous empirical work (Sak & Maker, 2006; Tabach & Friedlander, 2013). Our findings suggest that this may be less the case with respect to language. The difference in this pattern of findings provides further evidence of the domain-specific nature of creativity,[1] which may be more pronounced in well-structured domains (Sawyer, 1992; Simonton, 2009).

It may be the case that language-based problems do not require as high levels of academic achievement to be scored as creative on the CLISAT as seems to be the case with math. It is also possible that other factors – motivational and self-beliefs related, specifically domain-specific beliefs in the area of language and math – may play a role for these patterns as well. Even a brief look at scatterplots presented in Figure 1.4, for instance, clearly shows that in both cases – math and language – there were students who obtained very low scores in academic achievement tasks (in fact, they did not solve any of the closed-ended, knowledge-based tasks), while dealing quite effectively with creative tasks from the same tests. It seems unlikely that these students did not possess subject-relevant knowledge, rather other factors seem to be at play (e.g., stronger motivation to complete the creativity-related tasks). This is something we intend to explore in future phases of the longitudinal work.

Our study also provided some evidence for the mutually dependent relationship between creativity and academic achievement. As our quantile regression demonstrated, when CLISAT academic scores were regressed on CLISAT creative scores, creative scores served as statistically significant and robust predictors. Moreover, at least in the case of math, we observed a relatively stronger predictive relationship of creativity on academic achievement at lower quantiles of the distribution of achievement. Perhaps the creative solving of mathematical tasks is easier when the tasks are relatively basic, as many different solutions could be generated and tested, whereas it becomes more challenging when the complexity of the tasks grows. In the case of language, the links between creativity and academic achievement were relatively constant (and yet still robust) across the distribution of academic achievement. At this point, our findings are still preliminary and requiring replication, but they do provide some intriguing directions for future research, in particular, examining more complex cross-lagged links and patterns amongst a variety of factors to further untangle the relationship between creativity and academic achievement.

Limitations and Future Directions

Our findings should be interpreted in light of the limitations of this study. Perhaps the most prevalent is that the CLISAT tasks are not integrated or dynamic enough to measure creative learning (see Beghetto, 2020, 2016), and thereby, the CLISAT still provides a somewhat separate and static picture of the relationship between creativity and academic achievement. Moreover, the number of creativity-related tasks in the CLISAT was relatively limited (five in the case of language and only four in the case of math), and not all tasks were scored for originality and flexibility.

Although the reliability of our measurement was good, the limited number of items made it difficult to cover the broad range of language and math skills, and therefore, it is not appropriate to make strong claims about the creativity-relevant processes related to these broader encompassing academic skills. Also, as discussed, all CLISAT creative tasks were scored for fluency. However, the team members developing the scoring criteria decided that for some tasks, scoring for flexibility was more appropriate than attempting to score for originality, whereas for other tasks, scoring for originality was determined to be more appropriate than scoring for flexibility. Although the psychometric properties of the CLISAT creative items were found to be promising, we recognise that it is possible to score responses to these items differently and potentially improve the scoring of these items. It is therefore important to stress that results based on these items, albeit promising, are limited by the scoring approach and should be considered tentative. Subsequent work is needed to test the stability of these findings and consider what improvements need to be made, as well as work toward more closely exploring the role played by how approaches to measuring different aspects of creative thinking and academic learning influence the relationship between these constructs.

Members of this team plan to address these limitations in future studies. More specifically, when using the CLISAT as the main measure in the ongoing cross-sequential study and continuing to work on improving its psychometric properties, we plan to go beyond the purely psychometric studies and toward designing studies that examine the more mutually dependent nature of creativity and learning. This may involve putting CLISAT tasks in laboratory studies that use eye-tracking and thinking aloud methods (following the recent investigations into the creative process as part of the same research endeavour; see Jankowska, et al., 2018), as well as exploring the inter-psychological sphere of creative learning by classroom observations and diary studies (e.g., Beghetto & Schuh, 2020; Gajda, Beghetto, & Karwowski, 2017). Therefore, we emphasise that in order to be effective, the measurement of creativity and learning should examine the full spectrum of conceptualisations of creativity and learning, using blended methodologies, measures, and approaches, which combine quantitative studies on large samples, with smaller yet deeper laboratory studies and naturalistic situations.

Acknowledgement

This study was supported by the funding obtained from the National Science Centre (UMO-2016/22/E/HS6/00118).

Note

1. This is not to say that there are no cross-domain influences. Indeed, our results did indicate a modest relationship between academic achievement in math and language and creativity in these domains. This pattern warrants future studies given that this modest correlation could be caused by a common method factor as well, i.e., be driven by more methodological than substantial reasons. More focused, microgenetic studies, exploring the processes and mechanisms involved into solving specific tasks, are needed to better understand these links.

References

Alexander, P. A., Schallert, D. L., & Reynolds, R. E. (2009). What is learning anyway? A topographical perspective considered. *Educational Psychologist, 44*, 176–192.

Alexander, P. A., Singer, L. M., Jablansky, S., & Hattan, C. (2016). Relational reasoning in word and in figure. *Journal of Educational Psychology, 108*(8), 1140–1152.

Anderson, L. W., & Krathwohl, D. R. (Eds.). (2001). *A taxonomy for learning, teaching, and assessing: A revision of Bloom's taxonomy of educational objectives*. New York: Longman.

Anderson, R. C., Haney, M., Pitts, C., Porter, L., & Bousselot, T. (2019). "Mistakes can be beautiful": Creative engagement in arts integration for early adolescent learners. *The Journal of Creative Behavior*. https://doi.org/10.1002/jocb.401

Andiliou, A., & Murphy, P. K. (2010). Examining variations among researchers' and teachers' conceptualizations of creativity: A review and synthesis of contemporary research. *Educational Research Review, 5*, 201–219.

Baer, J. (2014). *Creativity and divergent thinking: A task-specific approach*. New York: Psychology Press.

Baird, B., Smallwood, J., Mrazek, M. D., Kam, J. W. Y., Franklin, M. S., & Schooler, J. W. (2012). Inspired by distraction: Mind wandering facilitates creative incubation. *Psychological Science, 23*(10), 1117–1122.

Beauducel, A., & Herzberg, P. Y. (2006). On the performance of maximum likelihood versus means and variance adjusted weighted least squares estimation in CFA. *Structural Equation Modeling, 13*(2), 186–203.

Beghetto, R. A. (2016). Creative learning: A fresh look. *Journal of Cognitive Education and Psychology, 15*(1), 6–23.

Beghetto, R. A. (2020). Large scale assessment, personalized learning, and creativity: Paradoxes and possibilities. *ECNU Review of Education, 2*, 311–327. https://doi.org/10.1177/2096531119878963

Beghetto, R. A., & Schuh, K. (2020). Exploring the connection between imagination and creativity in academic learning. In D. D. Preiss, D. Cosmelli, & J. C. Kaufman (Eds.), *Creativity and the wandering mind: Spontaneous and controlled cognition* (pp. 250–270). San Diego, CA: Academic Press.

Condon, D. M., & Revelle, W. (2014). The international cognitive ability resource: Development and initial validation of a public-domain measure. *Intelligence, 43*, 52–64.

Dollinger, S. J. (2011). "Standardized minds" or individuality? Admissions tests and creativity revisited. *Psychology of Aesthetics, Creativity, and the Arts, 5*(4), 329.

Dul, J. (2016). Necessary Condition Analysis (NCA) logic and methodology of "necessary but not sufficient" causality. *Organizational Research Methods, 19*(1), 10–52.

Dul, J., van der Laan, E., & Kuik, R. (2018). A statistical significance test for necessary condition analysis. *Organizational Research Methods, 23*, 385–395. https://doi.org/10.1177/1094428118795272

Dumas, D. (2018). Relational reasoning and divergent thinking: An examination of the threshold hypothesis with quantile regression. *Contemporary Educational Psychology, 53*, 1–14.

Dumas, D., & Alexander, P. A. (2016). Calibration of the test of relational reasoning. *Psychological Assessment, 28*, 1303–1318.

Freund, P. A., & Holling, H. (2008). Creativity in the classroom: A multilevel analysis investigating the impact of creativity and reasoning ability on GPA. *Creativity Research Journal, 20*, 309–318. https://doi.org/10.1080/10400410802278776

Gajda, A., Beghetto, R. A., & Karwowski, M. (2017). Exploring creative learning in the classroom: A multi-method approach. *Thinking Skills and Creativity*, *24*, 250–267.

Gajda, A., Karwowski, M., & Beghetto, R. A. (2017). Creativity and academic achievement: A meta-analysis. *Journal of Educational Psychology*, *109*, 269–299.

Gralewski, J., & Karwowski, M. (2012). Creativity and school grades: A case from Poland. *Thinking Skills and Creativity*, 7(3), 198–208.

Gralewski, J., & Karwowski, M. (2013). Polite girls and creative boys? Students' gender moderates accuracy of teachers' ratings of creativity. *Journal of Creative Behavior*, *47*, 290–304. https://doi.org/10.1002/jocb.36

Greiff, S., Wüstenberg, S., Molnár, G., Fischer, A., Funke, J., & Csapó, B. (2013). Complex problem solving in educational contexts – Something beyond G: Concept, assessment, measurement invariance, and construct validity. *Journal of Educational Psychology*, *105*(2), 364–379.

Guilford, J. P. (1950). Creativity. *American Psychologist*, *14*, 469–479.

Guilford, J. P. (1967). *The nature of intelligence*. New York: McGraw Hill.

Hu, L., & Bentler, P. M. (1999). Cutoff criteria for fit indexes in covariance structure analysis: Conventional criteria versus new alternatives. *Structural Equation Modeling: A Multidisciplinary Journal*, *6*(1), 1–55.

Jankowska, D. M., Czerwonka, M., Lebuda, I., & Karwowski, M. (2018). Exploring the creative process: Integrating psychometric and eye-tracking approaches. *Frontiers in Psychology*, *9*. https://doi.org/10.3389/fpsyg.2018.01931

Jauk, E., Benedek, M., Dunst, B., & Neubauer, A. C. (2013). The relationship between intelligence and creativity: New support for the threshold hypothesis by means of empirical breakpoint detection. *Intelligence*, *41*, 212–221.

Karwowski, M. (2018). The flow of learning. *Europe's Journal of Psychology*, *14*, 291–295.

Karwowski, M., Dul, J., Gralewski, J., Jauk, E., Jankowska, D. M., Gajda, A., . . . Benedek, M. (2016). Is creativity without intelligence possible? A necessary condition analysis. *Intelligence*, *57*, 105–117.

Karwowski, M., & Gralewski, J. (2013). Threshold hypothesis: Fact or artifact? *Thinking Skills and Creativity*, *8*, 25–33.

Karwowski, M., Kaufman, J. C., Lebuda, I., Szumski, G., & Firkowska-Mankiewicz, A. (2017). Intelligence in childhood and creative achievements in middle-age: The necessary condition approach. *Intelligence*, *64*, 36–44.

Kaufman, J. C., Plucker, J. A., & Baer, J. (2008). *Essentials of creativity assessment* (Vol. 53). New York: John Wiley & Sons.

Kim, K. H. (2008). Underachievement and creativity: Are gifted underachievers highly creative? *Creativity Research Journal*, *20*(2), 234–242.

Koenker, R. (2018). *Quantreg: Quantile regression. R package version 5.36*. Retrieved from https://cran.r-project.org/web/packages/quantreg/index.html

Koenker, R., & Hallock, K. F. (2001). Quantile regression. *Journal of Economic Perspectives*, *15*, 143–156.

Krathwohl, D. R. (2002). A revision of Bloom's taxonomy: An overview. *Theory into Practice*, *41*, 212–218.

Lee, C. S., Huggins, A. C., & Therriault, D. J. (2014). A measure of creativity or intelligence? Examining internal and external structure validity evidence of the Remote Associates Test. *Psychology of Aesthetics, Creativity, and the Arts*, *8*, 446–460.

Leopold, C., Mayer, R., & Dutke, S. (2018). The power of imagination and perspective in learning from science text. *Journal of Educational Psychology*, Advance online publication. http://doi.org/10.1037/edu0000310

Mayer, R. E., & Gallini, J. K. (1990). When is an illustration worth ten thousand words? *Journal of Educational Psychology, 82*(4), 715–726.

McKay, A. S., Karwowski, M., & Kaufman, J. C. (2017). Measuring the muses: Validating the Kaufman Domains of Creativity Scale (K-DOCS). *Psychology of Aesthetics, Creativity, and the Arts*, 216–230.

McNeish, D., & Dumas, D. (2017). Nonlinear growth models as measurement models: A second-order growth curve model for measuring potential. *Multivariate Behavioral Research, 52*, 61–85.

Mooneyham, B. W., & Schooler, J. W. (2013). The costs and benefits of mind-wandering: A review. *Canadian Journal of Experimental Psychology/Revue Canadienne de Psychologie Expérimentale, 67*, 11–18.

Rosseel, Y. (2012). Lavaan: An R package for structural equation modeling. *Journal of Statistical Software, 48*, 1–36.

Rubenstein, L. D., Callan, G. L., & Ridgley, L. M. (2018). Anchoring the creative process within a self-regulated learning framework: Inspiring assessment methods and future research. *Educational Psychology Review, 30*, 921–945.

Runco, M. A., & Jaeger, G. J. (2012). The standard definition of creativity. *Creativity Research Journal, 24*(1), 92–96. http://doi.org/10.1080/10400419.2012.650092

Sak, U., & Maker, C. J. (2006). Developmental variation in children's creative mathematical thinking as a function of schooling, age, and knowledge. *Creativity Research Journal, 18*(3), 279–291.

Sawyer, K. (1992). Improvisational creativity: An analysis of jazz performance. *Creativity Research Journal, 5*(3), 253–263.

Silvia, P. J., Martin, C., & Nusbaum, E. C. (2009). A snapshot of creativity: Evaluating a quick and simple method for assessing divergent thinking. *Thinking Skills and Creativity, 4*(2), 79–85.

Simonton, D. K. (2009). Varieties of (scientific) creativity a hierarchical model of domain-specific disposition, development, and achievement. *Perspectives on Psychological Science, 4*(5), 441–452.

Simonton, D. K. (2017). Big-C versus little-c Creativity: Definitions, implications, and inherent educational contradictions. In R. Beghetto & B. Sriraman (Eds.), *Creative contradictions in education: Creativity theory and action in education*. Cham: Springer.

Skiba, T., Tan, M., Sternberg, R. J., & Grigorenko, E. L. (2016). Roads not taken, new roads to take: Looking for creativity in the classroom. In R. A. Beghetto & J. C. Kaufman (Eds.), *Nurturing creativity in the classroom* (pp. 108–130). New York: Cambridge University Press.

Tabach, M., & Friedlander, A. (2013). School mathematics and creativity at the elementary and middle-grade levels: How are they related? *ZDM, 45*(2), 227–238.

Treffinger, D. J., Isaksen, S. G., & Firestien, R. L. (1983). Theoretical perspectives on creative learning and its facilitation: An overview. *Journal of Creative Behavior, 17*, 9–17.

Vygotsky, L. S. (2004). Imagination and creativity in childhood. (Trans. M. E. Sharpe, Inc.). *Journal of Russian and East European Psychology, 42*, 7–97 (Original work published 1967).

Wainer, H., Bradlow, E. T., & Wang, X. (2007). *Testlet response theory and its applications*. New York: Cambridge University Press.

Westby, E. L., & Dawson, V. L. (1995). Creativity: Asset or burden in the classroom? *Creativity Research Journal, 8*, 1–10.

Wüstenberg, S., Greiff, S., & Funke, J. (2012). Complex problem solving – More than reasoning? *Intelligence, 40*, 1–14.

2 Social Creativity in the Education Sector

The Case of Collaborative Design of Digital Resources in Mathematics

Chronis Kynigos, Nataly Essonnier, and Jana Trgalová

Introduction

Most researchers on human creativity would agree that it is highly context specific and context bound. Our research aimed to shed light on creativity generated amongst professionals in the field of education, specifically in the process of co-designing digital resources to inspire creativity in students' mathematical thinking. We call it *social creativity* (defined in Section 1). We adopted the recently recognised view (Laurillard, 2012; Jones & Pepin, 2016) that mathematics teachers can be considered amongst other stakeholders designing resources and activities for their students. We organised the collaboration of diverse groups of professionals, including teachers, for the design and development of innovative resources using innovative technologies (Kynigos & Kolovou, 2018). The research was carried out in the framework of the MC2 European project (www.mc2-project.eu/, 2013–2016), aiming at developing a socio-technical environment facilitating and enhancing the design of educational digital resources, called c-books (lowercase c for creative). A c-book is a digital book gathering activities aimed to foster students' creative mathematical thinking and learning. The technical part of the environment consisted of the so-called C-book (uppercase C) technology, embedding a collaborative tool named CoICode[1] and an authoring tool containing interactive multi-representational digital artefacts (widgets).

Four communities of designers established in four partner countries – France, Greece, Spain, and United Kingdom – constituted the social part of the environment. The French community, whose work is reported on in this chapter, brought together educational designers from diverse mathematical fields with a variety of expertise and knowledge (researchers, teacher educators, teachers, software designers, etc.) because the process of designing purposeful mathematical activities in a multi-representational technical environment is complex. An aspect of this complexity comes from the interrelated processes of

> learning to use a new technology for purposeful mathematical activity, designing tasks for students to initiate purposeful mathematical activity; collating the various artefacts that comprise the "document system" for

> the activity; supporting students to learn to use technology for purposeful mathematical activity; articulating the teacher's role in supporting the students to navigate their respective routes through the various artefacts that comprise the activity to include interaction with the technology.
>
> (Clark-Wilson & Timotheus, 2013, p. 48)

In this chapter, we aim at contributing to the study of resource designers' creativity by reporting how c-book design inspired social creativity. We also highlight factors that foster or hinder social creativity in the collaborative c-book design process. Studying these complex design processes required several theoretical perspectives that we tried to articulate. We start by explaining our theoretical framework and the conceptualisation of social creativity. We pursue by refining our research questions and by outlining our methodology before presenting an analysis of one case study. We discuss our results before concluding.

Theoretical Framework and Research Questions

In the educational sector, and more particularly in mathematics education, collaborative design of creative digital educational resources within a socio-technical environment is a complex human activity. It intertwines a multitude of interactions and elements that are difficult to capture without relevant lenses. The articulation of different theoretical approaches exposed in the sequel was not an initial goal or an end in itself. It rather played the functional role of employing existing knowledge to better understand and evaluate the elusive concept of social creativity within a socio-technical environment. This environment hosted and nurtured the collaborative design within a specific context, created by the challenge to develop a new kind of mediation fostering creativity in designers and students.

In order to understand the process of collaborative design of digital resources and the interactions between the designers, including not only face-to-face meetings but also mediated contact (Glăveanu, 2011), we found relevant to use, as a first lens, the *activity theory* (AT). Following Engeström (2001), the first generation of activity theory is built around Vygotsky's (1978) idea of *cultural mediation of action* according to which human activity is mediated by artefacts and signs available in the individual's social environment. It presents a limitation residing in the fact that "the unit of analysis remained individually focused" (p. 134). This limitation was overcome by the second generation, drawing on Leont'ev's (1978) perspective taking into account the social dimension of human activity (ibid.). The concept of activity became central, turning "the focus on complex interrelations between the individual subject and his or her community" (ibid., pp. 134–135). These complex interrelations are represented by the activity system model (Figure 2.1) proposed by Engeström (1987). This model brings to the

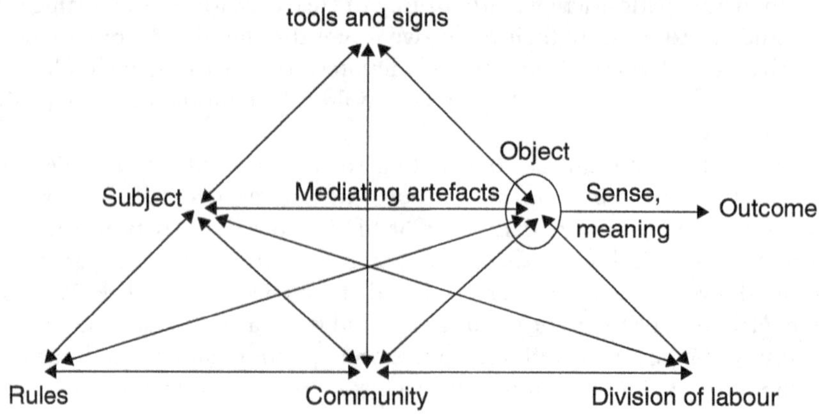

Figure 2.1 The structure of an activity system

Source: Engeström (1987, p. 78).

fore particular elements or entities implicated in the activity and the mediation between these entities.

The entities instantiated to our case of collaborative design activity are:

- the *subject* which can be a designer or a group of designers;
- the *object* which is the design of one or several c-books;
- the *community* with which the subject interacts;
- the *rules* which govern the design process;
- the *division of labour* which occurs among the designers;
- the *tools and signs* used by the designers; and
- the *outcome* which is the aim and the result of the design process being the designed resource or learning that can occur during the design process.

The third generation of activity theory expands the basic model "to include minimally two interacting activity systems" (Engeström, 2001, p. 136), as depicted in Figure 2.2.

According to Engeström (ibid.),

> the object moves from an initial state of unreflected, situationally given "raw material" (object 1 [. . .]) to a collectively meaningful object constructed by the activity system (object 2 [. . .]), and to a potentially shared or jointly constructed object (object 3 [. . .]).

The third generation of AT became the *cultural-historical activity theory* (CHAT) which copes with the global multidisciplinary research approach

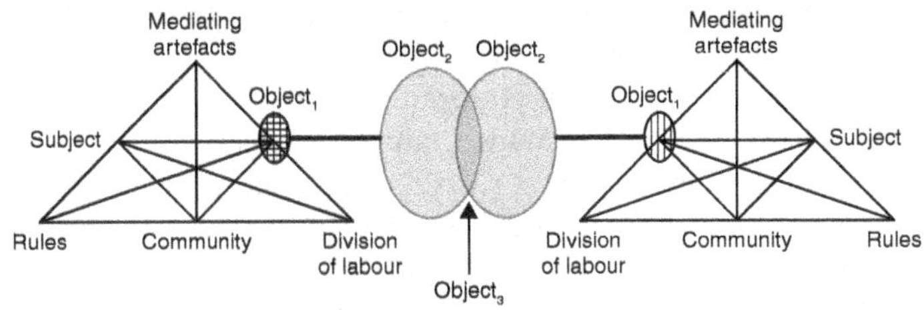

Figure 2.2 Two interacting activity systems

Source: Engeström (2001, p. 136).

(see Engeström, 1998; Chaiklin, Hedegaard, & Jensen, 1999) and which was also increasingly oriented toward the study of work and technologies (Nardi, 1996).

Instantiating the activity system to our case allows us to highlight the context of the design process. Likewise, it sheds light on and makes us aware of the interactions occurring between different individual activity systems that are characterised by a *subject* who represents only one designer.

However, CHAT does not allow us to understand either the nature of the entities or the kinds of interactions between these entities. In order to capture the nature of the *subject* and *community*, we draw on the concepts of *community of practice* and *community of interest.* Communities of Practice (CoP) are

> groups of people who share a concern, a set of problems, or a passion about a topic, and who deepen their knowledge and expertise in this area by interacting on an ongoing basis.
>
> (Wenger, McDermott, & Snyder, 2002, p. 4)

Three components characterise a CoP (Wenger, 1998): a shared *domain* that defines the CoP identity, a *community* of members who interact and engage in shared activities, help each other, and share information with each other, and a common *practice*; whilst Communities of Interest (CoI) "bring together stakeholders from different CoPs to solve a particular (design) problem of common concern" (Fischer, 2001, p. 4). CoI members thus represent multiple domains of knowledge and different practices. They are gathered together temporarily to solve a "particular (design) problem of common concern". Our choice of a CoI as designers' community was guided by the fact that the creative potential of a CoI is greater than the one of a CoP, as Fischer (2001) says: "CoIs, by bringing different CoPs together, provide unique opportunities to bring social creativity alive by transcending individual perspectives" (p. 11). Indeed, within a CoI of designers, each designer belongs to a unique "world" constituted by her culture, her history, and her knowledge bound to her domain of expertise.

Hence, within a CoI, there are several "worlds". These worlds have boundaries which can be seen as social and cultural dissimilarities, leading to discontinuity in action or interaction (Akkerman & Bakker, 2011, p. 133) between the designers. These discontinuities are what John-Steiner (2000, p. 3) called "shared struggles", which could lead to break down communication but also to new insight. It is therefore important, while studying collaborative resource design, to pay particular attention to what happens at those boundaries and to the boundary crossing mechanisms at stake. Thus, the *boundary crossing approach* (BC) (ibid.) enables us to enlighten the importance of boundaries and boundary crossing mechanisms in the creative design process. According to Akkerman and Bakker (2011), four dialogical mechanisms take place at the boundaries: *identification, coordination, reflection,* and *transformation*, defined in Table 2.1.

These mechanisms are related to the concepts of *boundary object* and *broker*. Star and Griesemer (1989) define boundary objects as "objects which are both plastic enough to adapt to local needs and the constraints of the several parties employing them, yet robust enough to maintain a common identity across sites" (p. 393), the word "site" meaning a particular social world. Boundary crossing is bound to interactions between different entities such as the *subject* – *community* – (*signs and tools* or *object* or *outcome*), or between two or more individual activity systems (Akkerman & Bakker, 2011, p. 140). It is also the matter of individuals or groups, called *brokers*, who act as a "bridge" between two worlds whose knowledge, practices, and language are different (ibid.).

Table 2.1 Overview of different mechanisms and related characteristic processes of boundary crossing

Dialogical Learning Mechanisms	*Meaning and Characteristic Processes*
Identification	Encountering boundaries (othering: delineating how a practice differs from another; legitimating coexistence: considering interferences between multiple memberships).
Coordination	Overcoming boundaries in order to facilitate future and effortless movements between social worlds (communicative connection, efforts of translation, increasing boundary permeability, routinisation).
Reflection	Realising and explicating differences between practices to emphasise comprehension, the formulation of distinctive perspectives (perspective making, perspective taking).
Transformation	Entailing the emergence of new in-between practices (confrontation, recognising shared problem space, hybridisation, crystallisation, maintaining uniqueness of intersecting practices, continuous joint work at the boundary).

Source: Adapted from Akkerman & Bakker (2011, p. 151).

Finally, in order to highlight the role of the teachers (*subjects*) involved in the design, in relation with their personal resources (*signs and tools*) brought into play in the design, and the trajectory of the digital resource being designed, we draw on the documentational approach to didactics (DAD) (Gueudet & Trouche, 2009). The notion of resource designates any "thing" with which the teacher interacts that can re-source the teaching practice, such as a textbook, a software, or a discussion with a colleague. DAD considers that teachers' resources are not isolated, but rather form a more or less structured system, called a resource system. From the DAD perspective, design of a c-book can be viewed as a resource that is collaboratively elaborated. The trajectory of such a resource can be observed through its different versions. The initial version is a set of resources coming from one or more designers' resource system(s), called *mother resources* (Hammoud, 2012). During the design process, these resources are transformed (instrumentalisation) and give rise to intermediate resources. The final version is the resource ready to be used by a teacher in the classroom, called *daughter resource* (ibid.). The different stages of a resource, from *mother resources* to *daughter resource*, enlighten the trajectory of the resource, its mediation from the *object* to the *outcome*. To sum up, the model of an activity system structure (Figure 2.1) was our main framework allowing to connect all the others through the entities of the activity system. Based on this, we have been able to conceptualise our understanding of social creativity.

As a matter of fact, different types of creativity are reported in literature. We have chosen the *little-c* creativity (Craft, 2000), which is when a person realises a new or improved way to approach an issue or accomplish a task. Moreover, creativity, social or individual, can be modelled through phases of divergent (novel ideas) and convergent thinking (appropriate and usable ideas; Csikszentmihalyi, 1996), constituting a creativity cycle. Hence, social creativity is characterised by the reification of creative ideas collaboratively elaborated, i.e., elaborated by at least two CoI members. We draw also on the concept of CoIs for characterising our communities of designers. Thus, within the MC2 project, we have defined social creativity as the generation of ideas which:

- stem from a combination of two or more individual activity systems;
- result from various interactions among the CoI members, the C-book technology, and tools;
- are externalised in and through specific digital artefacts (including the c-books); and
- are considered by the CoI members to be *novel*, *appropriate*, and *usable*.

(Daskolia, 2015)

It enabled us to address the following research questions. In the collaborative design of c-books,

- what interactions between *rules*, *community*, and *division of labour* promote or hinder social creativity?

- what types of objects have the potential to become *boundary objects*, under which conditions, and how can they stimulate social creativity?
- which members have the potential to become *brokers*, under what conditions, and what is their role in stimulating social creativity?
- how has c-book design inspired social creativity?

Methodology and Data

In the collaborative design of c-books, we have distinguished three levels of design. At a macro level, the design of c-books by a CoI within the MC2 project (15 c-books) is considered; at a meso level, the focus is on the design of one particular c-book within a CoI; and at a micro level, we study the re-design of a c-book by teachers for its use with students. Only the design process at a meso level is studied in this chapter.

The methodology comprises two main stages. The first stage consisted in analysing in detail the context of the activity of a c-book design by an in-depth study of the entities involved in activity, referring to the Engeström's (1987) model (Figure 2.1). This qualitative analysis was based on data collected by various instruments used in the project, such as

- the "CoI profile" intended to gather information about the identity of the CoI, both as a whole and as a configuration of individuals, and the undertaken procedures for its formation, as well as the CoI's intended role and aspired activity and production plan;
- the "CoI moderation" aiming at providing the rationale informing the process of CoI moderation, including the strategy to be used, suggested orchestrations of the CoI activities, and procedures for facilitating and supporting the CoI's creative performance.

These documents were completed by the CoI steering committee at the beginning of each of the three cycles of c-book design. Additional data come from the minutes of the meetings and the emails exchanged between the designers.

The second stage of the methodology consisted in studying social creativity taking place during the design process of each c-book produced, i.e., at the meso level. It was based on a five-level evaluation method elaborated within the MC2 project (Table 2.2). The method allowed the researchers to zoom on social creativity from general features to more specific ones. Its operationalisation was realised differently in the four partners' countries (Greece, France, Spain, and UK). In Table 2.2, we present the operationalisation done by the French researchers. The data on which this stage relies was mainly collected via the communication tool (CoICode) that keeps traces of interactions in the form of threaded map (see Figure 2.3) or of a forum. Each post made by a designer into CoICode is considered as an idea. Additional data was gathered through minutes of meetings (between the

Table 2.2 Method for evaluating and studying social creativity

Level	*Focus*	*Method and Data*
1	Overall social creativity rate	Quantitative analysis yielding a composite score (rate), based on four components (fluency, flexibility, originality, and social elaboration) automatically extracted from data registered in the workspace of the CoICode communication tool. More details are provided on these components in Section 3.
2	Creativity score (per idea)	Quantitative analysis providing an aggregate score of the registered votes of the CoI members on all ideas expressed in the workspace of the communication tool in terms of novelty, appropriateness, and usability. See Section 3 for some details.
3	Main stages of the design process	Qualitative analysis aiming at identifying and mapping out of the creativity cycles, i.e., divergent and convergent phases, and versions of the c-book during the design process. It was done by studying the flow of ideas in CoICode and their creativity score obtained in level 2.
4	Path of a creative idea	Qualitative analysis of selected cases of creative ideas in terms of critical moments in their timeline of development in the design process. The data collected in the communication tool in the form of the threaded map, correlated with the other data, is analysed with the lenses of boundary crossing approach to identify boundary objects and brokers and their role in the design and of DAD to highlight resources put into play in the design process.
5	Critical episode	In-depth qualitative analysis of selected segments of an activity (including discourse activity) focusing on the interaction between CoI members and with the socio-technical environment.

Source: Adapted from Trgalová (2016, p. 25).

designers, the CoI members), exchanged emails, and the designed c-books. It was completed by interviews when necessary.

The first two levels provide quantitative information: social creativity rate and scores of creative ideas generated during the c-book design that are automatically computed from the data collected in CoICode. These scores give an overall view of social creativity during the design process and a creative score per idea, in line with the *componential* and *consensual* tradition of creativity assessment (Hennessey & Amabile, 1999; see Section 3). These quantitative levels are detailed in Trgalová (2016, pp. 30–33). The next three levels are based on qualitative analyses and aim at getting a deeper insight into social creativity processes.

The third level aims at identifying the trajectory of the construction of a c-book in its different versions, drawing on the DAD to pinpoint recurrent patterns in the design process and their correlations with emergent forms of social creativity. It allows us to enlighten creative cycles (divergent and convergent phases) between two versions. This level of analysis is based on the "evolving system" approach to creative work (Gruber, 1988), viewing creativity as an evolving process over time, with various situational factors intervening and interacting with each other.

The fourth level focuses on the trajectory of creative ideas identified at the second level (creative ideas scores), leading to the study of the path of a creative idea chosen by the researchers. The analysis of the path of creative ideas enables us to highlight conditions for the emergence of creative interactions among CoI members, such as the role of specific resources (DAD), the role of *boundary objects* and *brokers* (BC), or the complementarity of the designers' background and culture.

At the fifth level, critical episodes identified from results of the previous levels are studied. The selection of an episode is related to one (or more) research question(s). This level of analysis focuses on highlighting and discussing aspects of social creativity and how they emerged in and were supported by the particular socio-technical environment.

Analysis of the Collaborative Design of C-books Within the French CoI

The Overall Creativity Rate of Seven C-books (Level 1)

The overall creativity rate[2] of the design process of one c-book is computed with four equally weighted components – fluency, flexibility, originality, and social elaboration – based on CoICode data. The rate is included between 0 and 100%. Fluency is defined as the total number of ideas generated during the design process. Flexibility is the ability to suggest varied perspectives for an idea towards a problem or situation. In CoICode tree representation (see Figure 2.6), expanding an idea is represented by a node stemming from the one in which the initial idea is posted. Thus, when several nodes stem from the same node, it means that the idea expressed in this node is further developed in various directions. Flexibility can thus be defined as a mean value of the out-degrees of the CoICode nodes. Originality is the ability to generate ideas that are novel, appropriate, and usable, at least to the minds of the CoI members, complying with the consensual assessment technique. In order to gather the CoI members' judgement about the creative character of ideas generated during the c-book design process, a voting mechanism has been integrated in the CoICode: for each idea expressed in the CoICode, each CoI member, except the author of the idea, can express his/her opinion on whether the idea is novel, appropriate, and usable. We therefore consider an idea as creative for that user if (s)he votes "yes" for the three indicators. Originality is thus defined as the sum of the originality votes divided by the number of votes. Finally, social elaboration represents the elaboration of an idea by two or more designers. In CoICode, we assume that an elaborated

Table 2.3 French c-books overall creative rate

c-book	*Fluency*	*Flexibility*	*Originality*	*Social Elaboration*	*Overall Creativity Rate out of 100 (%)*
Ski	110	1,56	0,41	0,63	**59,0**
Experimental geometry	75	2,46	0,33	0,57	**61,5**
Rearth (chap IX)	34	2,38	0,04	0,32	**46,3**
Maths for biology	110	1,93	0,44	0,86	**68,8**
Bicycle	31	1,87	0,75	0,14	**56,5**
Rearth (chap X)	11	2,25	0,43	0	**0**
Elementary algebra	27	1,46	1	0	**0**

Source: Trgalová (2016, p. 32).

idea corresponds to a branch having at least two nodes. Considering social elaboration, the branch should contain at least three nodes posted by at least two different CoI members. In order to guarantee that we do not count an idea elaborated just by one CoI member, we first collapse the CoICode graph regarding contributors: if an edge links two nodes from the same contributor, it will be collapsed. Social elaboration score is therefore based on the number of different contributors counted along the branch going up to the root multiplied by the depth of the branch. If the social elaboration score is 0, then the overall creativity rate is 0. Table 2.3 gives an overview of the scores for the c-books designed by the French CoI.

We observe that the overall creativity rate of the c-book "Ski" was 59 out of 100, one of the highest scores for a c-book. This c-book was also the only c-book intended to be used with students from the beginning. Therefore, we found it interesting to have an in-depth understanding of its design process. We wanted to point out what fostered social creativity guided by the questions formulated previously.

A Snippet of the Collaborative Design of the C-book "Ski"

In this section, we illustrate a snippet of our analysis of social creativity on the c-book "Ski". The c-book embeds mathematics into a story about ski touring and more particularly about the risk of provoking an avalanche while practicing ski touring.

Context of the Design of the c-book "Ski"

Drawing on the activity model, we can describe and analyse the context of the design activity (Figure 2.3).

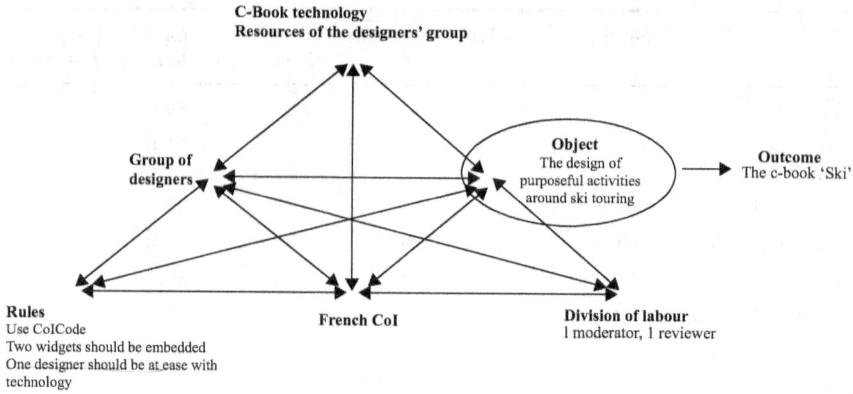

Figure 2.3 The structure of the design of the c-book "Ski"

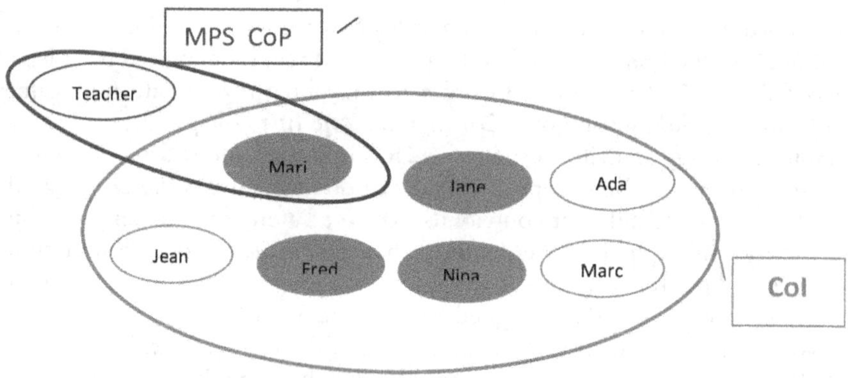

Figure 2.4 The designers of the c-book "Ski" and the CoI or CoP to which they belong

The aim (*object*) of the design process was to create meaningful mathematical activities linked to the risks of provoking an avalanche while practicing ski touring to foster students' mathematical learning and creativity (purposeful activities). The group of designers (Figure 2.4) was composed of seven members of the French CoI, all closely related to mathematics education with knowledge on mathematics, technology, and pedagogy and sharing a constructivist background.

Four members acted as the main designers: Nina (secondary mathematics and physics teacher and PhD student, with a good knowledge of the C-book technology), who moderated the group; Marie (researcher and mathematics teacher educator, expert in mathematical modelling); Fred (mathematics teacher educator, interested in real problems); and Jane (mathematics teacher educator, interested in digital technology in mathematics education), who played the role of a reviewer. The other three members, Marc (expert of digital technology such as dynamic geometry systems), Jean, and Adam, intervened on request or during CoI meetings (*division of labour*). The designers' group was constituted in a way that amongst the main designers, at least one was at ease with digital technologies and more particularly with the socio-technical environment (*rules*). The designed c-book (*outcome*) should be used by a teacher of an associated CoP, called MPS, to which Marie belongs (*rules*). This CoP reflects on the use of mathematics for solving interdisciplinary problems with Grade 10 students.

Analysis of the c-book "Ski"

This analysis follows the levels of the evaluation method described previously (see Table 2.2).

CREATIVITY SCORES PER IDEA (LEVEL 2)

Out of the 110 ideas posted in CoICode, 14 ideas were identified as creative. Table 2.4 shows some of these creative ideas and their scores.

We note that some creative ideas were related to the context of ski touring, such as

- "Picture of snowflakes", used in the c-book as a starting point for geometrical tasks, within an activity on snowflakes geometry. Indeed, the shape of snow crystals led to working on geometric figures, transformations, and sequences;
- "Measure the slopes with ski poles" and "Why slopes with more than 30 degrees are dangerous?" that gave birth to tasks requiring knowledge of trigonometry. The question about the angle of 30 degrees bound to the avalanche risk led to the design of a simulation of a snowy slope.

Other creative ideas were linked with the technology, such as "search with GeoGebra" which conducted to algorithms with programming of

Table 2.4 Examples of creative idea with scores extracted from CoICode

Author	*Title*	*Appropriate*	*Usable*	*Novel*	*Creative Score*
Marie	Why slopes with more than 30 degrees are dangerous?	5	5	5	5
Marie	Measure of the slope with ski poles	5	5	3	4
Marc	Simulation or programming?	5	5	2	3,5
Fred	Search with GeoGebra	3	2	2	2,25
Nina	Picture of snowflakes	2	2	2	2

an avalanche victim search device. The creative idea "Simulation or programming?" was linked to mathematics as it was a simulation enabling the reader to work on angles and programming or algorithms. Hence, the designers aimed at making sense of mathematical notions and concepts through these ideas. We observed that the c-book (*outcome*) was indeed making connections between the creative ideas and the activities. The designers took the opportunity to create meaningful and purposeful mathematical activities.

MAIN STAGES OF THE DESIGN PROCESS (LEVEL 3)

At this level, the trajectory of the c-book design process towards its versions is analysed, drawing on the framework described in Section 1. We identified four versions of the c-book. The initial version was constituted by Marie's personal resources on the theme of avalanche and skiing (*mother resources* = *object 1*), as she had already worked on this topic within the MPS CoP and experimented some activities with Grade 10 students. From her numerous resources shared within the MPS CoP, Marie selected several that she instrumentalised through ColCode posts (*object 2*) (*reflection mechanism* = *perspective making*). Then, a divergence phase was initiated by a brainstorming session amongst the CoI members. It generated nine new directions on real situations and mathematical notions (*reflection mechanism* = *perspective making*). Some of the creative ideas presented earlier emerged during this phase. This phase was followed by a phase of convergence (*identification*, *coordination*, and *transformation mechanisms*) characterised by the collective elaboration of some of these ideas. For instance, some artefacts already known within the French CoI, such as GeoGebra or Cinderella, were proposed to simulate an avalanche. Such a simulation was intended to encourage students to make conjectures about the risks, or to program an avalanche victim search device, which would allow introducing the notion of algorithm. In this cycle, no idea was rejected, but all ideas were transformed in shared perspectives (*mechanism of reflection* = *perspective taking*) or widgets (*objects 3*). We consider that the two phases of divergence – convergence constitute a *creativity cycle*. They led to the second version of the c-book pictured through a defined structure and content based on the preparation of a ski tour as a guideline for the story that would guarantee a unity for the c-book.

In the following creativity cycle, the creative ideas were mainly bound to the technology and the designers' technical knowledge. For instance, some suggestions were done about guidelines on how to use GeoGebra for creating snowflakes, or about relevant feedback for students to foster their interactions with the c-book. Some widgets, not familiar within the French CoI, were proposed. The copy/paste possibilities inside the Chat tool were added to facilitate interactions between students or between students and the teacher (social aspects).

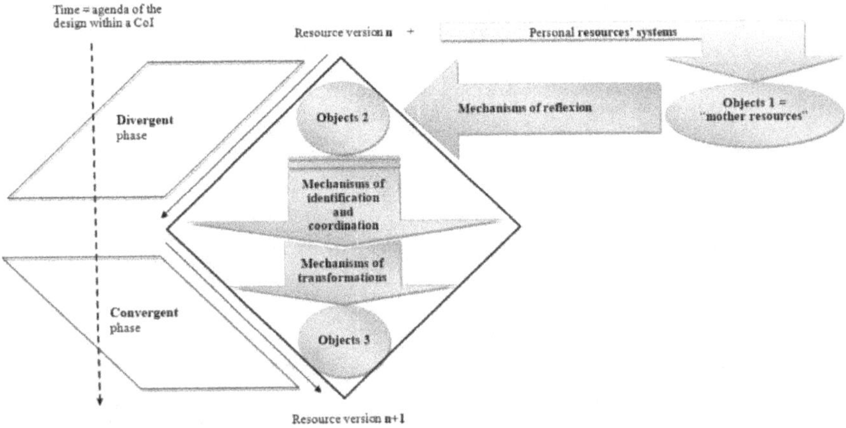

Figure 2.5 Model of versioning of the c-book collaborative design process

Source: Essonnier (2018).

During the third creativity cycle, the main concern of the designers was the usability of the c-book by the teachers and students from Grade 10 to 12. They were also interested in creating unity between all the activities thanks to a story on ski touring and avalanche risk. Hence, the focus of the designers changed from one cycle to the other. Regarding social creativity, we noticed that a divergent phase was often initiated by a review of the current c-book version by the reviewer or by critical feedback from some CoI members, less involved in the design (*reflection mechanism*). Each version was the result of a creativity cycle, i.e., a divergent phase followed by a convergent one as modelled in Figure 2.5.

PATH OF A CREATIVE IDEA (LEVEL 4)

We have chosen to analyse the path of the idea "Search with Geogebra"[3] (see Table 2.4) because of its strong collective elaboration. This creative idea (circled in Figure 2.6) was preceded by Marie's suggestion to create an activity on algorithms bound to the search of a victim of an avalanche (*mother resource*). From an interview with Marie, it appeared that within the MPS CoP, this activity was done outdoor in the playground of the school, where several cones were placed, one of them representing a hypothetical victim of an avalanche: the students were moving step by step one after the other, following a strategy (an algorithm) to find the victim as quickly as possible. The students were guided by the teacher who was telling them "you are closer" or "you are farther". Fred, who knows GeoGebra and the possibility it offers to program the movement of a turtle, has the idea to use it to create a simulation (*reflection mechanism*). This feature is not known to all,

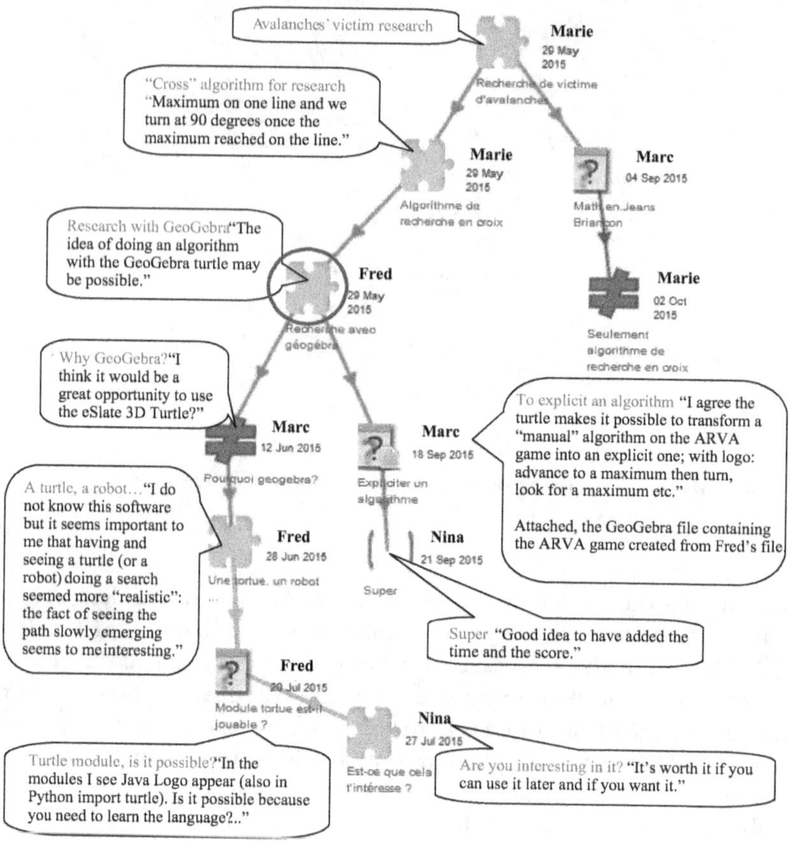

Figure 2.6 Extract of the ColCode workspace dedicated to the c-book "Ski" (in light grey, the title of the post; in quotes, the transcription of the content of the post)

especially Marc who does not know it, but turtle makes him think of "eSlate 3D turtle", software that uses a turtle too. Thus, Fred and Marc seemed to share a common frame of reference around the turtle, which enabled them to understand each other. The word "turtle" became a *boundary object* between them.

Nevertheless, from the meetings minutes we observe that Nina (moderator) noticed that Fred was in trouble because he could not manage to finalise his widget with GeoGebra (*creative idea*) that should allow students to work on algorithms without any programming language. Hence, Nina asked Marc to help Fred. She identified difficulties (*identification mechanism*), and to overcome them, she solicited another member of the CoI (*coordination mechanism*). Marc, expert of GeoGebra, designed the widget, adding time limitation and a score to foster affective aspects in students (*transformation *mechanism* = *hybridisation*, daughter resource). Moreover, Marc was eager to create an algorithm with "eSlate 3D turtle" designed within the Greek CoI, but he did not master the logo language required. He therefore asked the technological expert from the Greek CoI how to write the algorithm, and he eventually created a new widget showing the programming language used (*transformation mechanism* = *hybridisation*, daughter resource). He thus played a role of *broker* looking for knowledge in another CoI, part of the project *community*. Thus, although neither Fred nor Marc knew the widget evoked by the other, the idea of the simulator using the turtle displacement that would visualise the search path of the victim led to the development of two simulations.

CRITICAL EPISODE (LEVEL 5)

We choose here to evoke a critical episode related to the first creativity cycle during which ten creative ideas amongst the 14 creative ideas identified emerged, which is more than in the other cycles. It highlights a positive effect of the compulsory use of CoICode during brainstorming amongst the designers. Indeed, analysis of interactions among the designers during the different creativity cycles shows that CoICode was the main means of collaboration during the first one. This was not the case anymore during the other cycles when other media were also used (emails, minute from meetings). In fact, the designers had the feeling to spare more time for expressing their ideas in CoICode than with other classical media. That's why CoICode was not as strongly used in the other cycles. But, the explicit network of ideas recorded in the CoICode workspace seems to have triggered self-reflection and collaboration among the designers. Indeed, when the CoI members used CoICode, they had to read the ideas of the others and to react on them. Each post in CoICode obliged a designer to reflect on his/her own ideas. The latter had to choose if the idea was new or rather a reaction to another one, and furthermore, what kind of reaction (opposition, contribution, or alternative). Such a structured reflection turned out to boost social creativity.

Discussion

In this section the discussion is organised around our research questions.

- What interactions between *rules*, *community*, and *division of labour* promote or hinder social creativity?

In this study we looked for the conditions which might be conducive to the generation of creativity in the activity of resource design, meaningful in the education sector. We ourselves took part in the design of conditions to facilitate this kind of creativity. The cultural-historical activity theory provided us with tools to understand the process. For instance, we employed the rule of diversity within each main designer group. We perceived diversity as residing within the education sector and, even more closely, within the mathematics education community. So, in this context we found value in diversity with respect to knowledge about technology, mathematics, and mathematical pedagogy. This diversity should thus be understood in terms of complementary expertise of its members broadening the perspectives employed in the design. Particular attention was given to the roles of the actors which were either assigned a priori or emergent in the design process. Such roles for instance were those of moderator, designer, and reviewer. Indeed, the reviewer fostered a divergent phase, while the moderator facilitated a convergent phase, supporting the *creativity cycle* (Figure 2.5). In addition, the use of the communication tool CoICode during the brainstorming phase also seemed to enhance social creativity. Indeed, communicating within CoICode requires one to situate his or her own ideas in relation to the others already expressed, which stimulates both reflection and interactions. The increased number of creative ideas generated when CoICode supported exchanges evidences this observation. In this context, it thus seemed important to organise the moderation within a CoI.

- What types of objects have the potential to become *boundary objects*, under which conditions, and how can they stimulate social creativity?

During the process of collaborative design we noticed that some objects, for example digital artefacts, parts of a c-book, or even specific words, were used in a special way to generate communication and clarity regarding the diverse perspectives and expertise of the participant designers. These objects became critical in the exchange of various ideas which originally emerged from different frames of reference and contexts. They thus operated as objects around which the participants crossed boundaries of knowledge and experience. Such objects became *boundary objects* widening the CoI perspective. Therefore, within a CoI that designs c-books, we can say that potential *boundary objects* are malleable, transformable objects, compatible with the *object* of the design and belonging to the designers' common reference frame. *Boundary objects* helped to extend the common frame of reference between the designers (*coordination*) by enlarging their perspectives. Thus, boundary objects were addressed as facilitators to boundary crossing which revolved around the trajectory of an idea, and boundary crossing was perceived from the point of view of the designers.

- Which members have the potential to become *brokers*, under what conditions, and what is their role in stimulating social creativity?

We found that some members of the CoI played a particular role: they were able to cross boundaries, to bring new relevant knowledge during the design process, to identify missing knowledge for the c-book design, to look for it, and then to share this new knowledge within the CoI. We called them *brokers*. Thus, in our context, we can say that a *broker* is a member of the CoI who identifies missing knowledge within the CoI, then can find it in another related professional world in order to bring it to the CoI. Thus, the *broker* enables a *coordination mechanism* allowing the CoI members to extend their common frame of reference with new knowledge, fostering the generation of creative ideas. Thus, the application of the boundary crossing approach was directly made to help us understand the emergence and evolution of social creativity in the exchanges taking place in a CoI.

The notion of common frame of reference is in line with what Glăveanu (2011, p. 484) calls common representational space. According to the author, each member has a unique representational space. By exploring and communicating together, members come to realise other ways of understanding and doing things. This process enables the common representational spaces to grow. Hence, the enriched personal and common representational spaces foster novel outcomes, corroborating our understanding of the creative process.

- How has c-book design inspired social creativity?

We have been able to follow the transformation and reification of some ideas. We associated an idea reification with the instrumentalisation of resources through the boundary crossing mechanism of *reflection*, i.e., perspective taking and perspective making. We perceived the process of hybridisation as the transformation of an idea by its association with others through the mechanisms of *identification, coordination*, and *transformation*. Thus, a hybrid idea was the result of a creativity cycle and gained in creativity by means of changing as a result of new perspectives, expertise, and knowledge in order to augment the chances of students learning and engaging in creative mathematical thinking, through the use of the embedded affordances in the c-book.

Hence, the design of a c-book allowed us to better understand how ideas are ignited, how they evolve, how they are influenced by the social dynamics of such particular designer communities, and finally, how they are expressed through the instrumentalisation of resources with the available tools at hand.

Concluding Remarks

We have been able to elaborate an operational definition of social creativity to enlighten the collaborative design process of c-books, taking into account the educational context, a socio-technical environment where diversity within its social component should be understood in terms of complementary knowledge which generated creative processes and productions.

Then, the combined use of the five levels evaluation method within our theoretical framework provided a powerful explanatory lens to the nature of social creativity in the c-book design process. The theoretical frameworks were sometimes used as a whole and sometimes only partly to serve the evaluation of social creativity. They were rather perceived as explanatory tools. Hence, this work allowed to forge connections between theories which emerged in a functional way to facilitate the project's objective to elucidate social creativity. The *functional orientation* of the theories was employed to serve the researchers' concerns.

Finally, the designers tried to use CoICode at the beginning of the design process, but its instrumentation needed too many efforts from their part during the design process. That's why CoICode has not been used so significantly in the other cycles of creativity. Therefore, the complexity of the use of our communication tool, CoICode, has limited its utilisation during the design process by the designers.

Notes

1. CoICode is a communication environment part of the socio-technical environment, offering a workspace within which members of a community engaged in a c-book design can collaborate. A workspace is dedicated to each of the designed c-books. The designers' contributions can be viewed in a form of a threading map (see Figure 2.6) and a forum.
2. For more details, see Trgalová (2016).
3. GeoGebra is open access dynamic geometry software, www.geogebra.org/

References

Akkerman, S. F., & Bakker, A. (2011). Boundary crossing and boundary objects. *Review of Educational Research, 81*(2), 132–169.

Chaiklin, S., Hedegaard, M., & Jensen, U. J. (Eds.). (1999), *Activity theory and social practice*. Aarhus: Aarhus University Press.

Clark-Wilson, A., & Timotheus, J. (2013). Designing tasks within a multi-representational technological environment: An emerging rubric. In C. Margolinas (Ed.), *Task design in mathematics education. ICMI study 22* (Vol. 1, pp. 47–54). Oxford, UK: Oxford University Press.

Craft, A. (2000). *Creativity across the primary curriculum: Framing and developing practice.* London: Routledge/Falmer.

Csikszentmihalyi, M. (1996). *Creativity: Flow and the psychology of discovery and invention.* New York: HarperCollins.

Daskolia, M. (Dir.). (2015). *D2.2: Operational definitions and criteria for measuring social creativity in the design of digital educational resources for CMT.* Deliverable of the MC Squared project. FP7, ICT-2013.8.1. Retrieved 17 September 2016 from http://mc2-project.eu/index.php/dissemination

Engeström, Y. (1987). *Learning by expanding: An activity-theoretical approach to developmental research.* Helsinki: Orienta-Konsultit.

Engeström, Y. (1998). Innovative learning in work teams: Analyzing cycles of knowledge creation in practice. In Y. Engeström, R. Miettinen, & R.-L. Punamaki (Eds.), *Perspectives on activity theory* (pp. 377–404). Cambridge: Cambridge University Press.

Engeström, Y. (2001). Expansive learning at work: Toward an activity theoretical reconceptualization. *Journal of Education and Work, 14*(1), 133–156.

Essonnier, N. (2018). *Etude de la conception collaborative de ressources numériques mathématiques au sein d'une communauté d'intérêt*. Doctoral dissertation, Université C. Bernard-Lyon 1, France.

Fischer, G. (2001). Communities of interest: Learning through the interaction of multiple knowledge systems. *Paper presented at 24th Annual Information Systems Research Seminar in Scandinavia* (IRIS 24), Ulvik, Norway.

Glăveanu, V. P. (2011). How are we creative together? Comparing sociocognitive and sociocultural answers. *Theory & psychology, 21*(4), 473–492.

Gruber, H. E. (1988). The evolving systems approach to creative work. *Creativity Research Journal, 1*(1), 27–51.

Gueudet, G., & Trouche, L. (2009). Towards new documentation systems for mathematics teachers? *Educational Studies in Mathematics, 71*(3), 199–218.

Hammoud, R. (2012). *Le travail collectif des enseignants en chimie comme levier pour la mise en œuvre de démarches d'investigation et le développement de connaissances professionnelles*. Doctoral dissertation, Université C. Bernard-Lyon 1, Université Libanaise.

Hennessey, B. A., & Amabile, T. M. (1999). Consensual assessment. In M. A. Runco & S. R. Pritzker (Eds.), *Encyclopedia of creativity* (pp. 34–36). New York: Academic Press.

John-Steiner, V. (2000). *Creative collaboration*. Oxford: Oxford University Press.

Jones, K., & Pepin, B. (2016). Research on mathematics teachers as partners in task design. *Journal of Mathematics Teacher Education, 19*(2/3), 105–121.

Kynigos, C., & Kolovou, A. (2018). Teachers as designers of digital educational resources for creative mathematical thinking. In L. Fan, L. Trouche, C. Qi, S. Rezat, & J. Visnovska (Eds.), *Research on mathematics textbooks and teachers' resources*. ICME-13 Monographs. Cham: Springer.

Laurillard, D. (2012). *Teaching as a design science: Building pedagogical patterns for learning and technology*. London: Routledge.

Leont'ev, A. N. (1978). *Activity, consciousness, and personality*. Englewood Cliffs, NJ: Prentice-Hall.

Nardi, B. A. (Ed.). (1996). *Context and consciousness: Activity theory and human – Computer interaction*. Cambridge, MA: MIT Press.

Star, S. L., & Griesemer, J. R. (1989). Institutional ecology, "translations" and boundary objects: Amateurs and professionals in Berkeley's Museum of Vertebrate Zoology, 1907–1939. *Social Studies of Science, 19*, 387–420.

Trgalová, J. (Dir.). (2016). *D6.3: Report on the creative design process of CoI – Cycle 3*. Deliverable of the MC Squared project. FP7, ICT-2013.8.1. Retrieved 17 September 2016 from http://mc2-project.eu/index.php/dissemination

Vygotsky, L. S. (1978). *Mind in society: The development of higher psychological processes*. Cambridge, MA: Harvard University Press.

Wenger, E. (1998). *Communities of practice: Learning, meaning, identity*. Cambridge: Cambridge University Press.

Wenger, E., McDermott, R., & Snyder, W. M. (2002). *Cultivating communities of practice* (1st ed.). Watertown, MA: Harvard Business School Press.

3 Polyphonic Imagination

Understanding Idea Generation in Multidisciplinary Groups as a Multivoiced Stimulation of Fantasy

Ingunn Johanne Ness and Olga Dysthe

In order to survive fast-changing market environments, organisations need to stimulate creativity and become innovative. As firms continue to place a premium on new and novel product and service offerings, as drivers of their competitive success and survival (Baer & Oldham, 2006), there is a clear imperative for researchers to unpack the pathways leading to creativity. Consequently, organisations must have methods, toolboxes, and processes that can advance and support all the phases of the innovation process (Darsø, 2001). In today's knowledge societies, knowledge is key to innovation, and it is widely accepted that innovations are brought forward in an interactive process consisting of knowledge development and application. As a result, organisations engage in generating and applying new knowledge in order to achieve innovation.

As such, there is a need to understand the particular creative processes leading to innovation. Consequently, organisational creativity, defined as "*the production of novel and useful outcomes (products, services, processes, etc.) by people working together*" (Woodman, Sawyer, & Griffin, 1993, p. 293), has become an important focus in organisations.

Findings from the large ethnographic study this chapter is based on (Ness, 2017; Ness & Riese, 2015; Ness & Søreide, 2014) have shown that the generation of innovative ideas and the production of novel outcomes do not happen automatically. In the groups studied, it was not enough to bring together competent individuals from different disciplines. The creative processes were relational and, indeed, required a dynamic co-construction of knowledge and ideas between group members.

This relational formulation of creativity goes against the traditional view of this phenomenon, which typically considers it as an individual trait (Amabile, 1996, 2008; Barron & Harrington, 1981; Feist, 1998). Instead, this chapter is in line with more recent research on creativity that includes the dynamic relation between the self and others, promoted, among others, by John-Steiner (2000), Sawyer (2003), and Glăveanu (2010). In this chapter, we thus aim to formulate a relational and dialogical account of creativity and support it with research findings from a study of innovation in multidisciplinary groups.

We first briefly review the literature on creativity at an individual and social level and outline the need for a more dynamic approach. This is the rationale behind our sociocultural framework. Then the method of the study and a few key findings are presented. We use these analyses as a point of departure for the discussion on Polyphonic Imagination, a concept that characterises the creative processes in the groups that were investigated. We argue that innovative ideas emerge out of a Polyphonic type of Imagination – the relational and multivoiced stimulation of fantasy in which different voices acknowledge each other. Finally, we summarise the findings in a model focused on the characteristics of group creative processes.

Vygotsky used the notions of imagination, fantasy, creativity, and creative imagination almost interchangeably, stating that in psychology creative activity is called imagination or fantasy (Glăveanu, Karwowski, Jankowska, & de Saint-Laurent, 2016). In this chapter, we follow this and do not go into the distinctions and differences between these concepts.

Gaps in Our Knowledge of Group Creativity

When we look at organisational creativity in the literature, we see that there have been mainly two broad approaches to organisational creativity: one with a focus mainly on the individual, and another with a focus mainly on groups and group interactions (Diehl & Stroebe, 1991; Paulus, 2000; Paulus, Larey, & Ortega, 1995). In both these research streams, however, there is often a separation between the individual and the social and, thus, a need to investigate further the relational dynamics *between* the social and the individual – what happens in-between people as they engage in creative processes together?

In response to this gap, a third research stream has emerged, i.e., research that has increasingly tried to explore collaborative creativity (Hargadon & Bechky, 2006; John-Steiner, 2000; Kurtzberg & Amabile, 2001; Sawyer, 2006) and collaborative knowledge creation (Carlile, 2004; Dillenbourg, 1999; Hargadon & Sutton, 1997; Hämäläinen & Vähäsantanen, 2011; Mercer, 2010; Paavola & Hakkarainen, 2005; Tsoukas, 2009). These social and collective views claim that knowledge and creativity emerge in the interactions between people and, as such, focus more on the interaction than the skills and attributes of each individual.

This chapter explores further such a sociocultural viewpoint, which focuses on the dynamic between the social and the individual, between self and others, and in particular, on the collaboration itself (see Glăveanu, 2010; John-Steiner, 2000; Sawyer, 2003). Along with these authors, we acknowledge the need to investigate creativity as a relational process. In this chapter, relational processes include the collaborative and interdependent co-construction of meaning, knowledge, and ideas between group members from different disciplines. Furthermore, they also refer to the emotional or affective climate within an organisational context.

The point of departure for the theoretical framework is thus a sociocultural perspective on knowledge development with emphasis on how ideas are co-constructed in social interactions which include supportive as well as challenging dialogues.

A Sociocultural View on Knowledge Development

The theoretical framework rests primarily on sociocultural premises regarding knowledge development, and on the idea that knowledge emerges and develops through a process of dialogic co-construction. This co-construction is assumed to take place in the context of an active and dynamic relationship between the social and the individual. Humans exist and develop in intellectual interdependence and social interaction, and they co-construct their knowledge through this interaction (Linell, 2009; Valsiner & van der Veer, 2000).

In this chapter, we examine some basic assumptions of socio-cultural theory, and particularly the concepts of "imagination" and "dialogue and polyphony", by focusing on the scholarship of Lev Vygotsky (1886–1934) and Mikhail Bakhtin (1895–1975).

Imagination

Imagination is, according to Vygotsky (1930/2004), oriented towards the future:

> It is precisely human activity that makes the human being a creature oriented toward the future, creating the future and thus altering his own present. This creative activity, based on the ability of our brain to combine elements, is called imagination or fantasy in psychology.
>
> (pp. 9–10)

For Vygotsky, "imagination, as the basis of all creative activity, is an important component of absolutely all aspects of cultural life, enabling artistic, scientific, and technical creation alike" (Vygotsky, 1930/2004, p. 9). Even though Vygotsky's work on creativity remained incomplete (Moran & John-Steiner, 2003), his thoughts on imagination help us to understand the act of creation. Smolucha and Smolucha (1986) point to how Vygotsky saw imagination as a higher mental function and a consciously directed thought process. Creative thinking involves the collaboration of imagination and thinking in concepts, which is the case for both artistic and scientific creativity. Even though Vygotsky focused on adolescence as the phase when imagination first develops in all its complexity (John-Steiner, Connery, & Marjanovic-Shane, 2010), this ability continues to grow throughout a person's life span. Thus, it has relevance also in groups of adults.

This chapter conceptualises imagination as a higher mental function, mediated by psychological tools (for instance, the way the group members used language and terminology in their communication) but also other technological tools used to help them convey their meaning to the others. Vygotsky (1930/2004) considered imagination a process directly connected with meaning-making. Imagination is, according to Vygotsky, the process whereby the mind takes up known elements and uses and combines them in new ways. An individual's capacity to make connections between objects, events, and tools in his or her life is directly defined by how much that person can imagine someone else's experiences. Imagination "becomes the means by which a person's experience is broadened, because he has to imagine what he has not seen, can conceptualise something from another person's narration and description of what he himself has never directly experienced" (Vygotsky, 1930/2004, p. 17). As group members have different knowledge and experiences, the use of imagination can shed light on how they learn from each other's knowledge and experiences. Vygotsky postulated that imagination and the growth of creativity was shaped primarily by the amount and variety of a person's knowledge and life experiences (Vygotsky, 1930/2004).

Dialogue and Polyphony

In order to explore creative knowledge processes, we focus here on how the group members communicate and interact when generating new ideas. The notion of dialogue is thus crucial to examine meaning making processes and the development of new knowledge and understanding that often emerge in the tension between different perspectives (Dysthe, 2001; Igland & Dysthe, 2001; Morson & Emerson, 1990).

Dialogue is a central concept in the work of Mikhail Bakhtin, comprising both an ontological and an epistemological understanding. Dialogue was, according to Bakhtin, both a fact of life and, at the same time, an ideal to strive for. In this chapter, we draw on Bakhtin's notion of dialogue which focuses on how meaning, knowledge, and creativity are developed in the tension between different voices. Secondly, we draw on the way dialogue acknowledges different voices in order to avoid a mindset that is monological (i.e., dominated by a single perspective).

Bakhtin claimed that "A dialogue is a combination of voices, it is polyphonic. The voices in a dialogue are persons speaking "in concert", but a person engaged in a dialogue is not restricted to one voice" (Graumann, 1990, p. 108). The concept of dialogue is thus closely connected to that of polyphony. Polyphony is a concept borrowed from music which acknowledges the presence of many voices without any one voice being superior to the others. Bakhtin's perception of polyphony is normative in the sense that it implies that no authority is dominating, and everybody's voice is equally important. Polyphony, which literally means "many voiced", was used to describe literary writing that managed to liberate the voice of characters from the authorial or narratorial voice. In *Problems of Dostoevsky's Poetics*, Bakhtin (1984) referred to polyphony as a new kind of artistic thinking because what Dostoevsky did went against the grain of the traditional narration, privileging harmony and single voicedness. The reader of Dostoevsky, Bakhtin suggests, does not have the impression that he or she is dealing with a single, dominating author, but is, in fact, faced with a multiplicity of authors.

Polyphony refers, therefore, to the process whereby many voices interact together, and it acknowledges the tension between voices this interaction might lead to. For Bakhtin, this implies that participants in a dialogue must have an open mind in relation to others, as it is in the tension between different voices that knowledge and meaning are created.

> The idea *lives* not in one person's *isolated* individual consciousness – if it remains there only, it degenerates and dies. The idea begins to live, that is, to take shape, to develop, to find and renew its verbal expression, to give birth to new ideas, only when it enters into genuine dialogic relationships with other ideas, with the ideas of *others*. Human thought becomes genuine thought, that is, an idea, only under conditions of living contact with another and alien thought, a thought embodied in someone else's voice, that is, in someone else's consciousness expressed in discourse. At this point of contact between voice-consciousness the idea is born and lives.
>
> (Bakhtin, 1984, pp. 87–88)

The idea – as it was *seen* by Dostoevsky the artist – is not a subjective, individual, or psychological formation with "permanent resident rights in a person's head; no, the idea is inter-individual and intersubjective – the realm of its existence is not individual consciousness but dialogic communion *between* consciousnesses" (Bakhtin, 1984, pp. 87–88).

Bakhtin's view is that, in any idea generation process, dialogical relations are necessary. Different points of view can develop further and new ones emerge in the meeting between different perspectives, as Glăveanu and de Saint Laurent (in press) also explored. The concept of polyphony is relevant concerning the understanding of how an open dialogue enables creative processes instead of suppressing it and limiting the chance for innovative ideas to be generated. When multidisciplinary group members communicate and interact, there are challenges involved. Tudor Rickards and Christian deCock (2009) made an overview on brainstorming and concluded that this can be ineffective when it comes to problem solving because individuals often have more ideas than people working in groups.

In multidisciplinary groups, group members may have different terminologies which often leads to communication problems and may make it difficult to understand each other. Thus, it becomes crucial for the outcome of the group work that the members manage to have a dialogue and to overcome the obstacles involved in multidisciplinary collaboration. This is necessary in order to benefit from such group collaboration – combining knowledge that can lead to something new.

The sociocultural framework outlined here enables us to explore the creative processes in the multidisciplinary groups and to focus on the social interactions and how group members co-construct new knowledge and ideas across disciplines.

Methods in the Ethnographic Study

With the overarching research question "What characterises the creative processes in innovation work?" as a point of departure, the first author conducted an inductive and qualitative research study (for more, see Ness & Søreide, 2014; Ness & Riese, 2015; Ness, 2016). The empirical fieldwork focused on three purposefully selected groups (Flyvbjerg, 2006, p. 230), two located in an international oil and gas company, Statoil, and one located in a research institute. The sites were chosen due to the opportunity to follow authentic creative processes in leading innovation organisations. The groups were chosen due to their formal mandate on generating new ideas, strategies, or products. All the groups consisted of people with varied educational and experiential backgrounds, as follows:

- a Strategy group: based in the international oil and gas company, Statoil (now called Equinor). This group consisted of people with legal and on/offshore expertise, including logistics and engineering;
- an Innovation group: based in the Innovation Department in Statoil. This group had members with expertise in engineering, business, geophysics, and cyber technology;
- a Research Institute group: based in a Norwegian research institute, also with people with different competencies and expertise.

When investigating the characteristics of creative processes in these contexts, it was necessary to spend time with the groups, in their work environment, and "get a feel" for how they communicated and used artefacts. It was also crucial to see how the leaders facilitated creative teamwork. Since we aimed to observe how the group members communicated and interacted over time, an ethnographic approach was chosen for data collection. An ethnographic perspective can capture how new ideas are generated and operationalised in heterogeneous teams (Lund, Rasmussen, & Smørdal, 2010, p. 217), and this perspective was well suited to help us study both the visible and less visible processes of creativity. In addition to observations, we also conducted focus group interviews with the three groups and individual interviews with group leaders and other innovation leaders. In order to conduct the study, the first author had to pass courses on safety, since it was a requirement for getting access to buildings and meetings, and in order to freely come and go as "one of the group members". Since innovation is a highly business-sensitive field, it was necessary to sign confidentiality statements. These gave us some restrictions regarding reporting the content of the innovation processes, so that is why we often use "[. . .]" in quotes when reporting data. Using such brackets indicates that confidential content is removed, yet we are still able to report *how* the group members communicated and interacted and describe the creative processes.

The observations were audio or video recorded, and the interviews were audio recorded and transcribed before the analysis. The project has an empirical point of departure and is inspired by Hatch's (2002) inductive analyses, but it was also theory informed. In ethnographic research, theory plays an inductive role in the sense that theoretical insights inform the interpretations of data uncovered, not by testing prior theoretically driven hypotheses but in using the researcher's theoretical knowledge to make sense of the data uncovered in the field research (Wilson & Chaddha, 2009). In this inductive approach, we sought to identify different patterns which describe how the communication and interaction in the groups varied throughout the idea generation process. In this way it was found that there was indeed an overarching pattern across the groups indicating that creative processes took different forms and different levels of intensity at different times during the innovation work. When analysing further, six phases were identified: the initiation, knowledge distribution, polyphony, imagination, idea formulation, and consolidation phases. Microsoft Excel was used for coding and organising the material. This enabled us to organise the material according to descriptions of the identified phases in a structured manner. In this way of inductive analysis, data were investigated with the research question in mind as a point of departure, and when repeated ideas, concepts, and patterns became apparent, these were tagged with *codes*. The codes represented different categories or themes of meaning. For instance, code A3 would represent "Category A, Curious state of mind: communication and interaction where group members seem open and curious towards each other" and 3 indicating that this happened in phase 3 (polyphony) of the idea generation process. These categories became the basis for a new theoretical model. They allowed us also to see how communication and interaction varied from phase to phase, from the macro level of the entire collaboration to the micro level of the utterance. This inductive analytical approach (Hatch, 2002) was combined with an hermeneutical interpretation of meaning, and it was inspired by Kvale and Brinkmann (2009, pp. 213–218). Consequently, it was possible to write a description of the creative processes throughout the phases.

The identified phases and their characteristics were then used as a base for focus group interviews with the members of each group, which were conducted in order to discuss and elaborate our preliminary findings. The results from the analysis of focus group interviews resulted in a richer description of each of the six phases of creative processes. Finally, individual interviews with group leaders were also conducted in order to understand more of the leaders' role in the facilitation of the creative process.

Main Findings

Findings from this project showed that the creative process developed over time, and six phases had been identified for this initial innovation work. See Figure 3.1. These six phases could be divided into two separate processes in which (1) the groups, through knowledge sharing, build a common knowledge platform, and (2) this platform enables idea generation. The creative processes peaked in the three middle phases, and these phases have been metaphorically called the "Room of Opportunity". Within it, group members discussed different scenarios and ideas, and different views were put up against each other resulting in a polyphony where everybody's meaning was equally valuable; this dialogue stimulated group members' imaginations. Participants also used each others' experiences in order to learn and to think about new combinations. When doing this, they used a variety of technological tools. Knowledge was widely distributed among group members, and as such, they tutored each other.

The analyses also showed that, when group members from different disciplines construct a common knowledge platform and generate or develop innovative ideas, some relational skills become crucial in order to succeed. Most of all, they require the ability to recognise and build on each other's competences. This process was aided by openness, curiosity, and respect for each other's views. It is insufficient to simply assemble people with special expertise and from different disciplines. They need to exercise these additional relational skills in order to accomplish their task creatively (Ness, 2017; Ness & Riese, 2015).

An overall finding was that, across all three groups, discussions and disagreements stimulated group members' fantasies and imaginations, which were crucial for the creative process, particularly within the "Room of Opportunity". Next, we focus in particular on how a polyphonic form of imagination stimulated and gave direction to these creative processes.

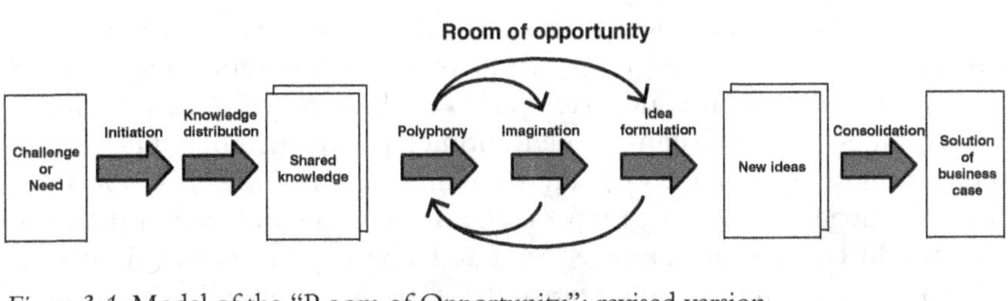

Figure 3.1 Model of the "Room of Opportunity"; revised version

Source: Ness (2018).

Idea Generation in Multidisciplinary Groups as an Expression of the Polyphonic Imagination

Findings from the first author's project showed that the groups' imagination was stimulated by the existence of multiple voices and perspectives within the team, and that these different perspectives acknowledged each other and didn't allow any particular voice to become dominant.

We will first discuss how imagination involved new ways of combining knowledge and ideas based on one's own and others' experiences and the way the groups made use of technological tools. Secondly, we will discuss how imagination was ignited by diversity and tension. Thirdly, we will elaborate on the importance of emotion and social support for stimulating and driving imagination in groups. Finally, we will sum up the discussion and present the concept of Polyphonic Imagination and a conceptual model.

Imagination: Combining Knowledge in New Ways

Being imaginative was observed in those moments in which group members combined their individual knowledge and experiences in new ways (Jovchelovitch, 2015, p. 79), and implied that group members listened to others' experiences and included what they heard in the repertoire of their own knowledge and experiences. We will explore this dynamic in more detail as follows.

Indeed, when observing how group members generated ideas, it became evident that they borrowed elements from the knowledge they already possessed and combined them in new ways in their discussions with other group members. This was especially noticeable during the many presentations in the groups where different terms and concepts were explained and demonstrated in detail. In particular, group members made use of a variety of technological tools as a supplement to their verbal explanations. This included different software systems, as well as the use of pictures, models, and figures. These presentations helped the members to combine knowledge in new ways since they learned from each other and developed a new perspective on their knowledge. They frequently expressed new insights derived from what they were explaining or demonstrating to the others.

A typical example on how the groups made use of technology in the idea generation, was when the group members in the Innovation group stood in front of a white board and Eric[1] started to draw and explain a particular system connected to drilling. Then another group member supplied his understanding by adding to the drawing and also making changes in what Eric had suggested. Other group members joined in and started drawing, building on each others' knowledge. The technological tool made it possible to save what they were doing, and the group could go back and forth between the different stages of the drawing. They were able to revisit their work and their ideas also at a previous state and to explore other ways by changing the drawings.

The group members also searched for new possibilities to build on each others' knowledge and perspectives. Hannah, another member of the Innovation group, expressed it like this (Ness & Søreide, 2014, p. 553):

> Participation and enthusiasm is important – and building on each other's ideas and perspectives. When there are several people in the group with different competences, you get this dynamics which is so important. You are challenged by others. You learn to think in a new fashion when you hear how others talk about matters you thought you knew.

Evidently, in these groups, the members were true experts within their field. However, this also means that they lacked equivalent knowledge in the others' fields of expertise. According to Vygotsky (1930/2004, pp. 14–15): "The richer a person's experience, the richer is the material his imagination has access to". Consequently, it was crucial that the group members could share knowledge and experiences in order to get a wider and richer individual knowledge, as well as a broader common knowledge platform to support their imagination. Vygotsky (1930/2004, p. 17) claimed that imagination is essential for all mental functioning and human behaviour because it also broadens a person's experience, thus, the person "can venture far beyond these boundaries, assimilating, with the help of his imagination someone else's historical or social experience". Indeed, the individual's capacity to make connections between objects, events, and tools is directly defined by how much that person can imagine someone else's experiences. Technological tools were used as mediation that enabled the group members to visualise their thoughts and invited others to add to these with their own ideas. Following Vygotsky, imagination is not only built on a person's own, real experience, but also on the experiences of others with whom he or she communicates about shared situations.

Imagination Ignited by Diversity and Tension

Tension and diversity can stimulate imagination, and Bakhtin's concept of polyphony highlights how knowledge and ideas are created in the tension between different voices acknowledging each other (Morson & Emerson, 1990). In order for meaning, new knowledge, and understanding to emerge, there must be a dialogue between several perspectives or voices, and it is particularly productive if these voices are in opposition. Previous research also shows that discovering how knowledge and assets, redefined and connected in novel ways, require heterogeneous networks of people. Such networks can expose people to a diversity that can inspire and enable creativity (Amabile, Conti, Coon, Lazenby, & Herron, 1996; Woodman, et al., 1993) as it can create a fruitful tension between positions and perspectives. This proposition is supported also by our ethnographic study.

In the present research project, we had seen that in the oil industry, groups could especially draw on differences in their operational and theoretical views. One of the group leaders made this comment about seeking new perspectives: "It was important to keep on seeking and not stop the discussion immediately when a solution came to the fore" (Helge). However, the leader emphasised that differences in perspectives were also present between group members who did not possess opposite perspectives: "It was nice that this group consisted of people from different departments. But even though some in the group normally work closely without many controversies, they still could propose different perspectives".

An example of difference in opinions between persons with similar backgrounds came to the fore when Birger – a member from the contract unit in the Strategy group – and the leader, coming from the contract unit, disagreed. Even though they both represented the contract unit, and therefore shared a common perspective, they had different opinions on what focus to have on drill string and assemblies. Through dialogical exchanges where they discussed different ideas, the group came further than what would have been the case if group members had sought an early agreement. Through such moments of tension, the group continuously created knowledge and ideas, without generating a conflict. We also found that group members did not automatically seek an agreement. According to Graumann (1990), group members do not have to agree – but they must be able to express an understanding for the other person's perspectives. As shown in the example with Birger and the leader, it is possible for the group members to disagree and still maintain an intersubjective field of mutual understanding. This is in line with Matusov's (1996) argument that the traditional conception of intersubjectivity is too narrowly defined and too static in order to fully account for the fact that individuals are different. It is not fruitful to focus on agreement only, and what individuals have in common. Matusov argues that intersubjectivity might also include lack of agreement or continuity in joint activities.

The way group members communicated implied disagreements since the perspectives and voices came from different practices and disciplines, but it was exactly this polyphony that allowed the groups to move beyond the existing knowledge of various experts and towards a territory new to all of them. In this way, the polyphony of disciplinary voices became a generative juxtaposition (Baerveldt & Cresswell, 2015) for each one of the groups.

Emotion Supports the Imagination

A sociocultural perspective sets out to examine learning and how common situations can trigger encounters that are not only socially and technologically mediated, but also emotionally charged. Understanding the emotional dimensions of the collective effort to collaborate on generating innovative ideas is important for organisational creativity and for the leaders working with these processes. When looking at the findings across the three groups, it became clear that emotions and social support were connected to how imaginative the groups became. We discuss in this section how emotions supported the Polyphonic Imagination.

From the interaction we could see how group members related to each other in humorous ways, sometimes using jokes to increase the affective bonds in the groups and to build positive relationships with each other. Emotional safety and respect were essential conditions for imagination and creative acts such as generating new ideas.

An example that shows how the social climate was seen as important for the imagination was when Eric explained, in a follow-up interview, that he wanted group members to have a good time:

> And I want laughter and fun! I want energy and activity and just notice: when everybody in the room is up on their feet, when there are voices and laughter blending together, then we are on to something!
>
> (Ness, 2017, p. 568)

When Eric said this, he shared his awareness of the connection between active participation, laughter, fun, and creativity. Bakhtin (1981) emphasised the creative energy embedded within polyphonic dialogues, and the leader acknowledged this by saying that they were "on to something" and agreed that laughter itself could contribute to generating innovative ideas.

According to Marjanovic-Shane, Connery, and John-Steiner (2010), the manner in which learning environments are organised fosters or dissuades the emotional and relational conditions for creativity. Positive relationships fuel risk-taking and creative engagement, resulting in novel insights and achievements for all the members of a teaching-learning community. When group members felt supported and safe, they seemed to relax around each other despite any tensions due to their different standpoints. Findings from our study also showed how the group members supported each other when someone dared to suggest something really radical and referred to it as "wild". This support can be understood as a form of emotional scaffolding (John-Steiner, 2000, p. 128) that included the sharing of risks in the presentation of new ideas. The group members created a safety zone in which challenging each other and also being critical or disagreeing were tolerated and were treated as constructive.

In long-term relationships between partners who work and live together, a great degree of emotional appropriation can take place (John-Steiner, 2000). John-Steiner claims that genuinely caring is especially important in high anxiety activities. Indeed, in the groups that comprise experts working with other experts and being selected to participate in innovative idea generation, group members tend to worry about not being creative enough or about saying something "wrong". Being recognised as experts implied that they were used to having control over certain subjects, so it was difficult for them to leave their comfort zone and discuss ideas about which they had little previous knowledge. This anxiety was often explicitly mentioned during meetings, and, for example, many of them hesitated to be the first to draw on the smartboard. Also, this nervousness seemed to be a barrier for imagining all kinds of possibilities, with no limitations, and for "being creative". This was clearly worrying for the group members and particularly evident when new people were brought into the groups. In those moments, group members became a bit self-aware and careful as they didn't know the newcomers. Newcomers, too, seemed equally careful and reluctant. It was crucial in such situations to have respect for each other and recognise each other as resources in the group. It took some time to reach a point where the new group members acted "freely" and began suggesting ideas outside the existing paradigms.

The combination of a supportive and challenging environment has been emphasised by many researchers as an important condition for creativity (Amabile, et al., 1996; Anderson & West, 1998; Ekvall, 1996; Mathisen & Einarsen, 2004; Siegel & Kaemmerer, 1978; West & Richards, 1999). Amabile, et al. (1996) argued that the creative climate consists of challenge, freedom, and support; in addition, it encourages openness and the tolerance of uncertainty. Our findings showed that, as the members of the group got to know each other, they trusted each other and achieved an emotional fine-tuning that helped to establish supportive relationships. This also helped them to be secure enough to challenge each other, as previously discussed.

Mahn and John-Steiner (2002, pp. 5–6) claimed that joint activities are enhanced when the interactions between participants are supported by "the gift of confidence". In this reciprocal emotional support offered by partners in collaboration – whether they are novice learners of a new language or individuals engaged in novel, creative endeavours – there is a dynamic interplay between their interactions and the ways in which they offer emotional support.

In the three groups, careful listening, intense dialogue, and emotional support sustained the cooperative construction of understanding. In this way, emotion became a condition of possibility for the Polyphonic Imagination to emerge.

Polyphonic Imagination

When summing up the characteristics of the creative processes presented in the discussion earlier, we return to the concept of *Polyphonic Imagination*. The groups' many voices and different perspectives can be conceptualised as a polyphony which stimulated the group members' imagination and in which everybody's voice was acknowledged. Polyphonic Imagination is, in

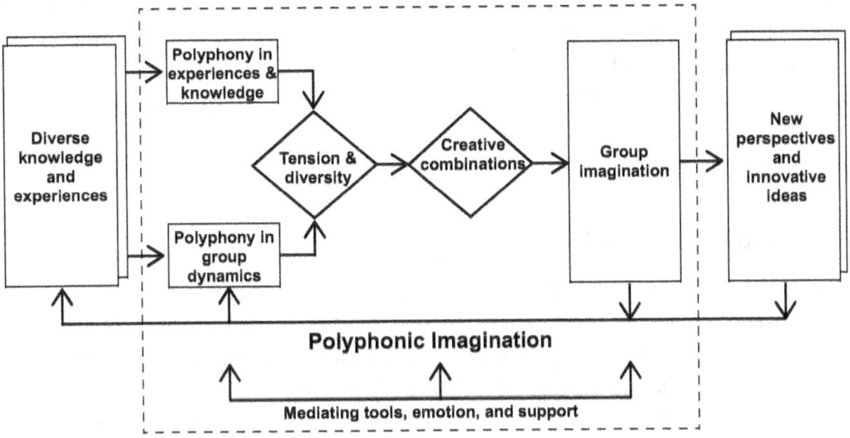

Figure 3.2 Polyphonic Imagination

other words, *a relational and multivoiced stimulation of fantasy*. The concept is derived from the processes between the group members using mediating tools, including technology, when co-constructing ideas. It is a collaborative, supportive, and creative act with an emphasis on the different voices and perspectives distributed among the group members.

The resulting model (see Figure 3.2) depicts how the multidisciplinary groups start from *diverse knowledge and experiences. Polyphony* exists both at the level of *experiences/knowledge*, as well as in the *group dynamics*. This polyphony stimulates the *groups' imagination* through *tension and diversity* leading to *creative combinations* of existing knowledge. The polyphony and group imagination were aided by *mediating tools, emotions*, and by *how the group members supported* each other. This multivoiced and supportive stimulation of fantasy, *Polyphonic Imagination*, was enabled in group creative processes. Such Polyphonic Imagination resulted in *new perspectives and innovative ideas*. The concept of Polyphonic Imagination is thus supported by empirical data and, especially, by the sociocultural lens that guided the interpretation of these data.

In particular, Bakhtin's dialogic polyphony focuses on how new knowledge is created in the tension between voices and openness to other views. It stands in contrast to a monologic position (Morson & Emerson, 1990). Thus, polyphony is an apt analytical tool to use in order to describe how imagination operates in the co-construction of innovative ideas by multidisciplinary groups. The polyphony among the group members was fuelled by a variety of shared experiences and perspectives, visualised and shared in the groups with the help of technological tools. As mentioned before, a Vygotskian view on imagination (John-Steiner, 2000; Vygotsky, 1930/2004) postulates that many voices co-construct knowledge together in supportive collaboration. Thus, this concept on Polyphonic Imagination is useful to highlight the importance of a wide experience base, tensions and complementarity, and the affective and supportive aspects of the imagination behind creative knowledge processes. We suggest that such Polyphonic Imagination is what most deeply and basically characterised the creative knowledge processes in the groups that were observed in the study.

Concluding Remarks

This chapter proposes Polyphonic Imagination as a concept that captures the characteristics of creative processes and the multivoiced stimulation of fantasy in multidisciplinary groups. The chapter goes against the traditional view on creativity as an individual trait (Amabile, 1996, 2008; Barron & Harrington, 1981; Feist, 1998). Our findings also differ from those social views on creativity (Diehl & Stroebe, 1991; Paulus, 2000; Paulus, et al., 1995) that see the "social" as a simple variable among others. Instead, our findings indicate that the dynamics between the social and the individual is important. This is in line with research promoted by Vera John-Steiner and Keith Sawyer, among others, who consider the "social" as including the dynamic relation between self and others (Glăveanu, 2010). As Moran and John-Steiner (2003) suggested, collaborators are not homogeneous people, but rather individuals with different perspectives, expertise, conceptualisations, working methods, temperaments, resources, needs, and talents. The interactions between these differences in the three groups studied here formed the foundation on which dynamic forms of collaboration and creativity could unfold.

Note

1. All names used in the chapter are pseudonyms.

References

Amabile, T. M. (1996). *Creativity in context.* Boulder, CO: Westview Press Inc.

Amabile, T. M. (2008). Within you, without you: Towards a social psychology of creativity, and beyond. In M. A. Runco & R. S. Albert (Eds.), *Theories of creativity* (2nd ed.). Newbury Park, CA: Sage Publications.

Amabile, T. M., Conti, R., Coon, H., Lazenby, J., & Herron, M. (1996). Assessing the work environment for creativity. *Academy of Management Journal, 39*(5), 1154–1184.

Anderson, N. R., & West, M. A. (1998). Measuring climate for work group innovation: Developing and validation of the team climate inventory. *Journal of Organizational Behavior, 19*, 235–258.

Baer, M., & Oldham, G. R. (2006). The curvilinear relation between experienced creative time pressure and creativity: Moderating effects of openness to experience and support for creativity. *Journal of Applied Psychology, 91*(4), 963–970. http://doi.org/10.1037/0021-9010.91.4.963

Baerveldt, C., & Cresswell, J. (2015). Creativity and the generative approach to culture and meaning. In V. P. Glăveanu, A. Gillespie, & J. Valsiner (Eds.), *Rethinking creativity: Contributions from social and cultural psychology* (pp. 93–109). New York: Routledge.

Bakhtin, M. M. (1981). *The dialogic imagination: Four essays*. Austin, TX: University of Texas Press.

Bakhtin, M. M. (1984). *Problems of Dostoevsky's poetics*. Minneapolis, MN: University of Minnesota Press.

Barron, F., & Harrington, D. (1981). Creativity, intelligence and personality. *Annual Review of Psychology, 32*, 439–476.

Carlile, P. R. (2004). Transferring, translating and transforming: An integrative framework for managing knowledge across boundaries. *Organization Science, 15*(5), 555–568.

Darsø, L. (2001). *Innovation in the making*. Fredriksberg, Denmark: Samfundslitteratur.

Diehl, M., & Stroebe, W. (1991). Productivity loss in idea-generating groups: Tracking down the blocking effect. *Journal of Personality and Social Psychology, 61*, 392–403.

Dillenbourg, P. (1999). What do you mean by collaborative learning? In P. Dillenbourg (Ed.), *Collaborative-learning: Cognitive and computational approaches* (pp. 1–19). Oxford: Elsevier.

Dysthe, O. (2001). Sosiokulturelle teoriperspektiv på kunnskap og læring. In O. Dysthe (Ed.), *Dialog, samspel og læring* (pp. 33–72). Oslo: Abstrakt forlag as.

Ekvall, G. (1996). Organizational climate for creativity and innovation. *European Journal of Work and Organizational Psychology, 5*(1), 105–123.

Feist, G. (1998). A meta-analysis of personality in scientific and artistic creativity. *Personality and Social Psychology Review, 2*(4), 290–309.

Flyvbjerg, B. (2006). Five misunderstandings about case-study research. *Qualitative Inquiry, 12*(2), 219–245.

Glăveanu, V. P. (2010). Paradigms in the study of creativity: Introducing the perspective of cultural psychology. *New Ideas in Psychology, 28*(1), 79–93.

Glăveanu, V. P., & de Saint Laurent, C. (in press). Taking the perspective of others: A conceptual model and its application to the refugee crisis. Special issue in *Peace and Conflict: Journal of Peace Psychology*.

Glăveanu, V. P., Karwowski, M., Jankowska, D. M., & de Saint-Laurent, C. (2016). Creative imagination. In T. Zittoun & V. P. Glăveanu (Eds.), *The Oxford handbook of imagination and culture*. Oxford: Oxford University Press.

Graumann, C. F. (1990). Perspectival structure and dynamics in dialogues. In I. Markovà & K. Foppa (Eds.), *The dynamics of dialogue* (pp. 105–127). New York: Harvester Wheatsheaf.

Hämäläinen, R., & Vähäsantanen, K. (2011). Theoretical and pedagogical perspectives on orchestrating creativity and collaborative learning. *Educational Research Review, 6*(3), 169–184.

Hargadon, A. B., & Bechky, B. A. (2006). When collections of creatives become creative collectives: A field study of problem solving at work. *Organization Science, 17*(4), 484–500.

Hargadon, A. B., & Sutton, R. I. (1997). Technology brokering and innovation in a product development firm. *Administrative Science Quarterly, 42*(4), 716–749.

Hatch, J. A. (2002). *Doing qualitative research in education settings*. Albany, NY: State University of New York Press.

Igland, M.-A., & Dysthe, O. (2001). Mikhail Bakhtin og sosiokulturell teori. In O. Dysthe (Ed.), *Dialog, samspel og læring* (pp. 107–128). Oslo: Abstrakt forlag as.

John-Steiner, V. (2000). *Creative collaboration.* Oxford: Oxford University Press.

John-Steiner, V., Connery, M. C., & Marjanovic-Shane, A. (2010). Dancing with the Muses: An cultural-historical approach to play, meaning making and creativity. In M. C. Connery, V. John-Steiner, & A. Marjanovic-Shane (Eds.), *Vygotsky and creativity: A cultural-historical approach to play, meaning making, and the arts* (pp. 41–59). New York: Peter Lang Publishing.

Jovchelovitch, S. (2015). The creativity of the social. Imagination, development and social change in Rio de Janeiro's favelas. In V. P. Glăveanu, A. Gillespie, & J. Valsiner (Eds.), *Rethinking creativity: Contributions from social and cultural psychology* (pp. 76–92). New York: Routledge.

Kurtzberg, T. R., & Amabile, T. M. (2001). From Guilford to creative synergy: Opening the black box of team level creativity. *Creativity Research Journal, 13*(Special Issue on Commemorating Guilford's 1950 Presidential Address).

Kvale, S., & Brinkmann, S. (2009). *Det kvalitative forskningsintervju* (2nd ed.). Oslo: Gyldendal Akademisk.

Linell, P. (2009). *Rethinking language, mind, and world dialogically: Interactional and contextual theories of human sense-making.* Charlotte, NC: Information Age Publishing, Inc.

Lund, A., Rasmussen, I., & Smørdal, O. (2010). Chapter 11: Joint design for working in wikis. A case of practicing across settings and models of work. In H. Daniels, A. Edwards, Y. Engeström, T. Gallagher, & S. R. Ludvigsen (Eds.), *Activity theory in practice: Promoting learning across boundaries and agencies.* London: Routledge.

Mahn, H., & John-Steiner, V. (2002). The gift of confidence: A Vygotskian view of emotions. In G. Wells & G. Claxton (Eds.), *Learning for life in the 21st century: Sociocultural perspectives on the future of education.* Oxford: Blackwell Publishing Ltd.

Marjanovic-Shane, A., Connery, M. C., & John-Steiner, V. (2010). A cultural-historical approach to creative education. In M. C. Connery, V. John-Steiner, & A. Marjanovic-Shane (Eds.), *Vygotsky and creativity: A cultural-historical approach to play, meaning making, and the arts* (pp. 215–232). New York: Peter Lang Publishing.

Mathisen, G. E., & Einarsen, S. (2004). A review of instruments assessing creative and innovative environments within organizations. *Creativity Research Journal, 16*(1), 119–140.

Matusov, E. (1996). Intersubjectivity without agreement. *Mind, Culture and Activity, 3*(1), 25–45.

Mercer, N. (2010). The analysis of classroom talk: Methods and methodologies. *The British Journal of Educational Psychology, 80*(1), 1–14.

Moran, S., & John-Steiner, V. (2003). Creativity in the making: Vygotsky's contemporary contribution to the dialectic of creativity & development. In R. K. Sawyer, V. John-Steiner, S. Moran, R. J. Sternberg, D. H. Feldman, J. Nakamura, & M. Csikszentmihalyi (Eds.), *Creativity and development* (pp. 61–90). New York: Oxford University Press.

Morson, G. S., & Emerson, C. (1990). *Mikhail Bakhtin: Creation of a prosaics.* Stanford, CA: Stanford University Press.

Ness, I. J. (2017). Polyphonic orchestration – Facilitating creative knowledge processes for innovation. *European Journal of Innovation Management, 20*(4), 557–577. https://doi.org/10.1108/EJIM-05-2016-0049

Ness, I. J. (2018). Behind the scenes: How to research creative processes in multidisciplinary groups. In I. Lebuda & V. P. Glăveanu (Eds.), *The Palgrave handbook of social creativity research.* London: Palgrave Macmillan.

Ness, I. J., & Riese, H. (2015, September). Openness, curiosity and respect: Underlying conditions for developing innovative knowledge and ideas between disciplines. *Learning Culture and Social Interaction, 6*, 29–39. http://doi.org/10.1016/j.lcsi.2015.03.001

Ness, I. J., & Søreide, G. E. (2014). The room of opportunity: Understanding phases of creative knowledge processes in innovation. *Journal of Workplace Learning, 26*(8), 545–560. http://doi.org/10.1108/JWL-10-2013-0077

Paavola, S., & Hakkarainen, K. (2005). The knowledge creation metaphor – An emergent epistemological approach to learning. *Science & Education, 14*(6), 535–557. http://doi.org/10.1007/s11191-004-5157-0

Paulus, P. B. (2000). Groups, teams, and creativity: The creative potential of idea-generating group. *Applied Psychology: An International Review, 49*(2), 237–262.

Paulus, P. B., Larey, T. S., & Ortega, A. H. (1995). Performance and perceptions of brainstormers in an organizational setting. *Basic and Applied Social Psychology, 17*(1–2), 249–265.

Rickards, T., and De Cock, C. (2009). Understanding organizational creativity: Toward a multiparadigmatic approach. In M. A. Runco (Ed.), *The creativity research handbook* (Vol. 2, pp. 1–31). Creskill, NJ: Hampton Press.

Sawyer, R. K. (2003). *Group creativity: Music, theater, collaboration*. Mahwah, NJ: Lawrence Erlbaum Associates, Inc.

Sawyer, R. K. (2006). *Explaining creativity: The science of human innovation*. New York: Oxford University Press.

Siegel, S. M., & Kaemmerer, W. F. (1978). Measuring the perceived support for innovation in organizations. *Journal of Applied Psychology, 63*, 553–562.

Smolucha, L. W., & Smolucha, F. C. (1986). L.S. Vygotsky's theory of creative imagination. *Spiel, 5*(2), 299–308.

Tsoukas, H. (2009). A dialogical approach to the creation of new knowledge in organizations. *Organization Science, 20*(6), 941–957.

Valsiner, J., & van der Veer, R. (2000). *The social mind: Construction of the idea*. New York: Cambridge University Press.

Vygotsky, L. S. (1930/2004). Imagination and creativity in childhood. *Journal of Russian and East European Psychology, 42*(1), 7–97.

West, M. A., & Richards, T. (1999). Innovation. In M. A. Runco & S. Pritzker (Eds.), *Encyclopedia of creativity* (Vol. 2, pp. 45–55). San Diego, CA: Academic.

Wilson, W. J., & Chaddha, A. (2009). The role of theory in ethnographic research. *Ethnography, 10*(4), 549–564.

Woodman, R. W., Sawyer, J. E., & Griffin, R. W. (1993). Toward a theory of organizational creativity. *Academy of Management Review, 18*(2), 293–321.

4 Networked Flow in Creative Collaboration

A Mixed Method Study

Andrea Gaggioli, Elvis Mazzoni, Martina Benvenuti, Carlo Galimberti, Antonio Bova, Eleonora Brivio, Pietro Cipresso, Giuseppe Riva, and Alice Chirico

Introduction

For many years, research on creativity focused on an individual level of analysis, following up the romantic image of the "lone genius" (e.g., Montuori & Purser, 1995; Eisler, Donnelly, & Montuori, 2016; Sawyer, 2007) and identifying key personal factors sparking unique and useful ideas. However, now, scholars are becoming increasingly aware of the importance of socio-cultural factors in shaping creativity (e.g., Glăveanu, 2010). Creativity viewed as an individual-level phenomenon emphasises more intrapersonal processes (Walton, 2003) compared to interpersonal ones, such as the role of social, cultural, and physical contexts.

The perspective on creativity as a systemic and context-dependent process is reinforced by the words of Csikszentmihalyi:

> We cannot study creativity by isolating individuals and their works from the social and historical milieu in which their actions are carried out. This is because what we call creative is never the result of individual action alone.
>
> (1988, pp. 325–326)

Creativity theories based on individual factors and on socio-cultural processes can appear as incompatible, yet a recent model proposed a feasible way to integrate both. The *We-paradigm*, introduced by Glăveanu, includes individual-based theories as part of a complex creativity system (Glăveanu, 2015) and relies on a distributed creativity concept (Hutchins, 2006) as a phenomenon dwelling beyond individuals' minds and consisting of a *network* of people, cultural and material artefacts, as well as their relationships across time.

Along this line of thinking, Gaggioli, Chirico, Mazzoni, Milani, and Riva (2017; Gaggioli, Mazzoni, Milani, & Riva, 2015; Gaggioli, Riva, Milani, & Mazzoni, 2013) have developed a theoretical and methodological framework – (*Networked Flow*) – which posits the concept of creative networks as a means to capture the complexity of collective creativity (Gaggioli, et al., 2013). The core of this model rests on three ideas.

First, the concept of "group creativity" is extended by introducing the notion of *networked creativity*, relying on the *structural* dynamics among individuals, material, and symbolic resources as part of the same creative collaboration process. That is, groups achieving optimal creativity levels also show a *peculiar network structure*, also including communication artefacts used by group members to collaborate – i.e., online collaboration platforms, groupware tools, social media, etc. (Gaggioli, et al., 2013). The NF model captures the "blended" side of communication prevailing in creative collaboration practices when people combine in-presence communication and mediated communication for achieving a common goal (e.g., Bell, Sawaya, & Cain, 2014; Hinds, Kiesler, & Kiesler, 2002; So & Brush, 2008). The NF model states that it is possible to achieve optimal group creative performances even in mediated communication exchanges, thanks to a peculiar *quality of group experience*. That is, when group members experience the highest levels of social presence (i.e., sense of being cognitively, behaviourally, attentively, and emotionally interconnected with other people in the real and virtual world; Biocca & Harms, 2011) and flow experience (i.e., an optimal psychological state associated to outstanding group performance; Diana, Villani, Muzio, & Riva, 2012; Jackson & Eklund, 2002; Jackson & Marsh, 1996), they enter a *Mutual Zone Of Proximal Development (MZPD)* (Goos, Galbraith, & Renshaw, 2002; John-Steiner, 2000) (i.e., members share the same frame of reference, and co-build a collective intention) at the base of optimal group creativity levels. Following up Vygotsky's model, John-Steiner and Mahn (1996) stated that the participation to group activities would allow sharing collective knowledge and its final internalisation in peoples' consciousness. All group members scaffold each other, and this process allows the network's ideas development. This collective space has been conceived as a "*Mutual Zone Of Proximal Development*" (Armstrong, 2008) where people can negotiate shared meaning and generate and pursue collective intentions (Sawyer, 2007).

Finally, to assess the emergence of the MZPD, the analysis of micro-level qualitative communicative interactions among group members is also required. The main goal of the present study was to investigate creative collaboration through the lens of the NF model, using a mixed-method approach. More specifically, we zoomed in on the relationship between the aforementioned key components of the model:

i. *Communicative structure* (to identify network markers of optimal creativity);
ii. *Quality of experience* (to investigate flow and social presence);
iii. *Communicative interaction* (to assess the collective zone of proximal development and dialogical style);
iv. *Creativity performance* (to assess the final product of the creative collaboration).

At the methodological level, these tenets can be translated into three main operative requirements. A first requirement is to consider both *structural* and *experiential* features of creative collaboration and its outcomes, thus focusing on the quality of group experiences, on the structural features, and on the creative product. The structural dynamics of group collaboration can be detected using Social Network Analysis (SNA) (Scott, 2000). Then, the experience of group involvement can be measured through group flow experience (Csikszentmihalyi, 1990; Diana, et al., 2012; Jackson & Marsh, 1996) and social presence (Biocca & Harms, 2011). Finally, the creative product should also be analysed through a domain-based approach, such as the *Consensual Assessment Technique* (Amabile, 1982). As a second requirement to examine the *evolution* of the creative collaboration, we should focus on micro, meso, and macro levels of interaction, that is, on the interaction patterns between group participants over time (micro-level); on the structural changes in internal group dynamics (meso-level); and on the outcomes of micro and meso interactions, i.e., transfer of the creative product (the artefact) over a larger socio-cultural context (i.e., a community: the macro level).

As a third requirement, in order to identify the possible links between the experiential features of NF (social presence, flow) and the inherent dialogical structure of group dynamics, qualitative and quantitative data need to be collected. A key prediction of this model concerns the role of a specific group structure in facilitating (or not) the emergence of an optimal group experience and creative performance.

To meet all these requirements in a consistent way, a longitudinal, mixed methodology, combining qualitative, quantitative, and topographical analysis of NF process (Galimberti, et al., 2015), has been developed. Here, the term "mixed methodology" refers to the procedure of collecting and analysing heterogeneous types of data within the context of a single study. Then, it was investigated that the emergence of the NF process in ten groups of university students tasked with the ideation of a videoclip over 11 weeks within the context of a university teaching course on "Enterprise Communication" at Università Cattolica del Sacro Cuore. They were not told explicitly to produce "creative" ideas. We assumed that a peculiar group structure was able to promote (or hinder) group optimal experience and group creative performance. We longitudinally analysed the groups' network structure by extracting online communication datasets from social media applications used by the teams to collaborate, and then we integrated.

Method

Sample

This study took place during the winter semester. It involved 111 undergraduate students (30 males and 81 females, mean age = 24.44; SD = 3.75) enrolled in a course on "Enterprise Communication" at the Università Cattolica del Sacro Cuore. The Ethical Committee of Università Cattolica del

Sacro Cuore assessed and approved the experimental protocol. Each participant provided written informed consent for study participation in accordance with the Helsinki Declaration. Students participated in the study on a voluntary basis, and they did not receive rewards or credits. They were aware of each stage of the research process.

Setting and Experimental Design

The course on "Enterprise Communication" at the Catholic University of Milan focuses on topics related to the design, management, and assessment of communication processes within groups and organisations. As part of the final assignment of the course, students worked in groups and created a multimedia project (i.e., including photographic, video, and audio materials) addressing the topic of improvisation in organisational settings. This is an open-ended task, related to a specific domain, in which students were trained during the course. During task execution, students were invited to collaborate both face to face or using two widespread and free social media applications (Facebook and WhatsApp). The course combined both frontal lessons and commentaries from experts in the field of improvisation.

The study consisted of a longitudinal design, in which social network data were collected from online group interaction over 11 weeks of project collaboration. The research protocol also: included (i) an assessment of group quality of experience in the last week of collaboration; (ii) a collection of conversational data; and (iii) the creative product assessment by independent experts in the domain (Figure 4.1).

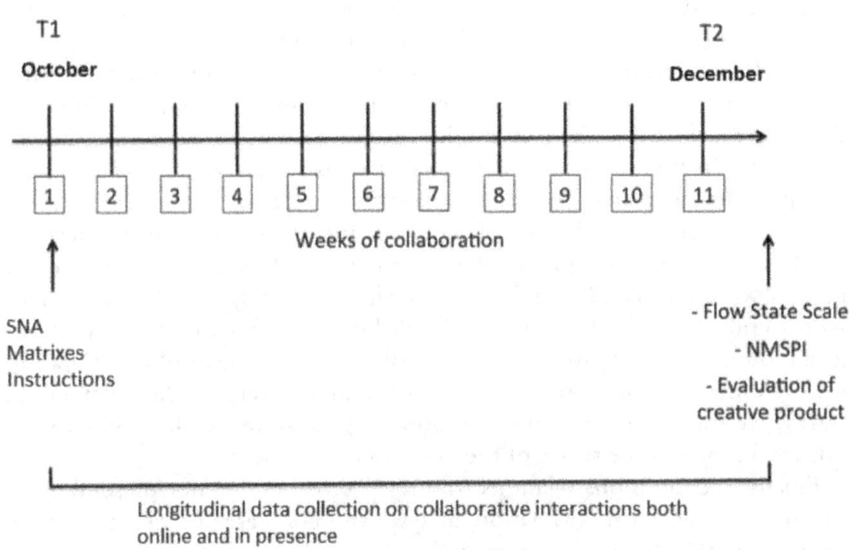

Figure 4.1 Graphical representation of the research flow

Measures

This mixed methodology integrated four measurements: (i) *communicative structure* (to identify network markers of optimal creativity); (ii) *quality of experience* (to investigate flow and social presence); (iii) *communicative interaction* (to assess mutual zone of proximal development and dialogical style); and (iv) *creativity* (to assess the final product of the creative collaboration).

Communication Structure

NF considers both processual and structural features of collaboration and its outcomes (e.g., the creative product). Therefore, the Social Network Analysis (SNA) technique was used to analyse communication exchanges as an index of group structure. This analysis has been already successfully implemented to study creativity and friendship (McKay, Grygiel, & Karwowski, 2017). SNA is a quantitative method to analyse real (Zohar & Tenne-Gazit, 2008) and virtual interactions (De Laat, Lally, Lipponen, & Simons, 2007; Palonen & Hakkarainen, 2013). Any kind of interaction among group members can be examined (e.g., money, friendship, information) and represented into two formats: numerical and graphical. The resulting group structure can be visualised as graphs (i.e., *sociograms*), representing the members as nodes of the graphs and the exchanges among them as lines in the graphs. Alternatively, group structural characteristics can be encapsulated into numerical indexes, which can be individual indices (i.e., based on relations and exchanges characterising each actor of the networks) or group indices (i.e., based on relations and exchanges characterising the network as a whole). To study the NF, different structural SNA indices have been proposed, such as *Density*, *Group Centralisation*, and *Cliques Participation index* (CPI) (Table 4.1) (for a full description of these indexes, see Gaggioli, et al., 2015). Furthermore, it is possible to carry out SNA either focusing on the group structure at a precise moment in time or adopting a longitudinal approach, thus taking multiple "snapshots" of the network structure over time. In this study, a longitudinal structural data analysis concerning group exchanges across 11 weeks was carried out. SNA data were collected every week, but we split the collaboration process in three phases according to the instructions provided to participants during the course. First, groups were created. Central weeks dealt with group collaboration. Last weeks concerned the final stages of collaboration after the delivery of the group product. Here, given the crucial role of central weeks of collaboration for the emergence of a specific group structural pattern (Galimberti, et al., 2016), we focused on the time window ranging from the 4th week to the 9th week, the middle stages of the collaboration process.

Finally, dichotomous relations (the relation is present/not present) were calculated to perform correlation analyses and comparisons, and to analyse the structural features of each group.[1]

Table 4.1 Metrics for social network analysis

Factors	*Measures*
Density	Represents the intensity of communication/collaboration within the group: the relationships expressed with respect to the maximum of possible relationships (percentage that describes how much in a group everyone has interacted or looked at all the other group members).
InDegree Centralisation	Represents the inequality in the intensity of incoming interaction; the more this value increases the more there are individuals who have received a greater intensity of communications/collaborations (i.e., the more a person receives relations or exchanges, the more he/she is relevant for the analysed dynamics).
OutDegree Centralisation	Represents the inequality in the intensity of outgoing interactions; the more this index increases the more there are students who have sent/started a greater intensity of communications/collaborations (i.e., the more a person activates relations or exchanges the more he/she is influent).
CPI (Cliques Participation Index)	Considers not only the number of cliques (i.e., subgroups) but relates it to the total number of members for each group. Identifies the average involvement of each subject in the existing subgroups.

Quality of Experience

We investigated group quality of experience in reference to the constructs of flow and social presence, as indicated by the NF model (Gaggioli, et al., 2013, 2015).[2]

Flow was assessed using the Italian version of the Flow State Scale (Diana, et al., 2012) initially developed by Jackson and colleagues (Jackson & Marsh, 1996; Jackson & Eklund, 2004), a widely used 36-item self-reported questionnaire on a 5-point Likert scale. Each item taps one of the nine dimensions of flow (Csikszentmihalyi, 1990; Jackson & Csikszentmihalyi, 1999). This scale showed an acceptable internal consistency (global mean Cronbach's alpha = 0.83) (Jackson & Marsh, 1996). A total flow score for each dimension (ranging from 4 to 20) was obtained by summing the scores of the single subscales. The range of scores for individual flow is from 36 (lowest flow) to 180 (highest flow). Global group flow score is computed by summing the average flow score for each of the individual team members.

Social presence was assessed using the *Networked Minds Social Presence Inventory* (NMSPI), a 34-item scale developed by Biocca and Harms (Biocca & Harms, 2003, 2011; Harms & Biocca, 2004) and adapted into Italian (Gaggioli, et al., 2017), also for non-mediated settings. Here, we focused on the first- and second-order constructs of social presence (Figure 4.2).

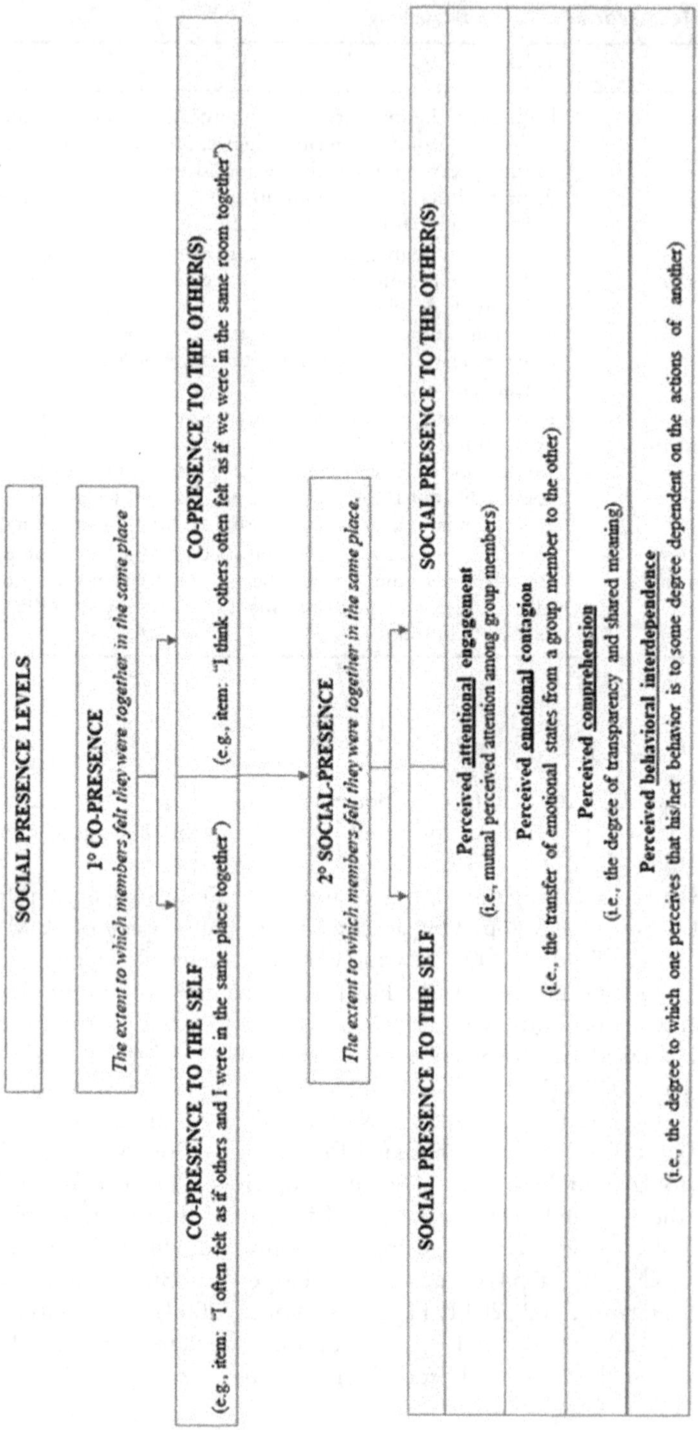

Figure 4.2 Social presence concept and Networked Minds Social Presence Inventory schema

The internal consistency of the scale is high (mean Cronbach's alpha = 0.83). Here, we computed a global level of social presence by summing the co-presence and second-order social presence dimensions scores for each team.

Communicative Interactions

We investigated communicative interactions in relation to the concept of *Mutual Zone Of Proximal Development* (MZPD) and dialogical style. The focus was on dialogical processes in conversations (i.e., dialogical patterns between participants during their group's activity; Galimberti, et al., 2016) analysed by means of Interlocutory Logic (Trognon & Batt, 2010). The qualitative analysis of macro-sequences of idea-generating processes is aimed at identifying potential dialogical markers of NF, such as:

- the ratio between conflicts produced and conflicts resolved;
- the number of group members that take part in the conversation;
- indicators of role fluidity: organisational/institutional roles, enunciative roles;
- team management processes (problem solving, decision making, etc.) supported by internal or external (material and/or human) resources;
- type of problems and the created ethnomethods used to solve them;
- number of subroutines that the group can/cannot solve;
- prevalence of dialogical continuity over monological coherence;
- the ratio between successful and satisfied speech acts and the total number of speech acts.

Creative Performance

Four expert judges in the domain of Enterprise Communication independently evaluated each group's creativity using the *Consensual Assessment Technique* (CAT) developed by Amabile (1982). This procedure involves participants with instructions for creating (in this case) group artefacts and asking experts to independently evaluate the creativity levels of those products (Amabile, 1982). Following this procedure, we asked four raters to judge the creativity levels of group artefacts on a 7-point scale, using their expertise on creativity in this domain.

Procedure

At the beginning of the course, ten self-selected student groups (size 8–11 members) were tasked with the creation of a multimedia product (time constraint: 11 weeks) on the theme of "improvisation" in organisational settings. The instructions were as follows:

> Please, get inspiration from experts, who talked during our lessons, or from other elements presented during our lessons and related to

the topic of "improvisation", to create a multimedia product (min 3 minutes – max 5 minutes length) in which the topic of "improvisation" is represented.

They were allowed to collaborate through (a) face-to-face meeting sessions in the classroom – video-recorded by students themselves and used to carry out qualitative analyses of dialogical interactions (2-hour session once a week), and (b) virtually – using two social media platforms (Facebook and WhatsApp as they chose – both or one), analysed by means SNA. Teams created either a WhatsApp group or a Facebook group to exchange information supporting their collaborative process. To collect data related to online interactions, a critical issue was how to safeguard students' privacy, following the recommendation of the Ethical Committee. To address this issue, we asked and taught students themselves to collect data related to their online conversations and create the adjacency matrixes, i.e., a square matrix used to represent relational data as a starting point for SNA.[3]

Data Analyses

Results

A global creativity score for each group was computed, given the high level of consistency among raters (Cronbach's alpha = .729). Considering the aim of this study and the longitudinal nature of SNA data, all analyses were carried out at group level (ten groups). First, the focus was on the relationship between SNA indexes, quality of experience, and group creativity scores. Then, the SNA analysis was deepened by considering the structure of communication exchanges in three groups, which showed the highest (Group A, Group B) and lowest (Group C) creativity scores. The choice of these groups was determined by the interactive dynamics showed by their members that were interesting and suitable for the following qualitative analysis. Finally, the analysis concerned verbal exchanges at quantitative levels – by means of SNA – and qualitative levels – through Interlocutory Logic analyses of conversation. Two normality tests (i.e., Kolmogorov-Smirnov and Shapiro-Wilk) showed that variables were normally distributed. Then, Pearson correlation coefficients indicated positive correlations between global and subdimensions of flow and social presence, as reported in Table 4.2. Results showed that Global Flow and Global Social Presence were positively and highly correlated. Moreover, $rwg_{(j)}$ indexes for Flow and Social Presence factors were computed in order to justify the aggregation of scores, as reported in Table 4.3. To test the relationship between structural dynamics (SNA), creativity, flow, and social presence, we carried out a Generalized Linear Model which can accept a violation of sphericity and collinearity (Agresti & Kateri, 2011; Mackinnon & Puterman, 1989). Therefore, three models were tested, including all SNA indexes (i.e., Density, Indegree Centralisation, OutDegree Centralisation, CVIndegree Centralisation, CVOutdegree Centralisation, CPI) for predicting creativity, group flow, and social presence

Table 4.2 Pearson's correlations between global and sub-dimensions of Flow and Social Presence

	Perception of the Self					*Perception of the Other*					
	Co-presence	*Attentional Engagement*	*Emotional Contagion*	*Comprehension*	*Behavioural Interdependence*	*Co-presence*	*Attentional Engagement*	*Emotional Contagion*	*Comprehension*	*Behavioural Interdependence*	*Global Social Presence*
Challenges Skills Balance	.58	.65*	.41	.74*	.81**	.59	.53	.49	.68*	.59	.67*
Action Awareness Merge	.91**	.66*	.49	.88**	.87**	.86**	.80**	.56	.82**	.62	.84**
Clear Goals	.73*	.44	.46	.77**	.83**	.68*	.59*	.56	.71*	.57	.73*
Unambiguous Feedback	.55	.32	.36	.67*	.81**	.53*	.58*	.53	.64*	.60	.64*
Concentration	.84**	.59	.65*	.86**	.93**	.75*	.70*	.75*	.83**	.71*	.87**
Paradox of Control	.69*	.41	.28	.73*	.78**	.65*	.70*	.46	.73*	.55	.67*
Loss of Self	.86**	.67*	.38	.78**	.75*	.82**	.83**	.51	.81**	.53	.77**
Time Transformation	.86**	.75*	.66*	.79**	.78**	.79**	.60	.61	.62	.48	.79**
Autotelic Experience	.57	.38	.68*	.69*	.75*	.53	.32	.63	.54	.55	.67*
Group Flow	.81**	.56	.54	.85**	.91**	.76*	.69*	.63	.79**	.65*	.82**

Note: N = ten teams.

*p < .05, two-tailed; **p < .01

Table 4.3 $rwg_{(j)}$ indexes for all Flow and Social Presence scores

Group	*Chall Skills Balance*	*Action Awareness Merge*	*Clear Goals*	*Unambiguous Feedback*	*Concentration*	*Paradox of Control*	*Loss of Self*	*Time Transformation*	*Autotelic Experience*	*Group Flow*	*Co-presence*	*Global Social Presence*
1	0.95	0.88	0.90	0.99	1.00	0.84	0.99	0.93	0.86	0.94	0.98	0.97
2	1.00	0.90	0.83	0.96	0.86	0.85	0.89	0.87	0.84	0.96	0.96	0.97
3	0.93	0.83	0.89	0.90	0.87	0.87	0.88	0.83	0.89	0.94	0.95	0.95
4	0.88	0.88	0.75	0.82	0.89	0.87	0.93	0.76	0.85	0.94	0.96	0.97
5	0.89	0.90	0.93	0.89	0.93	0.92	0.87	0.94	0.93	0.96	0.99	0.99
6	0.75	0.91	0.70	0.79	0.78	0.77	0.90	0.83	0.71	0.89	0.98	0.96
7	0.84	0.90	0.91	0.92	0.93	0.94	0.96	0.90	0.80	0.97	0.97	0.96
8	0.94	0.95	0.90	0.92	0.90	0.94	0.88	0.93	0.81	0.97	0.97	0.98
9	0.86	0.92	0.88	0.89	0.96	0.95	0.93	0.94	0.89	0.96	0.99	0.99
10	0.81	0.87	0.83	0.88	0.88	0.96	0.81	0.76	0.76	0.94	0.97	0.95

Note: We computed $r_{wg(j)}$ (>= .70) to calculate interrater agreement. All $r_{wg(j)}$ coefficients are reported in the table. We found all the groups had a $r_{wg(j)}$ value of .7 or higher for all of the scales.

Table 4.4 Generalised Linear Model: SNA indexes as predictors, Group Flow, Global Social Presence, and Group Creativity as measures

	Dependent Measures			
Predictors	*Statistics*	*Creativity*	*Group Flow*	*Global Social Presence*
Density	B	−4.455	−62.518	−159.562
	Wald χ^2	3.236	19.812	7.894
	Sign.	p = .072	p < .005	p = .005
InDegree Centralisation	B	62.151	−79.872	−721.133
	Wald χ^2	4.177	.164	.818
	Sign.	p = .041	p = .685	p = .366
CVInDegree Centralisation	B	.236	−.511	−5.510
	Wald χ^2	.445	.369	2.629
	Sign.	p = .118	p = 543	p = .105
OutDegree Centralisation	B	−62.494	90.761	785.197
	Wald χ^2	4.178	.212	.972
	Sign.	p = .04	p = .645	p = .324
CVOutDegree Centralisation	B	.193	.237	4.923
	Wald χ^2	1.720	.085	2.254
	Sign.	p = .190	p = .770	p = .133
CPI	B	.476	7.020	11.487
	Wald χ^2	.959	6.668	1.092
	Sign.	p = .327	p = .010	p = .296

levels. By calculating these SNA indexes, based on exiting literature (such as Freeman, 1978; Mazzoni, 2014), dichotomous data become continuous, as they represent interconnected dynamics of the entire network. In Table 4.4, all the tested models are reported. Group creativity was significantly and positively predicted by OutDegree Centralisation and InDegree Centralisation, although in an opposite direction. Flow was negatively predicted by Density, but positively by CPI. Finally, Density predicted Group Global Social Presence negatively. The analysis was deepened by focusing on three groups, which were selected because they showed the highest (Group A, Group B) and lowest creativity scores (Group C). Given the crucial role of central weeks of collaboration for the emergence of a specific group structural pattern (Galimberti, et al., 2016), only the time window ranging from the 4th to the 9th week was considered.

Analysis of Group Structural Dynamics

Because of the richness of SNA data available, we decided to focus the analysis on a subset of groups with well-defined profiles in terms of creativity outcomes, flow, and social presence. The selection criteria are detailed as follows. All groups were ranked based on creativity. Then, groups with the highest creativity scores (i.e., Group A and Group B) and the group that reported the lowest creativity score (i.e., Group C) were identified. Since the aim was to map out relevant structural dynamics involved in creative collaboration, communication exchanges among members were used to build a model of group interactions. However, Group A (highly creative) reported very few online interactions across the 11 weeks of collaboration. Therefore, in line with NF model requirements, we chose to balance this out in two ways. First, we included in the analysis another high-performing group whose exchanges were richer (Group B). Second, we deepened the analysis of Group A by focusing on the micro-level of interaction among members, using the Interlocutory Logic technique (Trognon & Batt, 2010). The analysis of dialogues allowed us to examine more closely the group dynamics and to provide a richer context for the interpretation of the relatively small number of online communication exchanges reported by this group.

In Table 4.5 Group A featured the highest global Creativity scores (i.e., 28) and Group Flow (326), as well as a high Global Social Presence (1038). In terms of SNA, Group A showed low Density and low InDegree Centralisation (Figure 4.2). The sequence of images in the line above showed the amount of interactions between the group across four weeks and during the ending phase (Figure 4.3). This group accrued all interactions between the 8th and the 9th week of collaboration. Images above showed sociograms of interactions during the ending phase (Figure 4.3). The left-bottom image showed the trend of Density, InDegreeCentralisation, OutDegreeCentralisation (we considered only dichotomous values indicating only the presence/absence of an interaction between members), and CPI during the same phase. The right-bottom image represented the same trend for InDegree and OutDegree Centralisation.

In Table 4.5 Group B showed a high Creativity score (23), as well as high levels of Group Flow (251) and Global Social Presence (851). SNA data indicated that Group B featured both high Density and high InDegreeCentralisation (Figure 4.4).

In Table 4.5 Group C, whose global Creativity score (i.e., 11), Group Flow score (225), and Global Social Presence score (824) were the lowest, showed lower Density but higher InDegree Centralisation indexes compared to the previous group (Figure 4.5).

Table 4.5 Group Creativity, Group Flow, and Global Social Presence of the selected groups

Groups	*Creativity*	*Flow*	*Social Presence*
A	28	326	1038
B	23	251	851
C	11	225	824

Note: Three out of ten groups are presented. Scores were computed as sums.

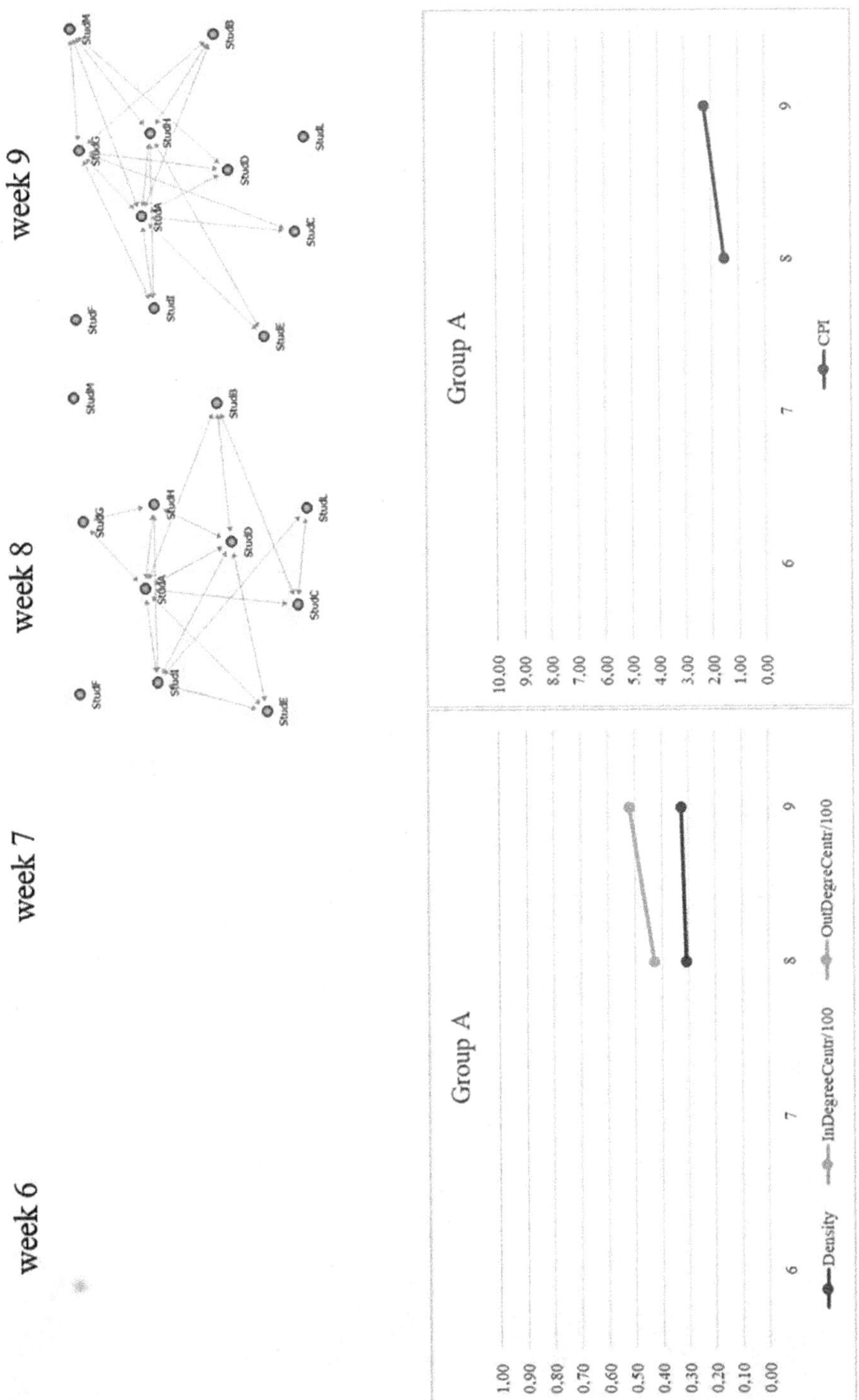

Figure 4.3 Group A SNA indexes across central weeks of collaboration

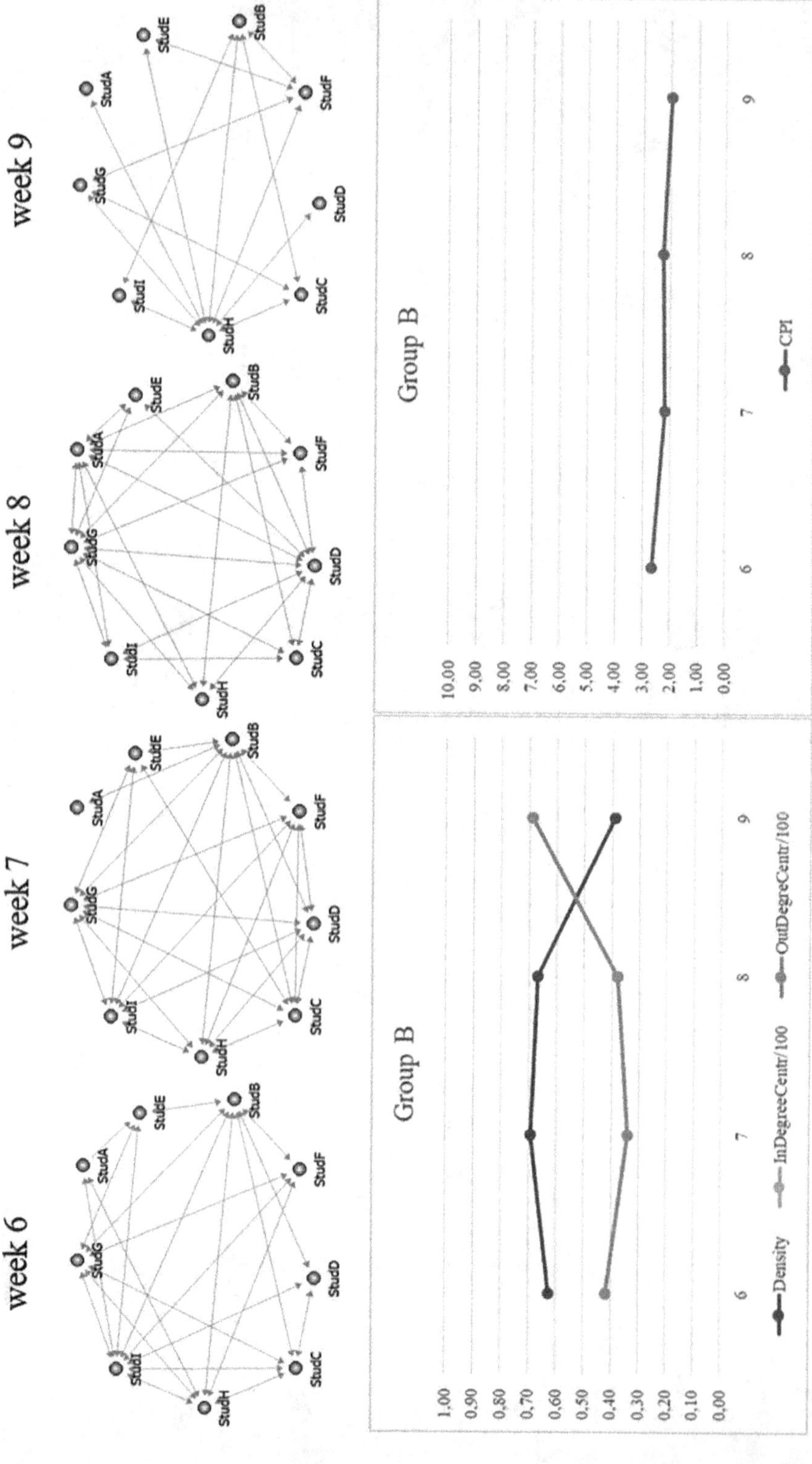

Figure 4.4 Group B SNA indexes across central weeks of collaboration

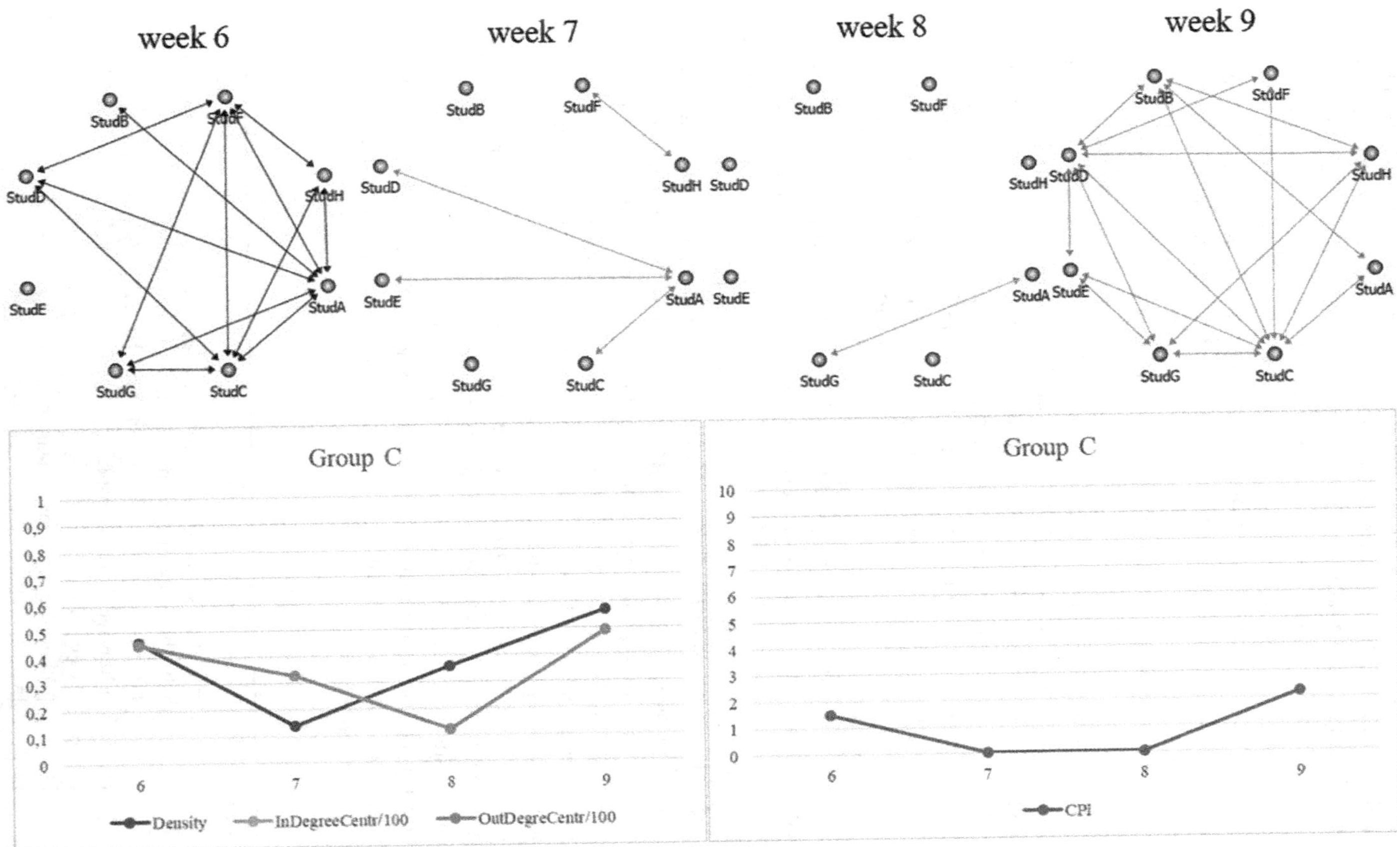

Figure 4.5 Group C SNA indexes across central weeks of collaboration

The analysis of interactions of Group A was deepened following the guidelines of the Interlocutory Logic method. This group was chosen since it was the most informative group, according to the NF model, because it scored highest on creativity. Two recordings of conversations from the first and central weeks of Group A's meetings were considered to find out prototypical macro-sequences of problem-solving or creative (idea-generating) processes. Three sequences from the first meeting and one from the half-way meeting were selected. These sequences were transcribed adopting the most commonly used conventions for transcribing vocal conduct in talk-in-interaction (Sacks, Schegloff, & Jefferson, 1974; see supplementary materials) and revised by two researchers until a high level of consent (agreement rate = 90%) was reached. Crucially, the analysis of the first off-line meeting reported group collaborative dynamics occurring in the "silent" phase of online group collaboration, that is, when no SNA data was collected. The analysis of these sequences identified specific patterns of communicative interactions that may help explain the high creativity scores obtained by Group A, as well as a high level of flow and social presence that were reported by its members.

Results of the analysis highlighted that Group A used the same pattern of "accumulation" of ideas across meetings and that two types of actors mainly managed this process. The first type of actor attended the first meeting and was the functional leader of the team. The second type of actor was absent but was "presentified" through the other participants' discourse. His "fictional" presence was used by the group to regulate decision-making processes. This second type of regulator could be either an absent team member or a person external to the group (in the following example, the regulating figure is the professor of their class). Two excerpts from the sequences are used here to support these analyses.

In this first meeting, group members accumulated and discarded ideas randomly and rapidly, with no specific time management and no clear goal. Members showed a low monological coherence across different topics, but looked for dialogical continuity, necessary to solve the assigned task. This strategy was crucial to mantain group dialogue, and to start shaping the quality of *group experience*.

Excerpt 1

1	G	= and we see ehm: different artists how they react, thus the: [= poet what he writes, the painter what
2		He paints and: [the dancer what he dances:[= and:: that all I think
3	H	[Otherwise you cannot hear
4	E	= th[e painter!
5	H	[Otherwise you cannot hear
6	E	[= Eh!
7		Correct

8	H	*[This is so nice!*
9	G	[= And:: then-
10	A	[Then (0.3) or we decide on a common theme, not music, a theme
11	G	A theme:
12	H	[But, that is:
13	-	[=
14	B	[Yeah one says to improv on something, instead a theme is focused
15	G	Then, what she is says is ok, but if you do that it's not real group work. I
16		Think that it depends, that i[s= – depends on how you sell it (0.4), meaning-
17	B	= [that is- (0.3) correct that in my opinion if-
18	C	*Then* in the end there is something made by the group, because everyone is influenced by the same thing
19		So if we rely on the fact that in the end the result is a – group thing (h) it is on point
20	G	In my opinion yes
21	A	Maybe we have to choose ehm: a theme – an idea

Students avoided starting an argumentative discussion to convince the other party to accept or retract his/her standpoint (van Eemeren & Grootendorst, 1992), which is clearly illustrated in line 15, when the student G advances an argument in support of his standpoint: *but if you do that it's not real group work*. Even though the argument advanced by the student was introduced by the linguistic marker "but", which typically indicates the beginning of a disagreement between the participant to a discussion (Schiffrin, 1987), it did not trigger any conflict among the students. Rather, all the students promptly showed their agreement with student G's argumentation. In this case, the absence of impulsive responses and rude behaviours during the argumentative discussions among group members may have played a crucial role in favouring group-creativity (Chiu, 2008; Chiu & Khoo, 2003; Hawlina, Gillespie, & Zittoun, 2017). Recently, several studies have demonstrated the link between the presence of argumentation among group members and the group-creativity levels. For instance, previous studies found that when group members value one another's diverse contributions they create more ideas and justifications (Larson, 2007; Paulus & Brown, 2003; Stasson & Bradshaw, 1995; Swann, Kwan, Polzer, & Milton, 2003). In the same line, De Dreu and West (2001) found that a disagreement among the members of the group might help them consider more aspects of a problem from more perspectives and, accordingly, increase the level of creativity of the group (in this regard, see also Nemeth & Chiles, 1988; and Nemeth & Rogers, 1996). In a similar vein, Gajda and her colleagues (Gajda, Beghetto, & Karwowski, 2017), using a micro-level interactional analysis to visually illustrate patterns of interactions between teachers and students, found more extended and exploratory interactions in classrooms where there was a positive association between students' measured creativity and academic achievement.

Excerpt 2

1	E	*But I think that he ((the professor)) wants us to use music because in my opinion because he* – (.) but we – he is
2		Introducing music to us, it's jazz and he linked jazz to organisations, to enterprises, to business
3		etcetera, etcetera – thus perhaps he – thus he brings in music bands for us, otherwise he could have brought in
4		even a painter – [and the painter would have done improv
5	G	[But maybe (0.4) ehm::: a way to demonstrate improv could be
6		I put – a musician and – a painter in the same room and see how they relate to each other = – and I just
7		Ask them "paint according to what you hear or play according to what you see:"

In the second excerpt, the group members accumulated ideas and proposals, analysed each possibility, and solved problems. Then, they moved to another point of the discussion. At that moment, the group had a specific goal in mind that needed to be reached. Hence, dialogical continuity was no longer a need to be fulfilled. On the contrary, the emergence of small oppositions in the dialogue in Excerpt 2 marked argumentative interactions among the members of the group. Accumulation of topics and ideas advanced as arguments in support of opinions was strictly linked to a sequence of problems and to the attempt to find their solutions. In this case, confrontation – the externalisation of disagreement on a certain standpoint – emerged as a necessary condition for an argumentative discussion to occur. Therefore, recalling how group members dialectically solved differences of opinion was useful to highlight dialogical choices, forms, and dynamics adopted by students.

In conclusion, the results of the qualitative analysis of two excerpts evidenced how Group A members exercised and managed both the *dialogic continuity* and the *monological coherence*, which is at the basis of the ability to manage both the group dynamics and the organisational dimension of the communication process within the group.

Discussion

A key finding concerns the relation between SNA indexes, creativity outcomes, and flow. All SNA indexes resulted as significant predictors of group creativity outcomes, flow, and social presence. These results are in line with a key hypothesis of the NF model on the role of group social network structure as a proxy of creative collaboration. However, as suggested by NF,

SNA remains a quantitative method providing rich data that needs to be complemented by an integrative approach (Gaggioli, et al., 2013; Wasserman, 1994) focusing on group performance, optimal experience, and dialogical dynamics.

On group performance, group centralisation indexes (i.e., InDegree Centralisation and OutDegree Centralisation) predicted teams' creative performance, even though in an opposite way. Specifically, the InDegree Centralisation index was positively related to creativity, while the OutDegree Centralisation index showed a negative link with group creative performance. OutDegree Centralisation and InDegree Centralisation indexes are measures of different kinds of groups' leadership dynamics. High levels of OutDegree Centralisation indicate a group structure with all interactions stemming from a specific member(s) – leader(s) – as a group "manager". InDegree Centralisation indicates the extent to which group exchanges are directed towards a specific member(s), intended as a reference point or as an inspirational source.

Consistently, several studies evidenced that network structural dynamics were crucial to achieve a shared goal (Brass, 1984; Burton & Carroll, 2001; Friedkin, 1993; Ibarra & Andrews, 1993; Molm, 1994; Sparrowe, Liden, Wayne, & Kraimer, 2001). Studies on small collaborative web groups showed that High Density and Low Centralisation were associated with better performances (Aviv, Erlich, Ravid, & Geva, 2003; Mazzoni & Gaffuri, 2009; Mazzoni, Gaffuri, & Selleri, 2013). Also, Cliques Participation Index (CPI), defined as the average individual involvement in the substructure (clique), can be conceived as an indicator of small groups' originality and creativity levels, when members are involved in a shared-goal task (Mazzoni, 2014). Here, we found only a significant relationship between group creativity outcomes and centralisation indexes, as a potential consequence of the small number of team members (Mazzoni, 2014). More, the density index was also not a significant predictor of creativity score. This may suggest finer processes underlying group creativity, thus requiring a more detailed approach of analysis. The NF model prescribes to deepen the analysis of the group creativity process by focusing on a micro-level of analysis, i.e., analysing single group exchanges.

As such, we chose to zoom in to three paradigmatic groups (which we called "Group A", "Group B", and "Group C") identified as the highly creative (vs. lowly creative) teams. First, we differentiated these groups on the base of the interactive dynamics represented by the sociograms. Then, we integrated the structural data from Group A with the dialogical ones achieved though Interlocutory Logic analysis. Group A – the most creative group – accrued interactions during last weeks, but several members interacted and participated. It showed low density and a low centralisation. Despite the lack of online interactions during the first two weeks, members might have been able to bring forth necessary exchanges to generate a creative artefact. Qualitative dialogical analysis showed that Group A proceeded randomly in the initial phases, but it ended with a high level of monological coherence. Once a collaborative frame has been established in the early stages of group work, members might have been able to focus on a common goal: the assigned task. Probably, they just need to interact to share ideas relevant to pursue the goal and be able to promote combination and "confrontation" of different points of view. Maybe, their overall approach led to low centrality and low density, as detected in the final stages of group collaboration. Similarly, Group B (the second most creative group) displayed low density, low CPI, and low centralisation. It also showed, in the final stages, a strong leader to whom information were oriented.

On the opposite side, Group C (the least creative group) displayed a higher centralisation of interactions oriented to specific members across the whole period (higher density and CPI). This pattern might have invalidated group creative performance.

According to findings on small groups and creativity (Aviv, et al., 2003; Mazzoni, 2014), a *democratic* sharing of information and a good but *thriftly* (i.e., the management of interaction was made only when necessary and not as a default control mechanism) managing of interactions could enhance creative performance. Therefore, despite Group C activating more interactions than Group A (i.e., it showed higher Density), its dynamics resulted as not well structured, and this might have lowered the final performance. To date, we adopted a vertical approach of analysis, from creative performance at the networked level (all groups) to the intra-group level (single groups). This investigation might seem exhaustive, but the NF model suggests also a horizontal plane of analysis. NF posited the need to investigate also the quality of group members' experiences.

As concerns group optimal experience, we found that Density and CPI predicted flow experience at the team level. Density, i.e., a measure of participation, was negatively related to group flow, while CPI (i.e., an indicator of members' involvement in different discussions) showed a positive relation with group flow. Therefore, less but diversified exchanges among group members could lead to an increased experience of group flow. Density was the only significant but negative SNA predictor of social presence. Groups with less exchanges reported a higher sense of co-presence, or a sense of mutual connectedness. At first sight, this result may seem rather unexpected, as one would anticipate that social presence is higher when members interact *more*. Despite previous research that has shown that dense groups are more socially cohesive, share different points of view, and show higher levels of satisfaction and stability (Saqr, Fors, Tedre, & Nouri, 2018), our quantitative findings were consistent with our analysis of dialogues. Only a few interactions were activated by highly creative groups, maybe because they did not need more relational effort to pursue the shared goal, since they have already achieved the right harmony among members. Once harmony was achieved, members, maybe, did not need to interact more; they were already "tuned" with each other.

Conclusions

Twenty-first-century survival skills should include also the ability to manage even complex interactions in a mediated context in a creative way (Kumpulainen, Mikkola, & Jaatinen, 2014). Technology and creativity have become a pervasive issue from the work (Turel & Zhang, 2010), to the artistic (e.g., Biasutti, 2015), to the pedagogical domain (e.g., Kumpulainen, et al., 2014). This work evidenced how creativity occurs even in blended environments when people interact physically and online. Starting from an idea of *networked creativity*, this study applied the NF model to unveil the experiential and structural dynamics of group creative process in blended environments. Here, we relied on two online social networks to introduce a "mediated" interaction component of analysis, that is, Facebook and WhatsApp. To our best knowledge, this study is a pioneer in the field of these two social networks and creativity. Crucially, since the NF model posited that both online and in presence interactions are useful for group creativity to emerge, an analysis integrating the physical exchanges among members with Facebook and WhatsApp-based interactions was adopted to achieve a more integrated and exhaustive group creative process view.

Practically, the core aspects of this research can be summed up as follows. First, we could assume that creative collaboration performance and group flow do not have a simple linear relationship, even though both experiences resulted related to specific group structural dynamics. Micro-communicative exchanges among members are crucial, and can be either frequent or not frequent, but need to be used to fuel group experience. Our results may suggest a three-stage process. It starts with group members building a common frame to settle a shared collaborative ground with a maximum level of group flow and social presence. This gives rise to a mutual zone of proximal development in which individuals just need to find the best ways to sustain the highest levels of group flow and social presence through specific interactions. This hypothesis is supported also by qualitative analysis of the dialogues among members in the early stages of group collaboration of Group A. Initially, members spend more time sharing ideas to enter a MZPD. At a second stage, they need less coordination effort. This would lead to artefact creation in the third phase. We may assume an initial phase of "closeness" promoting engagement in the creative process. Then, the network could have displayed more lax links among members, bringing forth an "open" network structure with a density no longer related to final creative outcomes (Porter, Keith, & Woo, 2018).

To complete the picture, our results may suggest that a formula for group creativity does not exist; instead, there could be potentially different pathways. Specifically, we found, at least, two possible interactive dynamics at the base of NF experience. NF might be either manifested in many interactions (i.e., "explicit" NF) or in fewer ones (i.e., a sort of "silent NF"). An effective metaphor to explain this process can be drawn from quantum physics regarding the wave-particle dualism. This posits that light can be shaped as a wave or particle, but it is always light. This could be the case of NF in creative collaboration teams. Optimal group experience of excellent creative teams might take two different forms: an explicit one (e.g., Group B: high Density and Centralisation indexes) or an implicit one (e.g., Group A: low Density and Centralisation indexes). The explicit form could be easily detected through SNA indexes, since it would result into a larger number of frequent interactions among members. The implicit form would be more difficult to measure by means of structural indexes since it would require a smaller number of interactions among team members. This depends on the group members' "maintenance" strategy to sustain NF.

A future step to test this hypothesis could be implementing measures of implicit communication such as eye contact exchanges, as it has been successfully done in previous studies but in different domains (e.g., Gaggioli, et al., 2017), overcoming the influence of social norms, and accessing a more authentic and sincere level of group dynamics. Finally, the aim of this study was explorative, and it focused only on ten groups with small size; therefore, it would be useful to replicate and extend the findings of this study with a wider sample. Moreover, in order to advance the implementation of the NF model in ecological and complex contexts, a future step could be to integrate our current longitudinal network analysis approach with a more sophisticated modelling technique such as SIENA (Simulation Investigation for Empirical Network Analysis) (Snijders, 2014).

Appendix

Transcription Conventions

– cut off of the prior word or sound
( ) description of situation / speaker's actions
word forms of stressing (pitch and/or volume)
(0.1) elapsed time in tenths of seconds
= lack of interval between the end of a prior and start of a next piece of talk
(h) explosive aspiration
°( ) low in volume
: prolonging of sounds
// // segments overlapped by the talk of another

Notes

1. In SNA, relations can be considered as dichotomous (the relation is present/not present) or reported as a range of values that indicate the strength, intensity, or frequency of a relationship. In this research, we calculated dichotomous relations to perform correlation analyses and comparisons, and to analyse structural features of groups. Specifically, dichotomous relations were entered in matrixes from which we calculated specific SNA numerical indexes.
2. The Networked Model posited that the sense of mutual connection among members (social presence) and a sense of group flow are experiential drivers for the emergence of mutual zone of proximal development.
3. The adjacency matrix is a square matrix used to represent relational data, in which the rows and columns represent different nodes or vertices of interactions inside their own group, with the technical supervision of an experimenter, who had no direct access to the contents of the conversations. We devoted two hours-lessons on basic principles of Social Network Analysis (SNA) in the course (second lesson). Specifically, students received instructions on data extractions from their own conversations online on Facebook and/or WhatsApp. Then, as part of their course program, they were taught to create the adjacency matrixes from their own interaction data. The digital instruction materials on how to build SNA adjacency matrixes, which were provided to students, are available upon request.

References

Agresti, A., & Kateri, M. (2011). *Categorical data analysis international encyclopedia of statistical science* (pp. 206–208). Berlin, Heidelberg: Springer.

Amabile, T. M. (1982). Social psychology of creativity: A consensual assessment technique. *Journal of Personality and Social Psychology, 43*(5), 997.

Armstrong, A. C. (2008). The fragility of group flow: The experiences of two small groups in a middle school mathematics classroom. *Journal of Mathematical Behavior, 27*(2008), 101–115.

Aviv, R., Erlich, Z., Ravid, G., & Geva, A. (2003). Network analysis of knowledge construction in asynchronous learning networks. *Journal of Asynchronous Learning Networks*, 7(3), 1–23.

Bell, J., Sawaya, S., & Cain, W. (2014). Synchromodal classes: Designing for shared learning experiences between face-to-face and online students. *International Journal of Designs for Learning, 5*(1).

Biasutti, M. (2015). Creativity in virtual spaces: Communication modes employed during collaborative online music composition. *Thinking Skills and Creativity*, 17, 117–129.

Biocca, F., & Harms, C. (2003). *Guide to THE NETWORKED MINDS SOCIAL PRESENCE Inventory v. 1.2: Measures of co-presence, social presence, subjective symmetry, and intersubjective symmetry*. East Lansing, MI: Michigan State University.

Biocca, F., & Harms, C. (2011). *Networked minds social presence inventory (scales only version 1.2): Tech. rep, MIND Labs*, Michigan State University, Michigan, 2002. Retrieved 11 March 2011 from http://cogprints.org/6742/

Brass, D. J. (1984). Being in the right place: A structural analysis of individual influence in an organization. *Administrative Science Quarterly*, 518–539.

Burton, J., & Carroll, M. (2001). *Journal writing as an aid to self-awareness, autonomy, and collaborative learning*. Doctoral dissertation, TESOL, Alexandria, VA.

Chiu, M. M. (2008). Effects of argumentation on group micro-creativity: Statistical discourse analyses of algebra students' collaborative problem solving. *Contemporary Educational Psychology, 33*(3), 382–402.

Chiu, M. M., & Khoo, L. (2003). Rudeness and status effects during group problem solving: Do they bias evaluations and reduce the likelihood of correct solutions? *Journal of Educational Psychology, 95*(3), 506–523.

Csikszentmihalyi, M. (1988). *Society, culture, and person: A systems view of creativity. The systems model of creativity*. Dordrecht: Springer.

Csikszentmihalyi, M., & Csikzentmihaly, M. (1990). *Flow: The psychology of optimal experience* (Vol. 1990). New York: Harper & Row.

De Dreu, C. K. W., & West, M. A. (2001). Minority dissent and team innovation. *Journal of Applied Psychology, 86*(6), 1191–1201.

De Laat, M., Lally, V., Lipponen, L., & Simons, R.-J. (2007). Investigating patterns of interaction in networked learning and computer-supported collaborative learning: A role for social network analysis. *International Journal of Computer-Supported Collaborative Learning, 2*(1), 87–103.

Diana, B., Villani, D., Muzio, M., & Riva, G. (2012). La validazione italiana della Flow State Scale – FSS. In M. Muzio, G. Riva, & L. Argenton (Eds.), *Flow, benessere e prestazione eccellente. Dai modelli teorici alle applicazioni nello sport e in azienda* (pp. 123–142). Milan: FrancoAngeli.

Eisler, R., Donnelly, G., & Montuori, A. (2016). Creativity, society, and gender: Contextualizing and redefining creativity. *Interdisciplinary Journal of Partnership, 3*(2).

Freeman, L. C. (1978). Centrality in social networks conceptual clarification. *Social Networks, 1*(3), 215–239.

Friedkin, N. E. (1993). Structural bases of interpersonal influence in groups: A longitudinal case study. *American Sociological Review*, 861–872.

Gaggioli, A., Chirico, A., Mazzoni, E., Milani, L., & Riva, G. (2017). Networked flow in musical bands. *Psychology of Music, 45*(2), 283–297. https://doi.org/10.1177/0305735616665003

Gaggioli, A., Mazzoni, E., Milani, L., & Riva, G. (2015). The creative link: Investigating the relationship between social network indices, creative performance and flow in blended teams. *Computers in Human Behavior, 42*, 157–166.

Gaggioli, A., Riva, G., Milani, L., & Mazzoni, E. (2013). *Networked flow: Towards an understanding of creative networks*. Dordrecht, Netherlands: Springer.

Gajda, A., Beghetto, R. A., & Karwowski, M. (2017). Exploring creative learning in the classroom: A multi-method approach. *Thinking Skills and Creativity, 24*, 250–267.

Galimberti, C., Chirico, A., Brivio, E., Gatti, F., Mazzoni, E., Riva, G., . . . Gaggioli, A. (2016). Networked flow in blended learning settings: A longitudinal mixed-method study. *Annual Review of Cybertherapy and Telemedicine 2016*, 39.

Galimberti, C., Chirico, A., Brivio, E., Mazzoni, E., Riva, G., Milani, L., & Gaggioli, A. (2015). Bridging minds: A mixed methodology to assess networked flow. *Stud Health Technol Inform, 219*, 33–36.

Glăveanu, V. P. (2010). Paradigms in the study of creativity: Introducing the perspective of cultural psychology. *New Ideas in Psychology, 28*(1), 79–93.

Glăveanu, V. P. (2015). Creativity as a sociocultural act. *The Journal of Creative Behavior, 49*(3), 165–180.

Goos, M., Galbraith, P., & Renshaw, P. (2002). Socially mediated metacognition: Creating collaborative zones of proximal development in small group problem solving. *Educational Studies in Mathematics, 49*(2), 193–223.

Harms, C., & Biocca, F. (2004). *Internal consistency and reliability of the networked minds measure of social presence*. Retrieved 11 March 2011 from http://cogprints.org/7026/

Hawlina, H., Gillespie, A., & Zittoun, T. (2017). Difficult differences: A socio-cultural analysis of how diversity can enable and inhibit creativity. *The Journal of Creative Behavior*, Special Issue, 1–12.

Hinds, P., Kiesler, S. B., & Kiesler, S. (2002). *Distributed work*. Cambridge, MA: MIT Press.

Hutchins, E. (2006). The distributed cognition perspective on human interaction. *Roots of Human Sociality: Culture, Cognition and Interaction, 1*, 375.

Ibarra, H., & Andrews, S. B. (1993). Power, social influence, and sense making: Effects of network centrality and proximity on employee perceptions. *Administrative Science Quarterly*, 277–303.

Jackson, S. A., & Csikszentmihalyi, M. (1999). *Flow in sports*. Champaign, IL: Human Kinetics.

Jackson, S. A., & Eklund, R. C. (2002). Assessing flow in physical activity: The flow state scale-2 and dispositional flow scale-2. *Journal of Sport & Exercise Psychology, 24*, 133–150.

Jackson, S. A., & Eklund, R. C. (2004). *The flow scales manual*. Morgantown, WV: Fitness Information Technology.

Jackson, S. A., & Marsh, H. W. (1996). Development and validation of a scale to measure optimal experience: The Flow state scale. *Journal of Sport and Exercise Psychology, 18*, 17–35.

John-Steiner, V. (2000). *Creative collaboration*. Oxford: Oxford University Press.

John-Steiner, V., & Mahn, H. (1996). Sociocultural approaches to learning and development: A Vygotskian framework. *Journal of Educational Psychology, 31*(3–4), 191–206.

Kumpulainen, K., Mikkola, A., & Jaatinen, A. M. (2014). The chronotopes of technology-mediated creative learning practices in an elementary school community. *Learning, Media and Technology, 39*(1), 53–74.

Larson, J. R. (2007). Deep diversity and strong synergy. *Small Group Research, 38*(3), 413–436.

Mackinnon, M. J., & Puterman, M. L. (1989). Collinearity in generalized linear models. *Communications in Statistics-theory and Methods, 18*(9), 3463–3472.

Mazzoni, E. (2014). The Cliques Participation Index (CPI) as an indicator of creativity in online collaborative groups. *Journal of Cognitive Education and Psychology, 13*(1), 32.

Mazzoni, E., & Gaffuri, P. (2009). Personal learning environments for overcoming knowledge boundaries between activity systems in emerging adulthood. *E-Learning Papers, 15*(5), 1–10.

Mazzoni, E., Gaffuri, P., & Selleri, P. (2013). Is it better to be alone or in company?: The impact of the structural profile of interpersonal skills on computer-supported group-based learning. In *Cases on online learning communities and beyond: Investigations and applications* (pp. 37–67). Hershey, PA: IGI Global.

McKay, A. S., Grygiel, P., & Karwowski, M. (2017). Connected to create: A social network analysis of friendship ties and creativity. *Psychology of Aesthetics, Creativity, and the Arts, 11*(3), 284.

Molm, L. D. (1994). Dependence and risk: Transforming the structure of social exchange. *Social Psychology Quarterly*, 163–176.

Montuori, A., & Purser, R. E. (1995). Deconstructing the lone genius myth: Toward a contextual view of creativity. *Journal of Humanistic Psychology, 35*(3), 69–112.

Nemeth, C. J., & Chiles, C. (1988). Modeling courage: The role of dissent in fostering independence. *European Journal of Psychology, 18*(3), 275–280.

Nemeth, C. J., & Rogers, J. (1996). Dissent and the search for information. *British Journal of Social Psychology, 35*(1), 67–76.

Palonen, T., & Hakkarainen, K. (2013). *Patterns of interaction in computer-supported learning: A social network analysis*. Erlbaum: Oxford, UK.

Paulus, P. B., & Brown, V. (2003). Ideational creativity in groups. In P. B. Paulus & B. A. Nijstad (Eds.), *Group creativity* (pp. 110–136). New York: Oxford University Press.

Porter, C. M., Keith, M. G., & Woo, S. E. (2018). A metaanalysis of network positions and creative performance: Differentiating creativity conceptualizations and measurement approaches. *Psychology of Aesthetics, Creativity, and the Arts, 14*(1), 50–67.

Sacks, H., Schegloff, E., & Jefferson, G. (1974). A simplest systematics for the organization of turn-taking for conversation. *Language, 50*(4 Pt 1), 696–735.

Saqr, M., Fors, U., Tedre, M., & Nouri, J. (2018). How social network analysis can be used to monitor online collaborative learning and guide an informed intervention. *PLoS One, 13*(3), e0194777.

Sawyer, K. (2007). *Group genius: The collective power of collaboration*. New York: Basic Books.

Schiffrin, D. (1987). *Discourse marker*. Cambridge: Cambridge University Press.

Scott, J. (2000). *Social network analysis: A handbook*. London: SAGE Publications.

Snijders, T. A. (2014). Siena: Statistical modeling of longitudinal network data. *Encyclopedia of Social Network Analysis and Mining*, 1718–1725.

So, H.-J., & Brush, T. A. (2008). Student perceptions of collaborative learning, social presence and satisfaction in a blended learning environment: Relationships and critical factors. *Computers & Education, 51*(1), 318–336.

Sparrowe, R. T., Liden, R. C., Wayne, S. J., & Kraimer, M. L. (2001). Social networks and the performance of individuals and groups. *Academy of Management Journal, 44*(2), 316–325.

Stasson, M. F., & Bradshaw, S. D. (1995). Explanation of individual-group performance differences. *Small Group Research, 26*(2), 296–308.

Swann, W. B. Jr., Kwan, V. S. Y., Polzer, J. T., & Milton, L. P. (2003). Fostering group identification and creativity in diverse groups. *Personality and Social Psychology Bulletin, 29*(11), 1396–1406.

Trognon, A., & Batt, M. (2010). Interlocutory logic. A unified framework for studying conversational interaction. In J. Streeck (Ed.), *New adventures in language and interaction* (pp. 9–46). Amsterdam: John Benjamins.

Turel, O., & Zhang, Y. (2010). Does virtual team composition matter? Trait and problem-solving configuration effects on team performance. *Behaviour & Information Technology, 29*(4), 363–375.

Van Eemeren, F., & Grootendorst, R. (1992). *Argumentation, communication, and fallacies a pragma-dialectical perspective*. Hillsdale, NJ: Routledge.

Walton, A. P. (2003). The impact of interpersonal factors on creativity. *International Journal of Entrepreneurial Behavior & Research, 9*(4), 146–162.

Wasserman, S. (1994). *Social network analysis: Methods and applications* (Vol. 8). Cambridge: Cambridge University Press.

Zohar, D., & Tenne-Gazit, O. (2008). Transformational leadership and group interaction as climate antecedents: A social network analysis. *Journal of Applied Psychology, 93*(4), 744.

5 The Expression of Users' Creative Potential in Virtual and Real Environments

An Exploratory Study

Samira Bourgeois-Bougrine, Peter Richard, Jean-Marie Burkhardt, Benjamin Frantz, and Todd Lubart

Introduction

In the past few years, users have been increasingly involved in the development of new products, services, and technologies. This trend is mainly motivated by the idea that users have knowledge of their own needs and are able to develop solutions that fit those needs (Kujala, 2003; Kristensson, Magnusson, & Matthing, 2002; Kristensson & Magnusson, 2010). In their research paper titled "Harnessing the creative potential among users", Kristensson, Gustafsson, and Archer (2004) indicated that professional developers and advanced users created significantly less original and valuable ideas than ordinary users when given the task of creating ideas for future mobile phone services. The authors suggested that aspects of earlier knowledge and experience might inhibit divergent thinking in terms of what was more or less technically feasible (p. 12). In addition, studies in ergonomics and management sciences have suggested difficulties related to the collaboration between users and experts such as divergences in perceived roles and interests (Cahour, 2002), difficulties for users to consider things in a long-term perspective, and the tendency of experts to reject systematically users' propositions due to their supposed lack of capacity (Buur & Matthews, 2008). A loss of productivity has been repeatedly reported in collective brainstorming and co-design situations, associated with the effect of being in "groups". This has been explained by referring to several socio-cognitive mechanisms like the apprehension of evaluation (social inhibition), the impossibility to express two ideas aloud at the same time (production blocking), the tendency to suggest ideas too similar to others (fixation), and the tendency to rely on the group to suggest ideas (social loafing) (see Diehl & Stroebe, 1987, for a review).

One way to support the exchange of ideas without production blocking is to hold ideation tasks in partially or totally computer-mediated environments (i.e., electronic brainstorming) that warrant against the aforementioned socio-cognitive biases, for example, by enabling the sharing of proposed ideas simultaneously amongst the participants while preserving anonymity (Dennis, & Williams, 2003; Michinov, Jamet, Métayer, & Le Hénaff, 2015). Multi-User Virtual Environments (MUVEs) are new types of computer-based environments that bring, in addition to the anonymity of the participants, the possibility to customise their avatars' appearance as well as their virtual environment. Recent research has, indeed, shown that MUVEs hold the potential to support greater creative collaboration due to behavioural modulation in situations of physical isolation, anonymity of the participants, and the appearance of their avatar (de Rooij, van der Land, & van Erp, 2017; Guegan, Buisine, Mantelet, Maranzana, & Segonds, 2016; Buisine, Guegan, Barré, Segonds, & Aoussat, 2016; Thornhill-Miller & Dupont, 2016). Guegan, et al. (2016) found, for example, significantly higher fluency and idea uniqueness when engineering students embodied an "inventor" avatar as compared to the same situation using an uncreative-stereotypical avatar. The second finding deals with the impact of the content and the visual appearance of the virtual environment. Using an ideation task, Bhagwatwar, et al. (2013) investigated the effect of providing a visually creative vs. neutral virtual environment. They obtained a significantly higher performance in the visual creative environment than in the neutral 3D environment, both in terms of number of ideas (fluency), originality (uniqueness), and relevance and workability of ideas. They interpret the results in terms of a priming mechanism. A limit of current research is that the way that MUVEs features may interact with the participants' individual characteristics has not been investigated in the context of creativity.

Indeed, research on collaboration within groups or teams of participants in virtual environments has assessed the creative performance at the team level with no analysis of individual differences regarding the team members' creative potential. Creative potential, which is the capacity to produce original ideas that have value in their context, refers to a latent state, which may be considered part of an individual's "human capital" and may be put to use if a person has the opportunity. Each person can be described as having more or less potential in a domain of work and, more specifically, in a given task. Creative potential remains latent, and the individual may be aware of his/her potential or may be blind to it. Recent advances suggest that creative potential stems from numerous factors (cognition, personality, emotional, environmental context); it can be defined, measured, and improved (Lubart, Zenasni, & Barbot, 2013). Assessing the extent to which a person is able to engage in creative work could (a) explain why some teams outperform others and what type of resources are involved, (b) be used to identify team members who may benefit from training programmes that develop specific cognitive or conative factors relevant to creativity (Lubart, et al., 2013), and (c) allocate creative avatars and/or hold creative session in stimulating virtual environments.

RESEARCH QUESTION

The aim of this study, which is exploratory in nature, was to examine (a) whether MUVEs improve everyone's creativity regardless of their creative potential profile and (b) the type of creative resources that facilitate fluency in a brainstorming task and the production of original ideas. For this purpose, our study involved brainstorming sessions in two conditions: a real meeting room (RE) and a similar meeting room in a virtual environment (VE). The participants, all users of public transport, were asked to provide solutions to improve the mobility in Paris's Île-de-France region. Because of the effect of the avatar appearance and virtual environments on creativity, behaviour, and attitude, we controlled the avatar appearance as well as the meeting room features to be able to explore the expression of creative potential in VE. Therefore, participants in VE were allocated neutral avatars and were not allowed to choose or personalise them or their settings.

Method

Participants

A group of 60 psychology undergraduate students participated in this study in exchange for course credit. The sample included 45 females and 15 males who were distributed equally between the two conditions (VE: 22 female and 8 male; RE: 23 female and 7 male). The average age was 22 ± 2.1 years. The participants did not know each other prior to the experiment, and there were no significant differences between the participants in the two conditions (VE and RE) in terms of age and creative potential. They were all users of public transport in Paris. One participant in each condition, VE and RE, did not complete their measure of creative potential and thus were excluded from the analysis.

Study Design/Procedure

The participants were divided randomly in 20 groups of three participants and were randomly assigned to one of the settings: face-to-face vs. 3D virtual room. The participants were asked to perform the brainstorming task for ten minutes and were strongly encouraged to collaborate. This study, which was a part of a large project that investigated individual creativity and group interaction and collaboration, will focus on the brainstorming task only.

Regardless of the condition, all participants were given the same following information and instructions about the task and rules of brainstorming:

> Every day, urban populations face many problems in their mobility: congestion of road traffic, lack of parking spaces, significant expenses related to transportation, saturation of public transport, delays, etc. In this context, the Paris Île-de-France region has called on its citizens

as well as engineers to find solutions that address these mobility issues (new modes of transport, new services, etc.). It is in this context that you were asked to participate in this workshop. You will perform this task as a group of three and together, you will have to imagine new solutions to improve the daily mobility in Paris Île-de-France region. Here are some rules to respect for the production of ideas: Do not judge others' ideas, do not judge your ideas/Do not restrict yourself: wild ideas are welcome/Do not hesitate to use others' ideas to improve them/Produce as many ideas as possible without worrying about quality.

Face-to-Face Condition

The participants were seated around a table with the experimenter in the physical meeting room of our lab. Each participant was handed a block of sticky notes of a particular colour: green, yellow, or pink (to trace the number of ideas per participant). They had to write one idea per note and say it out loud, before handing the post it to the experimenter. Reading or hearing others' ideas would theoretically have a stimulating effect of sharing ideas.

Virtual Environment Condition

We designed a virtual meeting room similar to the physical meeting room used for the face-to-face condition (Figure 5.1) using the Second Life environment from Linden Lab, one of the most widely used "sandbox" virtual worlds. The participants in the VE condition were installed in individual small rooms each equipped with a computer, were assigned neutral avatars, and communicated textually (chat) with each other. As none of the participants used Second Life before, they were made familiar with their avatars and trained to move in a virtual building to access the meeting room and to communicate with each other using the built-in Second Life chat. On the basis of the results of a previous study (Guegan, et al., 2016), the avatars assigned to the participants were neutral. They were asked to sit in the virtual meeting room with their avatars and to read the instructions given by the virtual leader (one of the experimenters), who was in another room. The brainstorming task lasted ten minutes. Before the task, the participants spent more time in the experimental box getting familiar with their avatars, moving in a virtual building to access the meeting room, and learning how to communicate with each other using the built-in Second Life chat.

Measurement of Creative Performance

Creative performance was measured threefold. Fluency was evaluated by counting the number of distinct ideas produced by each participant within

Figure 5.1 Brainstorming sessions in virtual and real environment with three participants and one experimenter

each team. Originality and utility of proposed ideas were evaluated through the following specific procedure based on expert judgements.

All the collected ideas in both conditions were randomly presented in an Excel sheet to eight analysts (postgraduate students in social sciences) who were blind to the conditions and hypothesis. Each analyst rated independently the ideas according to two criteria, originality and utility, on a 5-point Likert scale from 1 (not at all original/not at all useful) to 5 (extremely original/extremely useful). Then, two of them were given a new file to code the ideas in six categories: Improving existing public transport; Providing information and incentives; Promoting existing modes of travel; New urban developments; Futuristic/Science fiction ideas; and Changing work patterns. Each category was illustrated by examples of ideas. The coding framework was developed by the authors and was data driven. The aim was to assess not only the fluency of the participants in general, but also the number of ideas per category for each participant and team in the two conditions. Cronbach's alpha coefficients were 0.87 for originality and 0.62 for utility. The moderate level of agreement for utility may be explained by the fact that some judges considered utility as feasibility. As a consequence, some divergence was observed for a few original solutions that were useful to the problem at hand but not feasible in the short term. For the coding, Cohen's Kappa analysis showed a high degree of agreement between the two analysts (0.94).

Measurement of Individual Dimensions of Creative Potential and Profile of Participants

We evaluated the creative potential of participants, using the online version of the Creative Profiler (Lubart, et al., 2013; www.creativeprofiler.com). One of the paths to measure creative potential is resource-based, which consists of presenting an individual with a series of tasks and questionnaires to assess the components or the resources underlying creative work. Lubart, et al. (2013) proposed a tool that assesses the creative potential profile through a set of five cognitive and five conative measures based on their importance as identified in the literature (Table 5.1). The five cognitive components are: Divergent thinking, Mental flexibility, Analytic thinking, Associative thinking, and Selective combination. The cognitive resources, which refer to preferred ways of behaving, include five components: Openness, Tolerance of ambiguity, Intuitive thinking, Risk taking, and Motivation to create.

Statistical Analysis

Correlations and analysis of variance (ANOVA) were used to test our hypothesis regarding the link between creative potential and creative performance. The distributions of ideas categories was analysed using Cramer's V2 (Corroyer & Rouanet, 1994) and Relative deviations (Bernard, 2003). Cramer's V2 estimates the magnitude of the association between two categorical variables presenting more than two modalities. Relative deviations (RD) measure the association between the modalities of two nominal variables.

Table 5.1 The definitions of the ten dimensions of creative potential

Cognitive resources
Divergent thinking: It is defined as the ability to generate alternate ideas based on a single initial piece of information, which may be a word, an image, a story. A high level of divergent thinking indicates great ideational productivity and a certain degree of cognitive flexibility. Measure: Two tasks – generate ideas
Mental flexibility: It is the ability to change points of view and to change initial cognitive frames in order to explore new directions. It is synonymous to mental suppleness and to the ability to alternate between processing several kinds of information. Measure: Ambiguous images (morphing task) presented every 3 seconds, participants must list all the perceived interpretations of the image
Convergent or analytic thinking: It is defined as the global ability of individuals to reason and to complete various kinds of logical tasks. Intelligence is primarily measured by analytical thinking abilities. Measure: Matrices-type problems
Associative thinking: It is the ability to process and to put together elements or sets of elements that are not connected to one another. Measure: An association task
Analogical thinking or selective combination: It indicates the ability of individuals to create metaphors, to transpose information from a specific domain to another domain that is a priori independent, in order to find useful matches. Measure: Analogies search
Cognitive resources
Openness: It determines the tendency to seek out or to prefer novelty, to try out new things, and to have new experiences. It is opposed to dogmatism and conformism. Measure: Questionnaire
Tolerance of ambiguity: It is characterised by the ability to solve, or at least to tolerate situations and/or information that are ambiguous, unclear, contradictory, or absent. Measure: Questionnaire
Intuitive thinking: It qualifies the ability of individuals to rapidly grasp the real world, to experience situations in an instinctive manner, to have immediate knowledge of things without necessarily thinking about the target problem. Measure: Scenario-based (multiple choice between more or less intuitive alternatives)
Risk taking: It refers to the tendency of some individuals to take well advised and relatively suitable risks. Measure: Scenario-based (multiple choices between different probabilities more or less acceptable to engage in this new social and design activities)
Motivation to create: It is the will to create to respond to a demand or to satisfy a personal desire. It is an engine for the activation of knowledge involved in creation. Measure: Questionnaire

Results

The first section compares creative performance, e.g., fluency, originality, utility, and the type of ideas produced in the VE and RE conditions. The scores obtained by the participants for the dimensions of creative potential are presented in the second section. The association between the creative potential and performance is analysed in the third section.

Creative Performance

Fluency

A total of 456 ideas were produced by the 60 participants (Table 5.2). We did a qualitative analysis of the content of ideas produced by participants. This analysis showed no repetition of the same idea within each team, indicating that the team members paid attention to the ideas of each other. However, we found similar ideas across different teams. Furthermore, we coded all the ideas according to six mutually exclusive categories elaborated from the iterative reading and parsing of the whole set of ideas, in order to summarise the main "types" of ideas (Table 5.2). The participants (students in psychology) favoured solutions related to the improvement of existing public transport and services or in providing information and incentives. In contrast, the low rate of ideas related to changing work pattern may be due to the fact that our participants were students and thus did not identify themselves with actual workers.

Participants in VE produced more ideas than those in RE (Table 5.3), respectively 254 (56%) and 202 (44%). The average number of ideas produced by each team in VE was higher than in RE (e.g., VE: average = 25.5 ± 3.6, min = 21 and max = 32 ideas; RE: average = 20.2 ± 4.5, min = 14 and max = 28 ideas). At the individual level, the average number of

Table 5.2 Idea categories, examples, frequency, and %

	Idea Categories	*Examples of Solutions*	*Freq.*	*%*
A	Improving existing public transport	Increase capacity, speed, frequency, automation . . .	136	30%
B	Providing information and incentives	Reduction of the ticket prices, carpooling . . .	131	29%
C	Promoting existing modes of travel	Bike, skate, speed boat/river traffic . . .	70	15%
D	New urban developments	New networks that avoid the city centre/ more transports means in the suburbs/ dedicated roads/"flying" highways/ overhead buses and subways . . .	54	12%
E	Futuristic/Science fiction ideas	Flying cars/teleportation/"mini-haul" flights/space station like the city hub in orbit/propulsion cannons . . .	53	12%
F	Changing work patterns	Sleeping in the office, telework, compressed week (3-day work week)/ widening the window of the jobs start and end times . . .	12	3%
	Total		456	100%

Table 5.3 Creative performance

	RE	*VE*	*Total*
Number of participants	30	30	60
Number of ideas:			
Total	202	254	456
Average ideas/participant	**6.73 ± 2**	**8.27 ± 2.5**	7.5 ± 2.4
Median/participant	6.54	8	7.12
Min & Max/participant	4 & 11	5 & 15	4 & 15
Average ideas/team	**20.2 ± 4.55**	**25.5 ± 3.66**	22.8 ± 4.88
Min & Max per team	14 & 28	21 & 32	14 & 32
Idea categories:			
Improving existing public transport	63	73	136
Providing information and incentives	59	72	131
Promoting existing modes of travel	32	38	70
New urban developments	23	31	54
Futuristic/Science fiction ideas	**15**	**38**	53
Changing work patterns	10	2	12
Originality	**1.83 ± 0.9**	**2.43 ± 0.7**	2.27 ± 0.9
Utility	2.75 ± 1	2.60 ± 0.7	2.77 ± 0.9

Note: Significant differences between virtual and real environment (VE & RE) are in bold. Originality and utility 5-point Likert scale from 1 (not at all original/not at all useful) to 5 (extremely original/extremely useful).

ideas per participant was significantly higher in VE than in RE (respectively 8.27 ± 2.47 and 6.73 ± 2.01; F (59,1) = 7.7, p = .007). One could argue that this result might be linked to the differences in response execution (typing vs. writing): it is faster to type ideas (and you don't get interrupted doing so) rather than write them down and read them as you give the sticky notes, one by one, to the leader in the "real" environment. However, because some participants in VE did not outperform those in RE, we consider that response execution is a secondary cause. In addition, we did a study comparing voice chat and text chat, all with neutral avatars, same task as this study (Bonnardel, et al., unpublished creativeness report) and found that text chat is better than voice chat, probably due to the anonymous aspect of text chat. In general, it is "normal" for avatars to text chat, and for "live" people to write on sticky notes, or talk.

The distributions of categories of ideas differed significantly between the VE and RE conditions (χ^2 (5) = 13.2822, p < .021), although the mean strength of the association is weak (Cramer's V^2 = 0,029). The analysis of Relative deviations (RD) highlights the specifically strong attractions and repulsions between E and F idea categories and conditions. Indeed, there is a strong attraction (RD = +0.9) between F ideas (Changing the work patterns) and the RE setting condition, whereas there is a strong repulsion (RD = −0.7) between these ideas and the VE condition. Conversely, the E ideas (futuristic and science fiction) are strongly associated with the VE condition (RD = +.29), whereas a strong repulsion is observed with the RE setting condition (RD = −0.36). There are no noticeable RD for any of the other ideas categories, suggesting a similar distribution in both RE and VE conditions. A possible explanation refers to the priming effect of the futuristic-oriented features of the virtual environments (avatars, synthetic place and objects, etc): whereas participants in the RE setting are more likely to think with the space and time constraints of real setting, participants in the VE condition are more likely to think about emerging technologies and futuristic solutions due probably to the "sci fi" nature of VR.

At the team level, eight teams in VE and four teams in RE, respectively, came up with at least one idea in this category leading to significantly ($F_{(52,1)} = 3.9$, $p = .05$) more E-ideas produced by participants in VE (72% of E-ideas). However, the virtual environment did not favour everyone (Table 5.4). Indeed, 50% of participants in VE (vs 70% in RE) did not come up with any E-idea. Interestingly, when a team came up with two or more E-ideas, these ideas were produced by two to three different members of the team, suggesting a potential stimulating effect of idea sharing. Indeed, in the two most creative teams in VE, members seemed to have a "conversation or chat" building on each other's ideas within lengthy sentences. For the other teams in RE or VE, we observed most of the time lists of unrelated ideas suggesting that although they paid attention, they seemed to work in parallel.

A variation of brainstorming technique as well as individual rewards (Paulus, et al., 2015) or performance feedback should be considered in future studies.

Originality and Utility

As Table 5.3 shows, 74% of the produced ideas are in categories A, B, and C, hence the average level of originality and utility of the ideas (respectively 2.27 ± 0.9; 2.77 ± 0.9). The most original ideas were those in category E: Futuristic/Science fiction ideas (E average originality: 4.21 ± 0.9). The average originality per participant was significantly correlated with the total number of ideas produced ($r = .30$, $p = .02$). This significant relation between originality and fluency was positive as well for the number of ideas in categories E and C (respectively, $r = .29$, $p < .001$; $r = .41$, $p = .001$), but negative for categories A and B (respectively, $r = -.29$, $p = .02$; $r = -.38$, $p = .003$).

Whereas the utility of the produced ideas was similar in both conditions, the originality was significantly higher in VE ($F_{(455,1)} = 63.3$, $p < .001$). This was linked to the production of more ideas in the category "Futuristic/Science fiction ideas".

Table 5.4 Creative fluency per team (T 1–10) and participant (X, W, Z) for E: Futuristic/Science fiction ideas for RE (left) and VE (right)

		E Ideas (Total Ideas) Per Participant					*E Ideas (Total Ideas) Per Participant*		
RE Teams	*E IDEAS (Total) Per Team*	*X*	*W*	*Z*	*VE Teams*	*E IDEAS (Total)*	*X*	*W*	*Z*
RE T 1	**8** (23)	**1** (6)	**1** (6)	**6** (11)	VE T 1	**12** (26)	**7** (15)	**4** (6)	**1** (5)
RE T 7	**3** (28)	**2** (11)	**1** (9)	−(8)	VE T 3	**10** (32)	**5** (14)	**3** (8)	**2** (10)
RE T 6	**2** (14)	−(4)	**1** (5)	**1** (5)	VE T 6	**5** (27)	**3** (12)	−(6)	**2** (9)
RE T 10	**2** (21)	**1** (10)	0 (4)	**1** (7)	VE T 8	**5** (21)	**3** (6)	**2** (9)	0 (6)
RE T 9	−(23)	−(9)	−(6)	−(8)	VE T 7	**3** (21)	**1** (7)	−(6)	**2** (8)
RE T 3	−(22)	−(7)	− (9)	−(6)	VE T 4	**1** (25)	−(6)	−(8)	**1** (11)
RE T 2	−(21)	−(7)	− (6)	−(8)	VE T 5	**1** (25)	−(10)	**1** (7)	0 (8)
RE T 5	−(21)	(7)	− (6)	−(8)	VE T 9	**1** (22)	−(6)	−(7)	**1** (9)
RE T 4	−(15)	(4)	− (5)	−(6)	VE T 2	−(30)	−(15)	−(9)	0 (6)
RE T 8	−(14)	(4)	− (4)	−(6)	VE T 10	−(25)	−(6)	−(9)	0 (10)

Note: The total number of ideas produced is in between brackets. VE: Virtual environment; RE: Real environment.

Creative Potential

Analysis of the creative potential scores showed no significant difference between female and male participants or between the two conditions for any of the ten dimensions (Table 5.5). However, the minimum and maximum values suggest large variability within each sub group, particularly for divergent thinking (range: 4–100), mental flexibility (range: 20–99), and associative thinking (range: 1–18). The average scores for analogical thinking were relatively high, 11.7 ± 1.9 (Maximum possible 15), whereas intuitive thinking were low 5.5 ± 1.9 (Maximum possible 12). The scores for openness, motivation, risk taking, and ambiguity tolerance were average compared to the maximum scores possible.

Correlation analysis between the ten dimensions showed five significant positive correlations and two significant negative correlations. Within the cognitive domain, convergent and analogical thinking were positively correlated (r = .27, p = .04). In the cognitive domain, risk taking and intuitive thinking were positively correlated (r = .29, p = .03). The significant correlations between the cognitive and conative domains were as follows: divergent thinking was positively linked to openness (r = .43, p = .001) and intuitive thinking (r = .37, p = .004). Flexibility was positively correlated to tolerance for ambiguity (r = .37, p = .005) and negatively linked to associative thinking (r = −.29, p = .04) and openness (r = −.26, p = .049). These correlations, which confirm previous results, support the validity of the Profiler tool. They will be addressed in the discussion section.

Creative Potential and Performance

As the utility did not differ between the two conditions, we only consider fluency and originality in the analysis of the relationship between performance and creative potential. These two performance criteria were explored in the top 10% of participants and for the whole sample. We conducted various types of analysis: descriptive analysis for the top 10% of participants, and correlation and analysis of variance (ANOVA) for the two conditions. As the most significant results for the whole sample concerned fluency, originality was further analysed in the sub group that produced the most original ideas in VE.

Fluency and Creative Potential

Correlations were first calculated to investigate the relationships between the creative potential of the whole sample and the number of produced ideas. The results indicated no significant correlation between fluency and any of the ten dimensions for the whole sample and for each sub-group separately, VE and RE.

Second, we described in a qualitative way the most performing participants. To determine which participants were capable of outperforming

Table 5.5 Creative potential dimensions scores

	RE					*VE*					*Total*		
	Average	*SD*	*Median*	*Min*	*Max*	*Average*	*SD*	*Median*	*Min*	*Max*	*Average*	*SD*	*Median*
DIVERG	26.2	11.2	25.3	12	65	30.6	17.6	26.3	4	100	**28.4**	14.8	**25.9**
FLEX	66.9	14.5	68.3	36	97	66.1	18.6	68.0	20	99	**66.5**	16.6	**68.1**
CONVERG (0–12)	7.3	2.2	7.2	3	11	7.4	2.1	7.3	4	12	**7.3**	2.1	**7.2**
ASSOC	5.0	3.2	4.7	1	14	6.5	4.2	5.9	1	18	**5.7**	3.8	**5.3**
ANALOG (0–15)	12.1	1.9	12.4	7	15	11.3	2.0	11.7	7	14	**11.7**	1.9	**12.0**
OPENNESS (1–5)	3.5	0.5	3.6	3	4	3.3	0.7	3.4	2	5	**3.4**	0.6	**3.5**
AMBIG (1–5)	2.8	0.4	2.7	2	4	2.7	0.5	2.7	2	4	**2.7**	0.5	**2.7**
INTUIT (0–12)	5.4	1.7	5.2	2	9	5.5	2.0	5.5	2	10	**5.5**	1.9	**5.3**
RISK (0–24)	14.7	2.3	14.9	10	19	14.0	3.4	14.4	8	20	**14.4**	2.9	**14.6**
MOTIV (0–10)	7.1	1.2	6.9	5	9	6.9	1.1	6.8	5	9	**7.0**	1.1	**6.8**

Note: DIVERG: Divergent thinking; FLEX: Mental flexibility; CONVERG: Convergent thinking; ASSOC: Associative thinking; ANALOG: Analogical thinking; Openness; AMBIG: Tolerance of ambiguity; INTUIT: Intuitive thinking; RISK: Risk taking; MOTIV: Motivation.

others and which resources of the creative potential were involved, we used similar methods used frequently in the study of the sources of interpersonal differences in excellence (Gagné, 2004; Nijs, Gallardo-Gallardo, Dries, & Sels, 2014). To this end, we used a relative cut-off point: the 10% of participants who performed better than others in each condition and compared their creative potential profile to the average of the group. Indeed, the differentiated Model of Giftedness and Talent (Gagné, 2004) uses the top 10% of age peers. Talent designates the outstanding mastery of systematically developed abilities (or skills) and knowledge in at least one field of human activity to a degree that places an individual at least among the top 10% of age peers who are or have been active. Giftedness designates the possession and use of untrained and spontaneously expressed natural abilities (called outstanding aptitudes or gifts), in at least one ability domain, to a degree that places an individual at least among the top 10% of age peers.

However, because of the size of our sample (e.g., 10% corresponds to three participants in each condition), we explored the participants' profiles in a descriptive and qualitative way. Figure 5.2 shows the creative potential

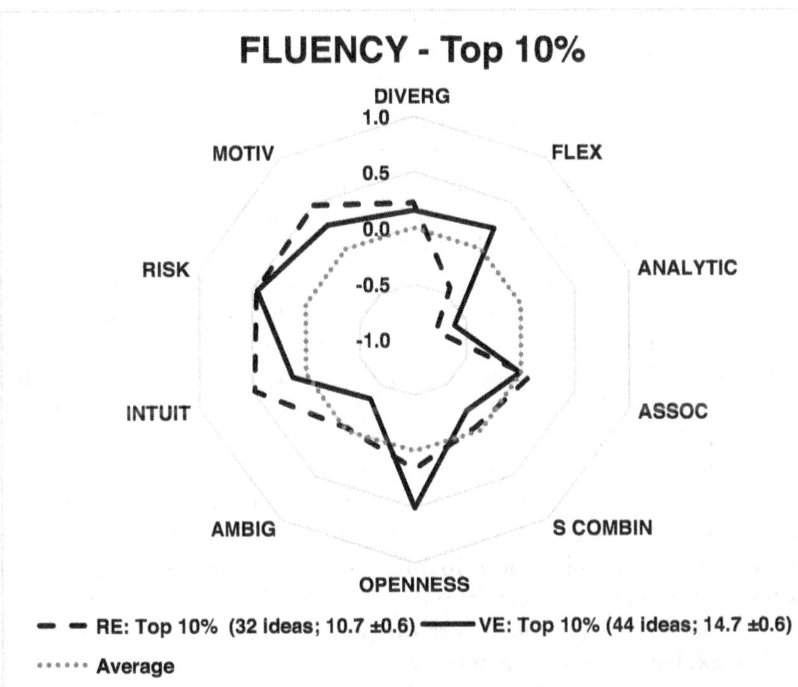

Figure 5.2 Creative profiles of the top 10% participants in each condition VE and RE compared to the sample's average

Note: DIVERG: Divergent thinking; FLEX: Mental flexibility; ANALYTIC: Analytic thinking; ASSOC: Associative thinking; S COMBIN: Selective combination; Openness; AMBIG: Tolerance of ambiguity; INTUIT: Intuitive thinking; RISK: Risk taking; MOTIV: Motivation; VE: Virtual environment; RE: Real environment.

profiles of the top 10% of participants in VE and RE compared to the sample average (z-scores). The average fluency of the top 10% of participants in each condition was respectively 14.7 ± 0.6 and 10.7 ± 0.6 ideas for VE and RE (respectively, a total of 44 ideas and 32 ideas produced by the top three participants in each condition, VE and RE). In the two conditions, high fluency is associated with relatively similar creative potential profiles in VE and RE: (a) scores higher than the average in risk taking, motivation, and divergent thinking; (b) scores below the average in analytic thinking; and (c) average scores on associative thinking and selective combination. The observed differences between the two profiles are related to mental flexibility, openness, tolerance of ambiguity, and intuitive thinking. Interestingly, the participant that scored maximum in divergent thinking (100) is not included in the top 10%: he produced a total of six ideas without any E ideas (Table 5.4: VE10 participant X).

Finally, in the third step we considered the whole sample (n = 58) to investigate in a quantitative way the resources of the creative potential that were involved in high creative performance. To this end, we used an absolute cut-off for each of the ten creative potential dimensions: each participant was considered as having high or low potential in a creative resource if his/her score was respectively above or below (or equal to) the median of the sample (n = 58) for this resource. We then compared the creative performance (number of ideas) between the groups for each dimensions and conditions. ANOVA results showed a significant difference for the fluency for several dimensions of the creative potential. We observed a significantly higher number of produced ideas in VE by participants with high scores in risk taking ($F_{(54,3)} = 4.29$; $p = .009$), divergent thinking ($F_{(54,3)} = 3.96$; $p = .013$), and (/or) mental flexibility ($F_{(54,3)} = 3.2$; $p = .029$). Figure 5.3 (left) shows this effect for risk taking; it suggests that in VE, participants with high scores in risk taking produce significantly more ideas than those with a similar profile in RE. No difference was observed between VE and RE for the low scores. This result suggests that VE benefited participants with high potential in the following resources only: risk taking, divergent thinking, and mental flexibility.

Interestingly, significant differences were observed for motivation ($F_{(54,3)} = 3.29$; $p = .027$), openness ($F_{(54,3)} = 3.29$; $p = .027$), and selective combination($F_{(54,3)} = 3.3$; $p = .027$). Figure 5.3 (right) shows this second trend for selective combination. In VE, participants with low scores in these resources produced significantly more ideas than those in RE with similar low scores. No differences were observed for high scores. These results could be explained to some extent by the correlation between some dimensions of creative potential. Indeed, the participants in VE with low scores on selective combination, motivation, and openness had, respectively, relatively high scores on risk taking, divergent thinking, and mental flexibility. This suggests a potential compensation between the dimensions of creative potential in VE (Lubart, et al., 2013).

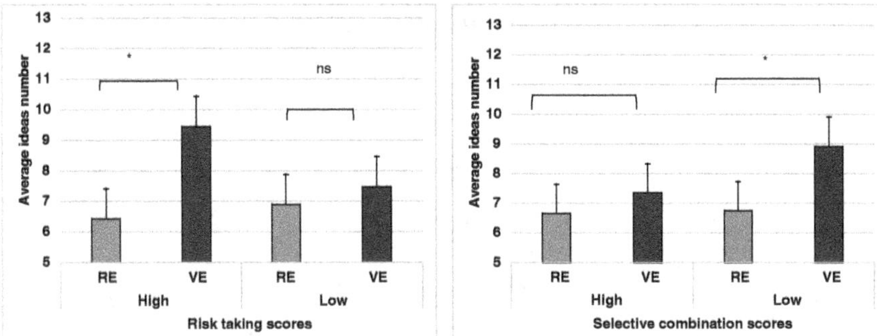

Figure 5.3 The fluency differences for risk taking (left) and selective combination (right) high and low scores for participants in VE and RE

Note: ns: no significant difference; ⋆: $p < 0.05$; VE: Virtual environment; RE: Real environment.

Originality and Creative Potential

A similar approach was applied to analyse the originality for each dimension of creative potential. Variance in originality was measured by comparing two factors: condition (VE/RE) and score level (H/L). ANOVA results showed a significant difference between the four categories for only one dimension of the creative dimension: analytic thinking ($F_{(54,3)} = 2.9$; $p = .04$). Average originality was significantly higher in VE for participants with low scores in analytic thinking compared to those with similar profiles in RE (average originality: 2.9 ± .57 for VE and 2.4 ± .67 for RE). There was no difference between VE and RE for those with high scores in analytic thinking.

To explore the resources involved in the production of original ideas such as "futuristic and science fiction solutions" (E ideas), we focused the analysis on the differences between the participants in VE because they produced 72% of the ideas in this category. Two sub-groups were created according to the number of E ideas per participant: low number of ideas (zero to one idea) and high number of ideas (two to seven ideas). The creative potential profiles of these two groups are presented in Figure 5.4. The analysis of variance of the ten dimensions of creative potential showed significant differences for two resources: risk taking ($F_{28,1)} = 11$, $p = 003$) and analytic thinking ($F_{(28,1)} = 5.3$, $p = .03$). The participants who produced higher numbers of original ideas (E category) in VE presented a significantly higher tendency to take risks and lower scores in analytic thinking. Similar analyses could not be performed for the real environment because of the low number of participants ($n = 2$) who produced a high rate of E ideas.

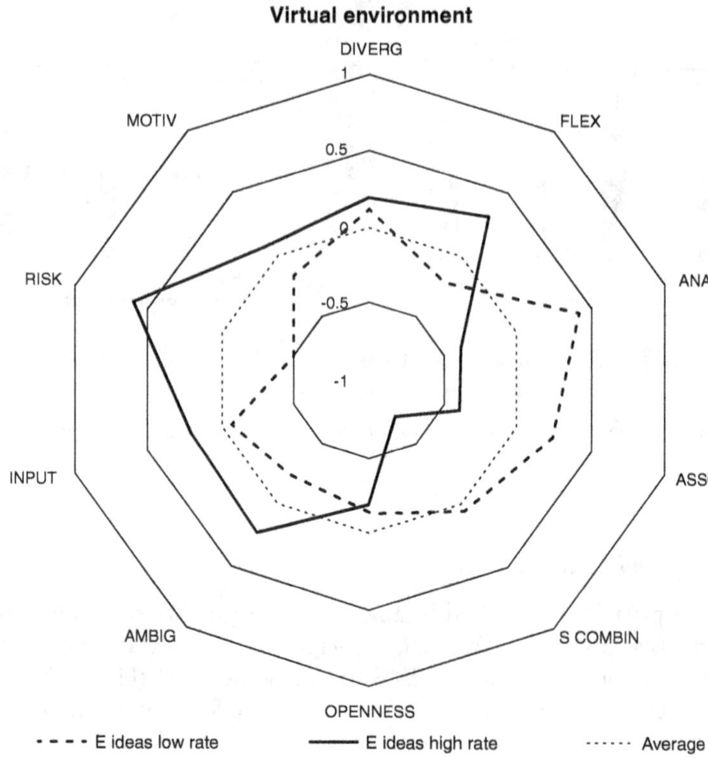

Figure 5.4 Creative profiles of the top 10% participants compared to the sample's average "futuristic and science fiction solutions" (E ideas)

Note: DIVERG: Divergent thinking; FLEX: Mental flexibility; ANALYTIC: Analytic thinking; ASSOC: Associative thinking; S COMBIN: Selective combination; Openness; AMBIG: Tolerance of ambiguity; INTUIT: Intuitive thinking; RISK: Risk taking; MOTIV: Motivation.

Discussion

This exploratory study of creative performance and potential confirms previous results regarding the role of virtual environment (VE) in promoting creative performance in an ideation task. However, because of the small size of the sample, these preliminary results need to be validated using larger samples. We, therefore, suggest some hypothesis to discuss the results that could be used in future studies.

At the team level, fluency was significantly improved in VE compared to the control situation, e.g., real environment (RE). Among the six categories of ideas produced by the participants, "futuristic and science fiction" (E ideas) are strongly associated with the virtual condition. The VE participants were probably less worried about expressing ideas, but the differences in this particular idea category is probably due to the "sci fi" nature of VE. Although, these E-category ideas were not feasible in the short term, they lead to a significant increase of originality in VE compared to RE. Pescovitz (2013), director of research at the Institute of the Future (IFTF), indicates that science fiction has always been a place of technological innovation, inspiring even the inventions of the submarine and the cell phone.

However, at the individual level, the results suggest that VE did not favour everyone: some VE participants performed as low as RE participants. The participants in the RE and VE expressed their ideas respectively in writing or typing with no instruction to take turns, therefore we cannot invoke "productivity blocks" due to forgetting an idea while waiting to speak to explain the loss of productivity.

The analysis of the participants' creative potential sheds light on potential causes for these inter-individual differences in brainstorming performance. Indeed, participants in VE with high risk-taking propensity were significantly more creative (fluency and originality) than the other participants (e.g., those with similar profile in RE, as well as participants with low scores in risk taking in VE). The same pattern was observed for divergent thinking and mental flexibility for fluency: high scores in divergent thinking and/or mental flexibility favoured the fluency in VE but not in RE. These last two resources have consistently been linked to a high creative performance (Lubart, Mouchiroud, Tordjman, & Zenasni, 2003; Beaty & Silvia, 2012; Beghetto & Kaufman, 2007; Carson, Peterson, & Higgins, 2005; Runco & Acar, 2012).

However, in this study, risk-taking propensity played a more significant role in the fluency and originality of produced ideas than any other dimension of creative potential. This finding confirms previous results regarding the positive relationship between sensible risk-taking propensity and idea generation (Lubart & Sternberg, 1995; Prabhu, 2011). Indeed, originality involves breaking from habitual ideas; risking social criticism, resistance, and idea rejection; as well as wasting personal resources, e.g., time, money, and energy (Lubart, et al., 2013). The idea of sensible or calculated risk taking is often associated with creativity, and several researchers have argued for the need to measure risk taking in a variety of domains to better capture its complex nature (Sternberg & Lubart, 1995; Sternberg, 1997; Runco, 2015; Steele, McIntosh, & Higgs, 2016). Recently, Tyagi, Hanoch, Hall, Runco, and Denham (2017) indicated that among six domains of risk taking (financial, health, safety, recreational, ethical, and social), only social risk taking (e.g., the willingness to challenge norms) showed strong evidence for correlations with ideation and creative achievements. For instance, the "idea of being different" and the willingness of creative individuals to risk the uncertainty of the unknown are more pertinent for creativity than risk taking in other domains, such as risky driving behaviour (e.g., violation of traffic rules, reckless driving, not using seat belt, drinking and driving).

The task used to measure risk taking in our study assessed the willingness of the users to take sensible risks while making a decision under uncertainty to engage in new social and design activities. The observed positive and significant correlation between risk taking and intuitive thinking suggests that these decisions under uncertainty rely on intuition. We assume that openness and intuitive thinking, which were correlated with divergent thinking and risk taking, might have facilitated creativity in VE via attentional mechanisms. It has been indeed suggested that high open-minded individuals have defective filters for irrelevant stimuli, which then leads to more ideas entering consciousness to be combined in interesting ways in order to form creative ideas (Batey & Furnham, 2006). Recently, Agnoli, Franchin, Rubaltelli, and Corazza (2015) established that attentive processing is a central psychological mechanism to explain the relationship between openness and creativity. Further, research has demonstrated an association between openness to experience and decreased latent inhibition. Kaufman (2013) examined recently the relationship between latent inhibition and individual differences in the tendency to rely on intuition to make decisions.

Based on these theories, we propose that the virtual environment offers a "liberating" atmosphere that disinhibits cognitively those participants with high risk-taking propensity, divergent thinking, and mental flexibility abilities. This disinhibition could be facilitated by high scores in intuitive thinking and openness that led to a broadening attentional scope (explorative global processing) and the activation of more remote concepts in explorative global processing. Future studies should investigate this assumption.

This study, which is the first to explore the relationship between the creative performance and the dimensions of creative potential, presents three major limits: (a) the limited size of the sample and the type of participants (students in psychology); (b) the use of the brainstorming task as the only measure of creativity; and (c) the use of neutral avatars and simple reproduction of our actual meeting room were probably not efficient in promoting the feeling of freedom and disinhibition in the less creative participants. Future studies should explore (a) whether the creative performance of participants with low creative potential will improve with the attribution of "creative avatars" instead of neutral ones, and (b) whether a visual creative environment will promote a feeling of openness and broaden the scope of attention at perceptual and conceptual levels.

Face-to-face meeting is very important in other contexts or at some other steps (e.g., convergence), and we should not avoid them. VE could be used when we would like to diverge from conventional wisdom, or when there is a strong hierarchical relationship. In sum, virtual worlds provide an opportunity to ask traditional questions about creativity in a new context (Ward & Sonneborn, 2009). Beyond merely measuring performance, satisfaction, and usability, identifying the mechanisms that come into play in the mutual interaction between participants' creative potential and the properties of these digital environments is a challenge for both creativity and ergonomics research. This kind of study has practical implications for predicting creative performance in virtual settings and optimising it by taking into consideration the nature of the individuals engaged in creative work within virtual (and non-virtual) environments.

Acknowledgement

This research was carried out as part of project CREATIVENESS (CREative AcTIvities in Virtual EnviroNmEnt SpaceS), funded by the National Research Agency (project ANR-12-SOIN-0005) in France. We would like to thank Mickael Cardoso and Maxime Preyssac for their assistance in data collection and Louise Bourgeois for proofreading the manuscript and for her insightful comments.

References

Agnoli, S., Franchin, L., Rubaltelli, E., & Corazza, G. E. (2015). An eye-tracking analysis of irrelevance processing as moderator of openness and creative performance. *Creativity research journal*, *27*(2), 125–132.

Batey, M., & Furnham, A. (2006). Creativity, intelligence, and personality: A critical review of the scattered literature. *Genetic, Social, and General Psychology Monographs*, *132*, 355–429.

Beaty, R. E., & Silvia, P. J. (2012). Why do ideas get more creative across time? An executive interpretation of the serial order effect in divergent thinking tasks. *Psychology of Aesthetics, Creativity, and the Arts*, *6*, 309–319.

Beghetto, R., & Kaufman, J. (2007). Toward a broader conception of creativity: A case for mini-c creativity. *Psychology of Aesthetics, Creativity, and the Arts*, *1*, 73–79.

Bernard, J. M. (2003, July). Analysis of local or asymmetric dependencies in contingency tables using the imprecise dirichlet model. *ISIPTA*, *3*, 14–17.

Bhagwatwar, A., Massey, A., & Dennis, A. R. (2013, January). Creative virtual environments: Effect of supraliminal priming on team brainstorming. In *2013 46th Hawaii international conference on system sciences* (pp. 215–224). IEEE.

Buisine, S., Guegan, J., Barré, J., Segonds, F., & Aoussat, A. (2016). Using avatars to tailor ideation process to innovation strategy. *Cognition, Technology & Work*, *18*, 583–594.

Buur, J., & Matthews, B. (2008). Participatory innovation. *International Journal of Innovation Management*, *12*, 255–273.

Cahour, B. (2002). Décalages socio-cognitifs en réunions de conception participative. *Le Travail Humain*, *65*, 315–337.

Carson, S. H., Peterson, J. B., & Higgins, D. M. (2005). Reliability, validity, and factor structure of the creative achievement questionnaire. *Creativity Research Journal*, *17*, 37–50.

Corroyer, D., & Rouanet, H. (1994). Sur l'importance des effets et ses indicateurs dans l'analyse statistique des données. *L'Année Psychologique*, *94*, 607–624.

Dennis, A. R., & Williams, M. L. (2003). Electronic brainstorming: Theory, research, and future directions. In P. B. Paulus & B. A. Nijstad (Eds.), *Group creativity: Innovation through collaboration* (pp. 160–178). London: Oxford University Press.

de Rooij, A., van der Land, S., & van Erp, S. (2017, June). The creative Proteus Effect: How self-similarity, embodiment, and priming of creative stereotypes with avatars influences creative ideation. In *Proceedings of the 2017 ACM SIGCHI Conference on Creativity and Cognition*, New York; NY; United States, pp. 232–236.

Diehl, M., & Stroebe, W. (1987). Productivity loss in brainstorming groups: Toward the solution of a riddle. *Journal of Personality and Social Psychology, 53*(3), 497.

Gagné, F. (2004). Transforming gifts into talents: The DMGT as a developmental theory. *High Ability Studies, 15*, 119–147.

Guegan, J., Buisine, S., Mantelet, F., Maranzana, N., & Segonds, F. (2016). Avatar-mediated creativity: When embodying inventors makes engineers more creative. *Computers in Human Behavior, 61*, 165–175.

Kaufman, C. B. (2013). Opening up openness to experience: A four-factor model and relations to creative achievement in the arts and sciences. *Journal of Creative Behavior, 47*, 233–255.

Kristensson, P., Gustafsson, A., & Archer, T. (2004). Harnessing the creative potential among users. *Journal of Product Innovation Management, 21*(1), 4–14.

Kristensson, P., & Magnusson, P. R. (2010). Tuning users' innovativeness during ideation. *Creativity and Innovation Management, 19*(2), 147–159.

Kristensson, P., Magnusson, P. R., & Matthing, J. (2002). Users as a hidden resource for creativity: Findings from an experimental study on user involvement. *Creativity and Innovation Management, 11*(1), 55–61.

Kujala, S. (2003). User involvement: A review of the benefits and challenges. *Behaviour & Information Technology, 22*(1), 1–16.

Lubart, T. I., Mouchiroud, C., Tordjman, S., & Zenasni, F. (2003). *Psychologie de la créativité*. Paris: Armand Colin.

Lubart, T. I., & Sternberg, R. J. (1995). An investment approach to creativity: Theory and data. In S. M. Smith, T. B. Ward, & R. A. Finke (Eds.), *The creative cognition approach* (pp. 269–302). Cambridge, MA: MIT Press.

Lubart, T. I., Zenasni, F., & Barbot, B. (2013). Creative potential and its measurement. *International Journal for Talent Development and Creativity, 1*(2), 41–51.

Michinov, N., Jamet, E., Métayer, N., & Le Hénaff, B. (2015). The eyes of creativity: Impact of social comparison and individual creativity on performance and attention to others' ideas during electronic brainstorming. *Computers in Human Behavior, 42*, 57–67.

Nijs, S., Gallardo-Gallardo, E., Dries, N., & Sels, L. (2014). A multidisciplinary review into the definition, operationalization, and measurement of talent. *Journal of World Business, 49*, 180–191.

Paulus, P. B., Korde, R. M., Dickson, J. J., Carmeli, A., & Cohen-Meitar, R. (2015). Asynchronous brainstorming in an industrial setting: Exploratory studies. *Human Factors, 57*(6), 1076–1094.

Pescovitz. (2013). *An aura of familiarity*. Retrieved from www.iftf.org/fileadmin/user_upload/downloads/th/IFTF_SR-1590C__AnAuraOfFamiliarity.pdf

Prabhu, V. P. (2011). Risk-taking. In M. A. Runco & S. R. Pritzker (Eds.), *Encyclopedia of creativity* (2nd ed., Vol 2, pp. 319–323). New York: Elsevier.

Runco, M. A. (2015). Meta-creativity: Being creative about creativity. *Creativity Research Journal, 27*, 295–298.

Runco, M. A., & Acar, S. (2012). Divergent thinking as an indicator of creative potential. *Creativity Research Journal, 24*(1), 1–10.

Steele, L. M., McIntosh, T., & Higgs, C. (2016). Intrinsic motivation and creativity: Opening up a black box. In M. D. Mumford & S. Hemlin (Eds.), *Handbook of research on creativity and leadership*. Norman, OK: University of Oklahoma.

Sternberg, R. J. (1997). *Successful intelligence: How practical and creative intelligence determine success in life*. New York: PlumeBooks.

Sternberg, R. J., & Lubart, T. I. (1995). *Defying the crowd: Cultivating creativity in a culture of conformity*. New York: Free Press.

Thornhill-Miller, B., & Dupont, J.-M. (2016). Virtual reality and the enhancement of creativity and innovation: Under recognized potential among converging technologies? *Journal of Cognitive Education and Psychology*, *15*(1), 102–121.

Tyagi, V., Hanoch, Y., Hall, S. D., Runco, M., & Denham, S. L. (2017). The risky side of creativity: Domain specific risk taking in creative individuals. *Frontiers in Psychology*, *8*, 145.

Ward, T. B., & Sonneborn, M. S. (2009). Creative expression in virtual worlds: Imitation, imagination, and individualized collaboration. *Psychology of Aesthetics, Creativity, and the Arts*, *3*(4), 211–221.

6 Malevolent Creativity and Social Media

Creating Anti-Immigration Communities on Twitter

Constance de Saint Laurent, Vlad P. Glăveanu, and Claude Chaudet

This chapter examines a rarely studied phenomenon, at least within creativity research: the creation of anti-immigration communities on Twitter. While the notion of "creation" should not be confused with "creativity" – as, indeed, something can be created without it being original or appropriate (Stein, 1953) – we will argue that, in this case, we are dealing with actual creative acts, specifically acts of malevolent creativity (see Cropley, Cropley, Kaufman, & Runco, 2010). What makes them so is the visible intent to negatively affect others, in this context, migrants and refugees. The exact motivations behind expressing oneself creatively, online, in a malevolent manner, are less relevant here. Independent of them, the pragmatic outcomes of engaging in anti-immigration rhetoric remain the same: building less tolerant, less inclusive, and less open communities.

What is particularly interesting is that the creative processes we are concerned within this chapter share three main characteristics: they are (primarily) linguistic in nature, they are *collective* in their expression, and they take place essentially online. The advent of the Internet and, in particular, social media marked a sharp increase in interconnectivity and, with it, brought new hopes for an age of communication, mutual understanding, and co-creation (for utopian but also dystopian views of the impact of technology on democracy see Grosswiler, 1998). Many of these hopes have been questioned in today's social and political climate (Keen, 2015; Vaidhyanathan, 2018). What we collectively came to discover is the fact that social media might stimulate exchanges, but these exchanges are generally shallow and not conducive for the kind of debates that are vital for functional democracies. That it can connect us to people the world over, yet often creates "information bubbles" and "echo chambers" that radicalise rather than relativise existing opinions. These troubling phenomena foster forms of malevolent creativity by giving social media users both the opportunity to gather together and to engage in groupthink (Janis, 1982), scapegoating social groups such as immigrants.

In this study, we are focusing on the micro-blogging platform Twitter to examine how exactly anti-immigration communities are constituted and maintained through linguistically creative means. As a point of comparison, we collected data about both pro- and anti-immigration tweets and focused on hashtags given their two important features for a discussion of creativity: high shareability and continuous generativity. This explorative study of linguistic, malevolent, and collective creative expression marks also a methodological premiere by using some data science techniques within creativity research. Its main objective is to shed light on the forms of expression and functions of malevolent linguistic creativity employed on social media in relation to migration. Before describing the methodology in more detail, we offer a brief overview of research done on Twitter as a social media platform.

Twitter: The Good, the Bad, the Ugly

Twitter is undeniably one of the most influential social media platforms, distinguished by the fact that it restricts the length of messages or tweets (currently to 280 characters). While in the first quarter of 2010 Twitter had about 30 million users, in the second quarter of 2018 that number increased to 335 million (according to statista.com). Founded in 2006, the history of this micro-blogging platform includes two broad "periods" (see Chaudhry, 2015). The first Twitter generation used it as an urban lifestyle tool to send friends updates and let them know about their whereabouts and activities. Reflecting this, Twitter's tagline was "What are you doing?" In 2009, this tagline was changed to "What's happening?", capturing a significant shift towards sharing news and following events. This Twitter II period was assumed by authors like Chaudhry to give room nowadays to Twitter III – a period in which the platform becomes appealing to researchers. This chapter is a case in point for this trend.

The fact that Twitter is establishing itself more and more as a news network is a rather alarming development given the high degree of misinformation circulating on this and other social media platforms like Facebook (Ehrenberg, 2012; Zollo & Quattrociocchi, 2018). The common use of Twitter by journalists and politicians, and the existence of official accounts for governmental and supra-governmental actors, cements this new reality. On the surface, this usage and the fact that it allows responses also increases Twitter's status as a democratic, conversational tool. However, "just because people are tweeting under the same hashtag, this does not mean they are conversing with each other in the traditional sense" (Murthy, 2013, p. 4). Another important social psychological question thus arises: tweets and hashtags indicate interest and offer constant forms of evaluation for current events, but are they fostering or hindering actual debates?

Research on Twitter is extensive nowadays and highly interdisciplinary (for an overview of research topics see Shapp, 2014, p. 11), but it rarely addresses the issue of malevolent creativity and its societal consequences. When creativity is an explicit research variable, it is mostly to document marketing behaviours such as consumer engagement (Stathopoulou, Borel, Christodoulides, & West, 2017). The bulk of it focuses on self-branding and the emergence of micro-celebrity (Page, 2012), on the role of hashtags in the creation of ad hoc publics (Bruns & Burgess, 2011), or on Twitter as a technology for audiencing and fandom (Highfield, Harrington, & Bruns, 2013). When it comes specifically to hashtags, some of them have been more extensively studied than others (e.g., #JeSuisCharlie and #JeNeSuisPasCharlie; Giglietto & Lee, 2016; or #Ferguson; Bonilla & Rosa, 2015). These studies move between an emphasis on media to one placed on politics. And, indeed, there is a growing literature available today on Twitter's use for activism and social change, especially in view of its role in popular mobilisation, including the Arab Spring (see Konnelly, 2015; Gerbaudo, 2018) or resisting Donald Trump's views and policies (Maas, et al., 2018). The "darker" side of Twitter has also been documented in studies of racism online, from hate speech to Islamophobia (see Chaudhry, 2015; Awan, 2014).

The focus of our research is *migration*, which is not only an important conversation topic on Twitter, but one that received considerable research attention in the past few years. The methodologies used to explore Twitter users' reactions to the migration crisis range from big data techniques to discourse analysis. For example, Ferra and Nguyen (2017) followed data related to #migrantcrisis on Twitter and identified the key actors and stakeholders that dominated the transnational debate around the crisis. They found that news agencies played a significant role, but also the fact that the discussions were much less about migrants and refugees (e.g., human experience or suffering) and much more about EU policies and Germany's position. A big data study conducted by Siapera, Boudourides, Lenis, and Suiter (2018) at the peak of the refugee crisis, between October 2015 and May 2016 and analysing almost 7.5 million tweets, pointed to the equivocal nature of Twitter contributions, which largely fell under two dominant discursive frames:

> a frame politicized from a far-right perspective, in which refugees were framed as terrorists or rapists, following along the lines of representations that mobilize security and safety; and a humanitarian frame, which revolved around human rights, and was created by humanitarian organizations, activists, and some mainstream media.
>
> (p. 17)

Interestingly, the authors also documented the fact that Twitter debates tend to be captured by pre-existing and quasi-organised groups that operate by using established hashtags and strategically retweeting influential users. For them, this is further evidence of the instrumentalisation of Twitter towards achieving certain political aims rather than its use for authentic, personal expression. More qualitative studies of particular hashtags, such as #refugeesnotwelcome, shed an even grimmer light on the kind of categorisations made on Twitter, in particular those that portray refugees as unwanted, criminal outsiders (Kreis, 2017). Overall, the same double framing – in terms of solidarity vs. xenophobic responses – has largely been documented using qualitative methods as well (see Gualda & Rebollo Díaz, 2016). Importantly, very few studies actually get to combine data science techniques (e.g., sentiment analysis; Pope & Griffith, 2016; Öztürk & Ayvaz, 2018) with discursive forms of analysis, a methodological gap we are trying to fill in the present chapter.

Methodology

We applied data science techniques, complemented by qualitative analysis, in order to examine the potential role played by the use of linguistic, malevolent creativity on Twitter in the construction and maintenance of anti-immigration online communities. More specifically, we aimed to explore the differences in tweet characteristics and content between anti- and pro-immigration users of social media and to understand how, when, and to what ends creative hashtags might be used by the former.

Data Collection

The data was collected at four different times in 2018 (28.06; 05.07; 28.08; 04.09), resulting in two continuous periods, one at the beginning of the summer and the other two months later. We used Twitter's free API and a Python script, allowing us to download seven days of tweets around specified hashtags: three pro-immigration (#WithRefugees; #RefugeesWelcome; #NoBorder) and three anti-immigration (#BuildTheWall; #IllegalAliens; #SecureThe-Border). Retweets were excluded to avoid going over the total number of tweets that can be downloaded with the free API, and only tweets officially categorised as in English by Twitter were included. A total of 112,789 tweets have been collected and included in the analysis (see Table 6.1).

The hashtags were chosen because they allowed us to infer the position of the author of the tweet (conversely to more general hashtags like #Immigration). For this reason, they are not fully comparable, as both sides of the debate focus on different issues: illegality and border crossing for anti-immigration tweets, and refugees and human rights for pro-immigration (also referred to as pro-refugee) tweets. However, this issue is unavoidable, given that social debates are never fully symmetrical and that how the problem is framed is part of the debate in itself. Moreover, as it clearly appears in these figures, the number of tweets per date and per hashtag is not balanced, nor could it be. First, anti-immigration discourses appear to be more present on Twitter than pro-immigration ones, at least in the four weeks during which we collected data. Second, there are not many partisan hashtags on

Table 6.1 Number of tweets collected per hashtag per day

Hashtag	*28.06*	*05.07*	*28.08*	*04.09*	*Total*
#BuildTheWall	28202	20596	18753	7358	74909
#IllegalAliens	4714	2698	2657	1027	11096
#SecureTheBorder	1127	424	297	76	1924
Total against	34043	23718	21707	8461	87929
#WithRefugees	12897	907	1809	1467	17080
#RefugeesWelcome	3345	1511	991	626	6473
#NoBorder	396	570	149	192	1307
Total pro	16638	2988	2949	2285	24860
Total	**50681**	**26706**	**24656**	**10746**	**112789**

immigration, which limited what could be chosen. Third, there is no (free) way to determine in advance how many tweets a hashtag corresponds to, making it a trial and error process. The hashtags we focused on were the main ones at the time when the two first batches of data were collected, using an iterative process: starting with the hashtags #RefugeesWelcome and #RefugeesNOTWelcome, we compiled the most frequent hashtags for which the orientation of the tweet could be inferred (e.g., #NoBorder but not #Immigrants), collected data for these, and then explored again the most frequent hashtags within these new tweets. We then selected, for each side, the three most frequent hashtags. Finally, our focus is on anti-immigration discourses and, thus, tweets and hashtags, and we are using here pro-immigration ones as a point of comparison.

Data Processing

The data was processed in several steps. The main ones involved: (1) feature engineering to carry out different statistical analyses, (2) hashtag processing, to analyse the topics of discussion, and (3) text processing, to analyse word frequencies and cluster the tweets. This chapter focuses on the two first analyses, which are most relevant for malevolent and linguistic creativity.

Feature engineering refers to adding several variables to the data for the purpose of statistical analysis (e.g., inferring if an account is official based on the presence of an official URL or classifying the author of the tweet as a bot based on the botsentinel.com classification). Because so much of the content of the tweet, for anti-immigration discourses, is contained in the hashtags used, it was decided to use hashtags to code the main topics of discussion. Thus, hashtag processing involved several steps:

1. Similar hashtags but spelled differently were automatically matched using the package "Fuzzy Wuzzy" in Python. This package uses the

Levenshtein Distance to calculate the proximity between two expressions. Each match was then manually checked to ensure that the hashtags were indeed identical (misspellings were easily identifiable);

2. Each group of hashtags was replaced by the corresponding expression (i.e., the text of the hashtag with spaces and consistent spelling);
3. Expressions were grouped by meaning (e.g., #enddaca and #nodaca were matched) and coded. At this stage, most groups of expressions/hashtags were searched both on Google and Twitter to check their meaning in context.

Of the original 29,375 unique hashtags in the dataset, 10,788 were hereby coded. The remaining hashtags were either irrelevant to the current study (e.g., #Bread or #MondayThought) or too ambiguous (e.g., generic first names or short and ambiguous acronyms). Because the remaining hashtags were scantly mentioned, of the 433,332 uses of hashtags in the data, we were able to code 393,691 of them, corresponding to 90.85% of instances.

Coding and Statistical Analysis

Each group of hashtags was coded using a combination of codes, corresponding either to their content or some of their characteristics. A total of 263 codes were developed in an iterative process by first developing codes based on the research questions and the reading of the hashtags (as part of hashtag processing), applying them to the data, considering the hashtags left uncoded, and proposing new codes until all the relevant hashtags had been coded (i.e., hashtags that were meaningful and unambiguous for the purposes of this study). Two types of codes were developed: characteristic codes (referring to the characteristics of the tweet independent of their content; e.g., support, threat, slogan, use of created words) and content codes (e.g., danger and crime; art and entertainment; conspiracies; economy). Last but not least, the codes were grouped in order to enable topic analysis. For example, references to Clinton was a grouped code including Benghazi, Clinton, Clinton-Family, Clinton-Scandal, Clinton-Emails. The categories presented in Table 6.2 correspond to the grouped codes used in relation to creative hashtags. The statistical analysis included descriptive statistics, two-way inferences (for continuous variables, a Mann-Whitney test and Cliff's delta were used; for categorical variables, a z-test was used to compare the proportions between the two groups) and logistic regressions (which allowed us to control for certain characteristics of the tweets and their authors, using the orientation of the tweets and their use of creativity as a response variable).

Coding for Creativity

In this chapter, the meaning of creativity is particular and constrained by what can be operationalised at the scale of the data we collected. Specifically,

Table 6.2 Created words and slogan variations for different categories of hashtags

Category	*Explanation*
America first	Variations of the slogan "America first" (e.g., "Britain first" or "American children first")
Amnesty	Created words using "amnesty" as a basis (e.g., "shamnesty")
Black lives matter	Variations of the slogan "Black lives matter" (e.g., "Black lies matter" or "All lives matter")
Brexit	Variations of Brexit (e.g., "Breshit")
Clinton	Created words and slogan variations around Clinton (e.g., "Shrillary"), not including variations of the "Lock her up" slogan
Democrats	Created words referring to democrats (e.g., "Demoncrazy")
Drain the swamp	Variations of the slogan "Drain the swamp" (e.g., "Drain the deep state swamp")
Hollywood	Created words and slogan variations around Hollywood and the associated conspiracy theories on paedophilia (e.g., "pedowood" or "hollyweird")
Immigrants	Created words using "immigrants" or "aliens" as a basis (e.g., "crimmigrants")
KAG	Variations of the slogan "Keep America Great" (e.g., "Keep America Safe")
Liberals	Created words referring to liberals (e.g., "Libtard")
Lock her up	Variations of the slogan "Lock her up" (e.g., "Lock democrats up")
MAGA	Variations of the slogan "Make America Great Again" (e.g., "Make America Sane Again")
Media	Created words using "media" or media outlets as a basis (e.g., "slime magazine")
Obama	Created words and slogan variations around Obama (e.g., "Ovomit"), not including variations of the "Lock her up" slogan
Other	Various created words that would not fit in other categories but were not common enough to have a category (e.g., "killuminati" or "moronlabe")
Red wave	Variations of the expression "Red wave" to refer to the upcoming elections (e.g., "Red tidal wave")
Refugees	Created words using "refugees" as a basis (e.g., "techfugees")
Trump	Created words and slogan variations around Trump (e.g., "Trumpists" or "SCROTUS")
USA	Created words referring to the USA or American people (e.g., "Americunts" or "Corruptifornia")
Warren	Created words and slogan variations around Elizabeth Warren (e.g., "Lieawatha" or "Fauxcahontas")
Waters	Created words referring to Maxine Waters, usually as variations of the "mad Maxine" attacks from Trump (e.g., "impeach mad maxine"), not including variations of the "Lock her up" slogan

since most of our analysis is done on hashtags, we focused on linguistic markers of creativity within them which were (1) created words and (2) slogan variations. These comply with a basic view of creativity as a process that generates novelty through the modification and combination of existing elements (central for the mini and little c levels of this phenomenon; Kaufman & Beghetto, 2009). Most of these uses, as seen in Table 6.2, were malevolent and oftentimes insulting or vulgar in nature, aiming to threaten or ridicule a person, group, or political party.

An important observation is thus needed before proceeding to the findings. Identifying some hashtags as "creative" doesn't imply that the content of the tweet they appeared in was "creative" and, even more, that the user tweeting it is a creative person (or, by extension, that hashtags, tweets, or people who are not using the linguistic markers we identified here are "uncreative"). As we shall see further on, there are different ways in which creativity is expressed on Twitter and, importantly, outside Twitter, when it comes to the issue of migration. In order to contextualise the use of "creative" hashtags, we also conducted a qualitative analysis of the tweets these hashtags appeared in, presented towards the end. Moreover, many of the hashtags discussed here have appeared at one point or another on Fox News or have been mentioned in Donald Trump's discourses. It is often impossible to know where they appeared first, Fox News, Donald Trump, and Twitter being part of a common communication ecosystem where all parties tend to borrow from each other. But it does mean that some of the hashtags presented here may have been "created" as expressions elsewhere first. However, our interest in this chapter is in how these are used on social media and for what purpose, no matter whether they appeared there first or not.

Findings

Our aim in this chapter is to examine how the use of creativity might contribute to spreading anti-immigration discourses on Twitter, especially by creating "echo chambers" in which particular points of view are expressed without critical reflection or debate. Before presenting findings associated with creative hashtags, it is important to note some of the general characteristics of anti-immigration tweets when compared to pro-immigration ones. The results are presented in Figures 6.1 and 6.2 for the descriptive statistics and measures of central tendency, Figures 6.3 and 6.4 for the effect sizes, and Table 6.3 for the inferential statistics. In the text, we report only the effect sizes, using Cohen's delta (for categorical variables) and Cliff's delta (for continuous variables, as they are not normally distributed). They best represent the importance of each variable and the direction of the effect, allowing us to keep the text as light as possible. All the inferential statistics are significant for $p < 0.0001$ (see Table 6.3 for details).

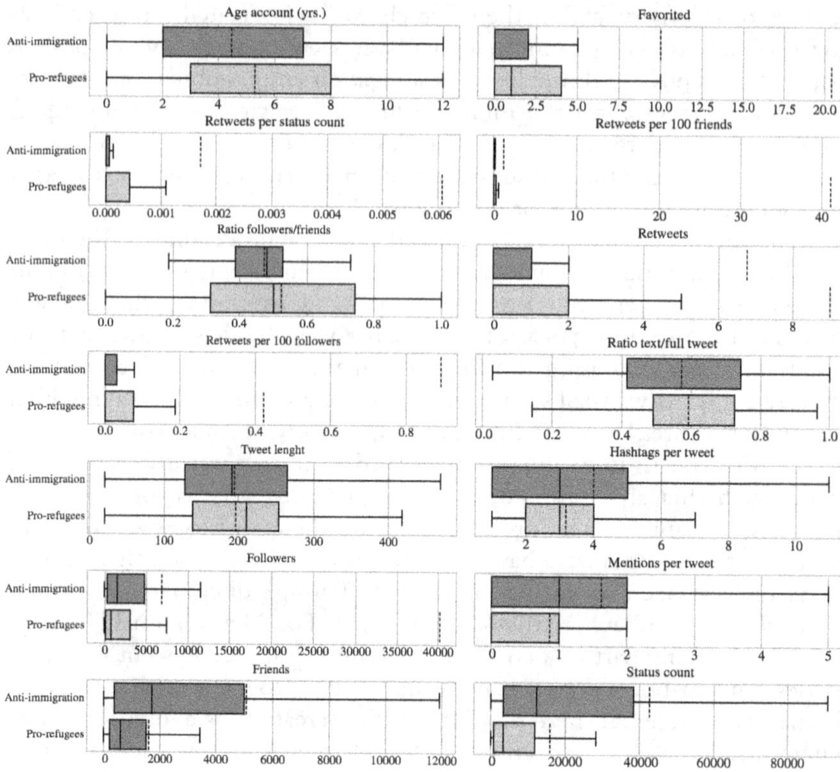

Figure 6.1 Distribution of the continuous variables for anti-immigration and pro-refugees tweets

Note: Dashed line: mean; full lines: quartiles; outliers not shown.

Pro-refugees tweets tend to come from older accounts (d = −0.150,[1] magnitude = small to medium) and that have been verified by twitter (d = −0.712, magnitude = medium to large) or include the URL of an official website (d = 0.596, magnitude = large, and d = 0.598, magnitude = large when considering together as official accounts that are verified and/or have an official URL). That is, pro-refugees content seems to come more often from official and established accounts, such as those of organisations or public figures, and to be more international. Indeed, all the tweets collected are in English, but pro-refugees tweets come more often from accounts that are not officially in English (d = 0.581, magnitude = medium to large). While they globally have fewer friends[2] (d = 0.319, magnitude = small to medium) and followers (d = 0.151, magnitude = small to medium) than users tweeting anti-immigration content, they are slightly more successful: their tweets are more retweeted (d = −0.077, magnitude = negligible) and more favourited (d = −0.143, magnitude = negligible), with effects slightly

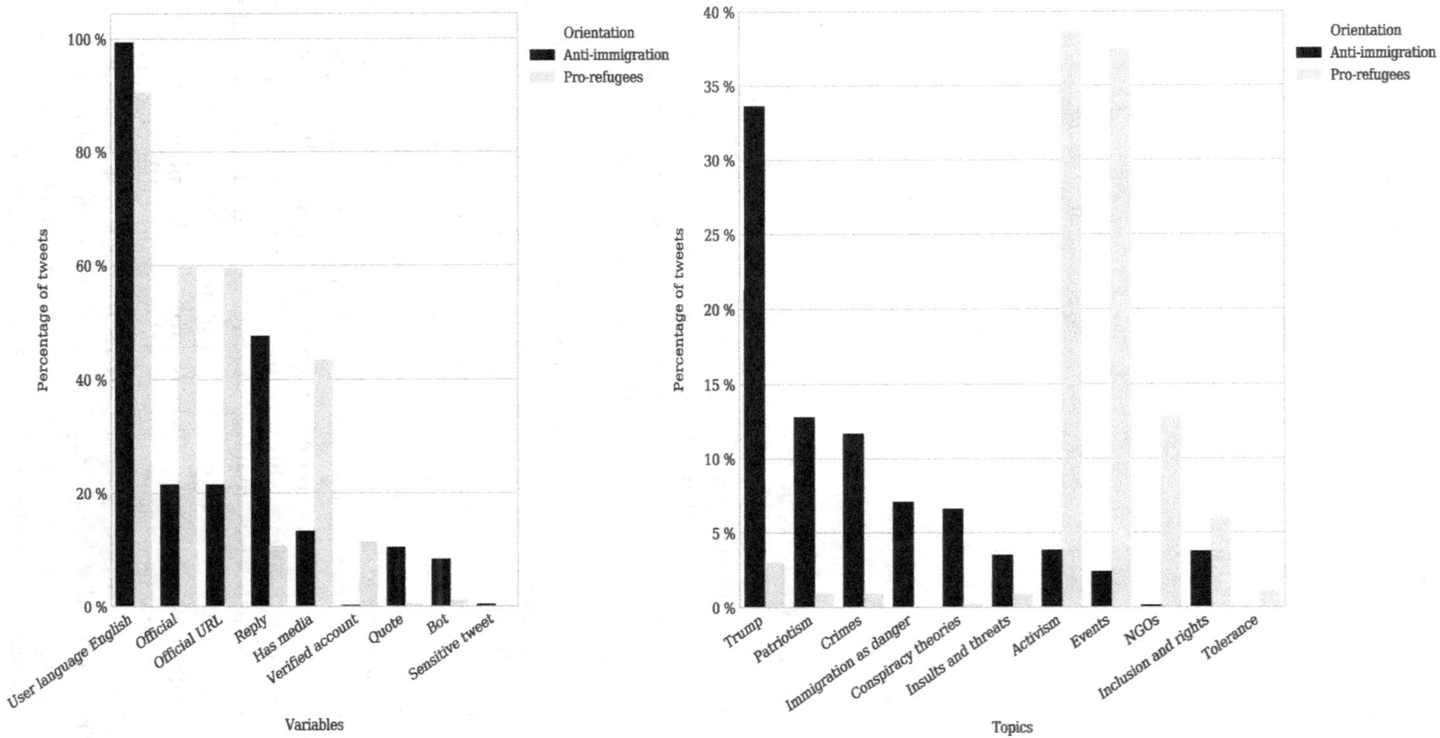

Figure 6.2 Frequencies of the main categorical variables and the topics of the tweets for anti-immigration and pro-refugees tweets

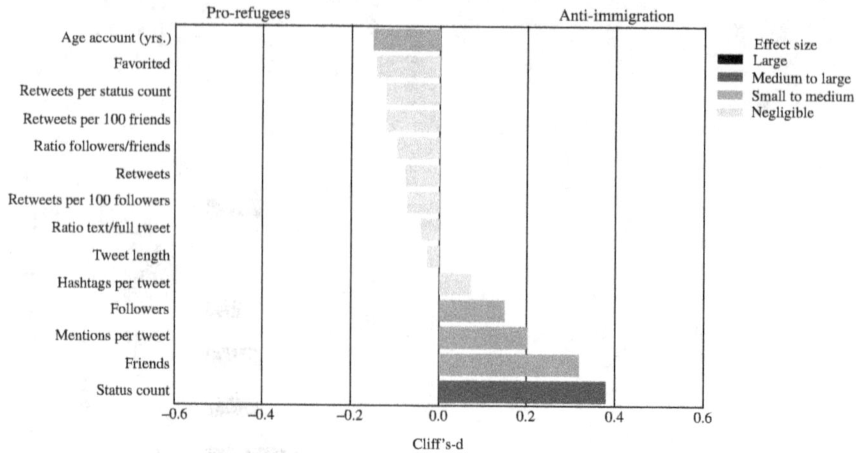

Figure 6.3 Effect sizes for the continuous variables for anti-immigration and pro-refugees tweets

more significant when taking into account how many friends (retweets per 100 friends: d = −0.121, magnitude = negligible) a user has or how active the person is on Twitter (retweets per status count: d = −0.121, magnitude = negligible). Pro-refugees tweets are also slightly longer (d = −0.028, magnitude = negligible), tend to contain more actual text (ratio actual text/full length of the tweet: d = −0.040, magnitude = negligible), and more media, such as videos or photos (d = −0.795, magnitude = medium to large). Although some of these effects are small, they globally paint a picture of pro-refugees tweets as being more likely to be coming from official sources or public figures with a more consistent "content" (either by having more actual text in the tweet or by including more media).

On the other side, anti-immigration tweets tend to come from much more active accounts, with users tweeting a lot more (d = 0.380, magnitude = medium to large), be-friending many more accounts and being much more followed in return. Moreover, looking at the friends/followers ratio – a more accurate measure of popularity (Wang, 2010) – shows that anti-immigration accounts who have more followers do befriend a lot of other accounts themselves, resulting in lower ratios than their pro-refugees counterparts (#followers/(#friends + #followers), d = −0.096, magnitude = negligible). While the effect is small, we did indeed observe that some users actively seek followers by friending many other users, especially those who are known to systematically follow back (e.g., hashtags such as #ArkTrumpers and #TrumpTrain were used during the period of data collection to flag such accounts and facilitate the practice). Anti-immigration tweets were more frequently replies (d = 0.795, magnitude = medium to

Table 6.3 Descriptive statistics and two-way inferences

	Continuous Variables					
			Mean Values		*Effect Size*	
	Mann-Whitney Scores[3]	*p-values*[4]	*Anti Immigration*	*Pro-Refugees*	*Cliff's Delta*[5]	*Confidence Interval*[6]
Age of the account in years	929099700	< 0.0001	4.470	5.310	−0.150	[−0.166; −0.134]
Favourited count	936426800	< 0.0001	10.030	20.400	−0.143	[−0.159; −0.128]
Followers	928363600	< 0.0001	6812.000	40089.400	0.151	[0.134; 0.167]
Friends	744277000	< 0.0001	5052.590	1582.640	0.319	[0.305; 0.333]
Hashtags per tweet	1012613000	< 0.0001	3.990	3.170	0.074	[0.059; 0.088]
Links per tweet	1084584000	< 0.0001	1.010	1.020	−0.008	[−0.011; −0.004]
Mentions per tweet	872069900	< 0.0001	1.630	0.870	0.202	[0.188; 0.216]
Ratio followers/friends	988399237.5	< 0.0001	0.47	0.52	−0.096	[−0.115; −0.076]
Ratio text/full tweet	1048697000	< 0.0001	0.570	0.590	−0.040	[−0.056; −0.025]
Retweets	1008630000	< 0.0001	6.780	9.020	−0.077	[−0.092; −0.063]
Retweets per 100 followers	1013264000	< 0.0001	0.890	0.420	−0.073	[−0.087; −0.058]
Retweets per 100 friends	960462100	< 0.0001	1.110	41.110	−0.121	[−0.136; −0.106]
Retweets per status count	960360900	< 0.0001	<0.001	0.010	−0.121	[−0.137; −0.106]
Statuses	677187900	< 0.0001	42628.830	15860.620	0.380	[0.366; 0.395]
Text length	1062579000	< 0.0001	194.400	196.830	−0.028	[−0.043; −0.012]

(Continued)

Table 6.3 (Continued)

Dichotomous Variables					
			Frequencies		*Effect Size*
	z-score	*p-values*	*Anti Immigration*	*Pro Refugees*	*Cohen's Delta*
			Main Variables		
English speaking users	80.937	< 0.0001	0.994	0.905	0.581
Has media	−110.704	< 0.0001	0.133	0.434	−0.795
Official accounts	−123.840	< 0.0001	0.216	0.598	−0.890
Quotes	50.274	< 0.0001	0.104	0.006	0.361
Replies	110.701	< 0.0001	0.474	0.107	0.795
Sensitive tweets	9.983	< 0.0001	0.046	0.003	0.072
User has official URL	−123.029	< 0.0001	0.216	0.596	−0.884
Users classified as bots	40.443	< 0.0001	0.083	0.011	0.291
Verified users	−99.147	< 0.0001	0.003	0.114	−0.712
			Topics		
Activism	−170.349	< 0.0001	0.038	0.387	−1.223
Conspiracy theories	40.171	< 0.0001	0.066	0.002	0.289
Crimes	52.044	< 0.0001	0.117	0.094	0.374
Events	−184.941	< 0.0001	0.024	0.376	−1.328
Immigration as danger	43.196	< 0.0001	0.071	<0.001	0.310
Inclusion and rights	−15.550	< 0.0001	0.037	0.060	−0.112
Insults and threats	21.524	< 0.0001	0.035	0.009	0.155
NGOs	−109.913	< 0.0001	0.014	0.128	−0.790
Patriotism	55.200	< 0.0001	0.128	0.095	0.397
Tolerance	−29.300	< 0.0001	0.003	0.011	−0.210
Trump	100.229	< 0.0001	0.336	0.030	0.720

large) or quotes of other tweets (d = 0.361, magnitude = small to medium) and contained more hashtags (d = 0.074, magnitude = negligible) and mentions of other users (d = 0.202, magnitude = small to medium). Finally, they were more likely to be classified as sensitive by Twitter (d = 0.072, magnitude = negligible) and as coming from bots (d = 0.291, magnitude = small to medium) – fake accounts, using BotSentinel classification. Thus, in contrast with pro-refugees tweets, anti-immigration messages tend to come from very active accounts who know how to use Twitter and its features to gain visibility (e.g., using hashtags, mentions, and replies to benefit from trending topics and users), but also more easily falling victims of the platform's moderation: not only are their tweets more likely to be classified as sensitive, but when we tried to explore certain anti-immigration accounts in more details, many had been closed – which never happened with pro-refugees accounts.

In terms of content, we found that pro-refugees tweets were more likely to refer to activism (d = −1.223, magnitude = large), events (d = −1.328, magnitude = large), and NGOs (d = −0.790, magnitude = medium to large). It seems, thus, that many pro-refugees tweets concerned campaigns and events proposed by different organisations – the hashtag #RefugeeWeek, for instance, was trending at the time – and may have been attempts to show support to refugees and migrants or to defend tolerance (d = −0.210, magnitude = small to medium) as well as human rights and the idea of inclusion (d = −0.112, magnitude = negligible).

In contrast, anti-immigration messages included more references to immigration as a danger (d = 0.310, magnitude = small to medium), to crimes (d = 0.374, magnitude = small to medium), and to conspiracy theories (d = 0.289, magnitude = small to medium), with an important part of the tweets devoted more or less directly to the idea that immigration is dangerous and/or criminal. They also evoked patriotism (d = 0.397, magnitude = small to medium) and Donald Trump (d = 0.720, magnitude = medium to large) much more often, and used threats and insults more frequently (d = 0.155, magnitude = negligible) – perhaps explaining why Twitter had in the meantime blocked quite a few accounts. Globally, they were thus more focused on the political debate around immigration – from what it represents, in their opinion, for Western societies (a danger) to those who promised to tackle these issues (Donald Trump).

Taken together, the characteristics of the tweets, of the users who wrote them, and of their content seems to indicate that pro-refugees tweets are the product of official accounts either launching or participating in campaigns to support refugees and their rights, on social media and outside of it, and to distribute content (i.e., media or text). In contrast, the anti-immigration tweets come from extremely active accounts who know how to use Twitter to increase the reach of their message (i.e., using Twitter's interactive functions and developing strategies to increase their number of followers), their message being that immigration is problematic. It thus seems that users with anti-immigration views may be actively trying to create echo chambers that will amplify their ideas and give the impression that they are more widespread than they actually are.

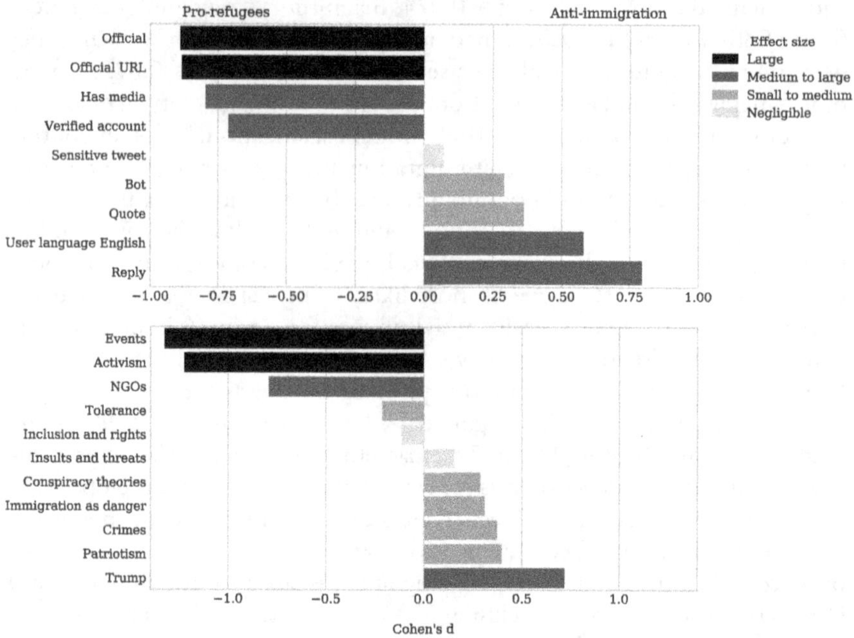

Figure 6.4 Effect sizes for the main categorical variables and the topics of the tweets for anti-immigration and pro-refugees tweets

Importantly for this chapter, it appears that anti-immigration users also tend to use more creative hashtags than pro-immigration ones (5.449% of anti-immigration tweets against 0.382% of pro-refugees tweets, d = 0.250, magnitude = small to medium). This is not difficult to understand given the restricted definition of creativity we are using here, which considers it in terms of word creation and slogan variation. Engaging in these practices, in particular in order to ridicule, insult, or threaten, seems to play an important role in creating echo chambers online and using social media to build identity and community rather than engage in debate or engage with events taking place outside of social media.

In order to control for the influence of other variables in understanding what characterises the use of creative hashtags (as compared to their absence from a tweet), we performed a logistic regression with creativity as a dependent variable and including only the variables that were not correlated to each other (Pseudo R-square = 0.2127, Log-Likelihood = −15837, LL-Null = −20116), presented in Table 6.4 and Figure 6.5.

What this analysis revealed is that creativity is much more likely in tweets that are anti-immigration (+700.93%, $p < 0.001$), showing that is much more a characteristic of that side of the debate. Creativity is also more frequent in replies (+33.72%, $p < 0.001$) and quotes (+50.77%,

Table 6.4 Logistic regression: creativity

	Coef	*Odds Ratio*	*Percentage Increase*	*Std err*	*z*	*P>|z|**	*Confidence Interval (0.95)*
Intercept	−2.9645	0.0516	−94.84	0.274	−10.808	< 0.001	[−3.502; −2.427]
Anti-immigration	2.0893	8.0792	707.93	0.109	19.233	< 0.001	[1.876; 2.302]
Reply	0.2906	1.3372	33.72	0.038	7.633	< 0.001	[0.216; 0.365]
Sensitive	0.1266	1.1350	13.50	0.207	0.612	**0.541**	[−0.279; 0.532]
Quote	0.4106	1.5077	50.77	0.048	8.624	< 0.001	[0.317; 0.504]
User language EN	−0.4823	0.6174	−38.26	0.158	−3.053	**0.002**	[−0.792; −0.173]
Bot	0.0166	1.0168	1.67	0.062	0.267	**0.789**	[−0.105; 0.139]
Official	−0.3825	0.6822	−31.78	0.040	−9.523	<0.001	[−0.461; −0.304]
Ratio text/full tweet	−4.3047	0.0135	−98.65	0.147	−29.341	< 0.001	[−4.592; −4.017]
Mention count	−0.1711	0.8427	−15.73	0.008	−20.581	< 0.001	[−0.187; −0.155]
Age account (yr.)	0.0414	1.0423	4.23	0.005	7.910	< 0.001	[0.031; 0.052]
Links count	−1.3528	0.2585	−74.15	0.199	−6.784	< 0.001	[−1.744; −0.962]
Hashtags count	0.0307	1.0312	3.12	0.007	4.495	< 0.001	[0.017; 0.044]
Retweet count (unit: 100)	0.0421	1.0430	4.30	0.012	3.573	< 0.001	[0.019; 0.065]
User statuses count (unit: 100)	−0.0003	0.9997	−0.03	< 0.001	−17.179	< 0.001	[< −0.001; < −0.001]
User friends count (unit: 100)	0.0010	1.0010	0.10	< 0.001	3.765	< 0.001	[< 0.001; 0.002]
User followers count (unit: 100)	−0.0005	0.9995	−0.05	< 0.001	−1.874	**0.061**	[−0.001; < 0.001]
Length text	0.0090	1.0090	0.90	< 0.001	22.610	< 0.001	[0.008; 0.010]
Before summer	−0.4145	0.6607	−33.93	0.033	−12.645	< 0.001	[−0.479; −0.350]
Tweet per user	0.0050	1.0050	0.50	< 0.001	39.168	< 0.001	[0.004; 0.005]

* Given that most results are significant, we marked in bold only those non-significant for p < 0.001.

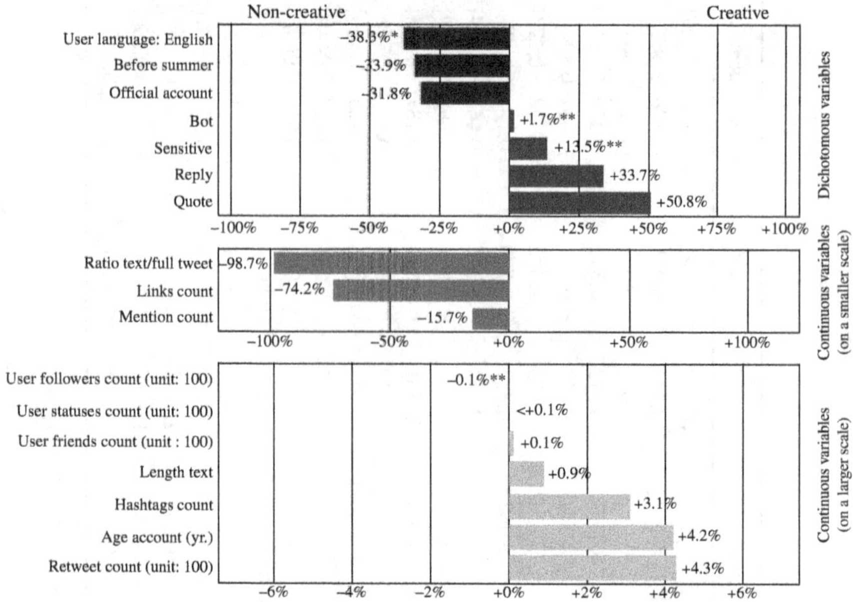

Figure 6.5 Percentage increase in the odds of a tweet being creative or non-creative for a unit increase in each variable

Note: **: not significant; *: significant at p < 0.01; else: significant at p > 0.001.

p < 0.001), and in tweets with more hashtags (+3.12%, p < 0.001). They also come from older accounts (+4.23%, p < 0.001) with slightly more friends (+0.10%, p < 0.001) and who posted more during the period of data collection (+0.50%, p < 0.001). Overall, they were a bit more successful, being retweeted more than their non-creative counterparts (+4.30%, p < 0.001). In contrast, creativity was less frequent in tweets coming from official accounts (−31.78%, p < 0.001), with more actual text (−95.65%, p < 0.001), and that contained more links (−74.15%, p < 0.001). It thus seems that creative hashtags came from users resembling most the prototypical anti-immigration tweeter described earlier – even when controlling for the orientation of the tweet – but who have been on Twitter the longest. They may thus represent the "heart" of the anti-immigration Twittersphere.[7] It should also be noted that linguistic creativity could be used as a strategy by active users (who tweet and follow more people) as a way to obtain retweets by offending specific social targets and signalling a particular identity online.

It is equally important to investigate the main content of the tweets using hashtags catalogued here as creative. Table 6.5 presents their use among different categories of topics identified in the data (see the data processing section). The top five categories centred around US politics, in particular slogans associated with Donald Trump or the Republican Party.

Table 6.5 Use of creative hashtag per different content categories

	Code	*Number of Uses*	*Number of Hashtags*	*Percentage of Creative Tweets*	*Percentage of All Tweets*	*Number of Tweets*	*Number of Users*
1	Red wave	1785	25	32.10	1.583	1714	721
2	Drain the swamp	1031	26	18.54	0.914	1026	256
3	Lock her up	899	9	16.17	0.797	895	235
4	KAG	624	17	11.22	0.553	623	100
5	MAGA	350	31	6.29	0.310	346	172
6	Black lives matter	295	24	5.30	0.262	294	145
7	Liberals	163	12	2.93	0.145	159	99
8	Democrats	111	16	2.00	0.098	110	71
9	Hollywood	52	7	0.94	0.046	50	28
10	Refugees	52	7	0.94	0.046	50	27
11	Warren	38	9	0.68	0.034	34	32
12	America first	34	5	0.61	0.030	34	17
13	Obama	36	4	0.65	0.032	36	5
14	Trump	23	9	0.41	0.020	23	18
15	Clinton	16	6	0.29	0.014	16	13
16	USA	11	7	0.20	0.010	11	7
17	Other	12	11	0.22	0.011	11	10
18	Immigrants	9	5	0.16	0.008	8	4
19	Amnesty	7	2	0.13	0.006	7	2
20	Waters	4	3	0.07	0.004	4	3
21	Brexit	5	3	0.09	0.004	5	2
22	Media	4	2	0.07	0.004	4	2
Overall		**5578**	**240**	**100**	**4.33**	**4886**	**1692**

Last but not least, in order to understand the function of these creative hashtags in context, we conducted a qualitative analysis of the tweets they belonged to by selecting the top 20 most re-tweeted such messages per category (see the 22 categories in Table 6.5), allowing us to focus in details on the most "successful" tweets per category. This analysis revealed that tweets using creative hashtags don't necessarily display any other signs of "creativity" (e.g., more invented words or variations of expressions or slogans). In fact, they sometimes simply offer a collection of hashtags without any particular order or meaning other than signalling the user's belonging to a particular Twitter community (the creative hashtags are in bold):

> @POTUS @realDonaldTrump #MAGA #TrumpArmy **#TrumpKick Hildebeast** #DrainTheSwamp **#LockThemAllUp** #LockHerUp #BuildTheWall ##KAG #WINNING #WINNING #GODSCHOSEN #WWGWGA #MAGAFORALL #Jobs#Jobs #OneNationUnderGod #AmericaFirst TRUMP2020 #PatriotFight **#REDTSUNAMI** #QArmy #InGodWeTrust[8]

It is in fact very common, even for those tweets that do have a specific message, to end in a list of anti-immigration and usually Trump-style slogans that help the user both perform a certain online identity and connect to like-minded people. This function is made clear, for example, by a tweet that includes the word "again" before going on to list generic hashtags, announcing the repetition of frequent hashtags:

> @AmericanFamily_1st @HillaryClinton @realDonaldTrump In #**Mexifornia**?? Ohhh I can GUARANTEE IT! #**Democraps** don't get #IllegalAlien voting they're gonna lose the state! #MandateEVerify #EndAmnesty AGAIN #SecureTheBorder #BuildTheDamnWall #RedWave2020 #MAGA #**MakeCaliforniaGoldAgain**

Rarely, and perhaps illustrating a higher degree of creativity, a few users succeeded in creating entire sentences completely made up of hashtags. This is further evidence of how anti-immigration users exploit to the maximum the affordances of social media by creating messages with a maximum likelihood of being tagged and thus visible:

> #FamiliesBelongTogether #**AmericanFamiliesFirst** #ReuniteFamilies at the #Border and #DeportThemAll then + there! Line the #Border with #Military + #BuildTheWall fast! @realDonaldTrump We'll help #SaveAmerica from #ILLEGALALIENS! #MAGA #DeportIllegals

In terms of the content of tweets using creative hashtags, it thematically fell under the following nine categories: (1) shifting the terms of the debate and pointing to the misdeeds of the other parts (typically Obama or the Democrats); (2) defending or praising Trump and his presidency; (3) restating current news; (4) sending political messages, typically in support of the Republican party for upcoming elections; (5) formulating one's worldviews, in particular warning about the dangers of migration up to stocking fear about it; (6) promoting fake stories and conspiracy theories; (7) giving advice or demanding things from politicians (from ending illegal migration to sealing the border); (8) normalising the harsh treatment of illegal migrants; and (9) formulating insults and slurs, some of them "creative", and denigrating people who share different views.

Further markers of creativity can be found in the use of sarcasm or even humour in promoting an anti-immigration agenda, although these instances are rare – the six instances that use this strategy from our corpus of 347 tweets used for qualitative analysis are reproduced here:

> I would buy ten bricks in a heartbeat. However I want the names of American citizens that have lost their life due to illegal immigration on my bricks. #BuildTheWall #MolliesWall #AmericaFirst #KAG #**AmericansLivesMatter**

@RealJamesWoods Shhh. Don't tell Obozo or #**Killary** . . . both have walls surrounding their estates. #BuildTheWall

#Democrats: Brave enough to kill our unborn children just not brave enough to kill our enemies. #prolife #Truth #LiberalismIsAMental-Disease #**Demonrats** #VoteThemOut #MAGA #BuildTheWall #VoteRed #RedWaveRising

@ABC. Send all them back home Together! #FamilyMatters #Build-TheWall #ChildrenTrafficking #**PedoWood** #VoteRedWave #QAnon #WWGWGA

Democrats don't really care about illegal immigrants only standing against Trump. I wonder if our #POTUS championed #guncon-trol higher taxes and #OpenBorder would #**libturds** then support #gunsense lower taxes and #BuildTheWall? #Dreamers #MAGA #TrumpTrain2020 #Hartford

HOW DARE YOU!? . . . want secure borders? . . . want immigrants to come legally? . . . want Congress to do its job? . . . want our home-less vets taken care of before illegal immigrants? WE WILL DARE AGAIN #**RedTsunami2018** #BuildTheWall #SundayFunday @Fuctupmind

In summary, the qualitative analysis of a reduced number of popular tweets using creative hashtags sheds light on the fact that the kind of linguistic creativity identified here doesn't apply to the rest of the text, and actually, its use is part and parcel of the general drive to signal identity and construct echo chambers with those who share the user's identity and set of beliefs. In fact, the lack of any other substantial message or attempt at having a debate are made clear by tweets such as:

> Profile hashtags that make me instantly follow: #Jesus #Conservative #MAGA #2ndA #Christian #Bible #MolonLabe #KAG #**Build-TheDamnWallTall** #**DrainTheDeepStateSwamp** #Trump #AmericaFirst #BuildTheWall #BackTheBlue Just to name a few . . .

This way of using hashtags, creative or otherwise, has been observed by other social media users who, ironically, started employing the tags of particular echo chambers on Twitter in order to attract their attention but for a different purpose:

> Remember . . . hashtagging #**Shrillary** #BuildTheWall #LockHerUp to an otherwise sensible and morally correct post is like stealing little pieces of a #Deplorables life and making them read something decent instead. #Trump #LGBTQ+ #Feminism #Love #Respect #Decency #America
>
> I'm so sorry you guys. 🙈🙉😱😌😂 #Trump #BuildTheWall #**TrumpAmerikkka** #**NazisAmerikkka** #KeepFamiliesTogether

#FatFuck #IMPEACHNOW **#LockHimUp** #TrumpsAnAsshole #MAGA #KAG #Resist #Resistance

In the end, the story of creativity online, including on social media, does not belong to a single community but defines exchanges between groups, particularly those with highly contrasting views and agendas. The broader question this kind of findings invites us to reflect on is whether social media can be a place for meaningful exchanges, one in which creativity is used for mutual understanding rather than (mainly) spreading intolerant, racist views.

Discussion

This chapter aimed to examine how malevolent creativity might contribute to the construction of echo chambers among anti-immigration communities on Twitter. This is, admittedly, an unusual topic given the largely positive societal effects creativity is supposed to have. And yet, acknowledging malevolent forms of creativity (Cropley, et al., 2010), those aimed at negatively affecting immigrants and their prospects, as well as recognising the creativity of language (a type of little c creativity that is often ignored; Kaufman & Beghetto, 2009) can bring valuable insights to understanding a global challenge, that of migration, and the role that social media, for better or worse, plays within it.

The relation between creativity and the Internet has been intensely debated in recent years (see Literat & Glăveanu, 2016, 2018) with a particular view to social media and what is largely assumed to be its positive association with creative expression. Indeed, it is not only the case that the use of social media revolutionised innovation management and vice versa (Ratten, 2017), but this relatively new milieu is often eulogised for affording increased creative possibilities (Peppler & Solomou, 2011). Social media users are supposed to draw on "collective intelligence" for need identification, idea generation, and evaluation (Wagner & Jiang, 2012). In this context, linguistic creativity on Twitter and similar platforms became a topic of interest for some researchers (see Gillen, 2018). In fact, the creativity of online communication is now an area of study within sociolinguistics, where specialists "can identify and investigate new sites of variation in phenomena that don't occur in spoken language but occur in Computer-Mediated Communication (CMC)" (Shapp, 2014, p. 2).

There are certainly many things to be excited about in relation to social media. For one, "mainstream media tell the stories of the powerful, social media are thought to involve generalized inclusivity and participation" (Siapera, et al., 2018, p. 2). This has major consequences for creativity, given its distributed and participatory nature (see Glăveanu, 2014; Clapp, 2016). The fact that everyone can express an opinion and gain "voice" on social media is empowering self-expression, including creative forms of it. Social media is also supposed to increase differences and diversity of perspectives, another pre-condition for creativity (Glăveanu & Gillespie, 2015; Glăveanu, 2015). Yet, these assumptions should not blind us to the fact that power and visibility are unequally distributed on platforms like Twitter. In fact, as Meraz and Papacharissi (2016) noted, about 10% to 20% of accounts on Twitter enjoy disproportionate influence over the network, and, even if power is more fluid and temporary on social media, it doesn't mean it doesn't work to restrict the access of marginal voices or perspectives resulting in stereotypes and discrimination. As Kreis (2017, p. 501) concludes, "although intentions such as raising awareness, expressing solidarity, or obtaining support may be for the common good, social media may also be used to disseminate racial and xenophobic opinions, resulting in 'anti-social media'".

Hashtags have a big part to play in both the positive and negative dynamic described earlier. Undoubtedly the result of a creative act, the use of hashtags has been proposed by a Twitter user named Chris Messina in August 2007 in order to create user groups and organise topics of discussion (see Shapp, 2014, pp. 3–4). Twitter incorporated the hashtag function in 2009 and Facebook followed in 2013, and, for about a decade now, we have all been experiencing an online space (over)populated by these quick means of communication. While Twitter has several other conventions, such as retweeting, favouriting, and replying, hashtags remain one of its most powerful creative and cultural tools, a position cemented by the fact that, for instance, in 2014 the American Dialect Society voted #BlackLivesMatter its Word of the Year (Konnelly, 2015). Hashtags are of particular interest for media experts and should be equally so for creativity researchers. This is because hashtags capture something essential about the dynamic between constant novelty (through variation), transmission (through reuse), and creative appropriation. Tying different online memes together, hashtags thus illustrate well the two dimensions of creativity: emergent novelty and clear significance. "People learn about the hashtag and then use it themselves to add their own contribution to a funny or thought-provoking idea" (Shapp, 2014, p. 6). The fact that these processes can support malevolent forms of creativity is the reality evidenced in this chapter.

In order to start understanding and addressing these issues, we need be mindful about the main functions of hashtags. Besides organising information (as meta-data), they play an even greater social role, as documented also in our research. This community-building property has been discussed at length by Zappavigna (2011), who theorised it as "ambient affiliation" – the invitation to search for and affiliate with like-minded people. Exercising this possibility results in virtual communities or "social aggregations that emerge from the Net when enough people carry on those public discussions long enough, with sufficient human feeling, to form webs of personal relationships in cyberspace" (Rheingold, 1993, p. 5). The identity work performed on social media and the resulting virtual communities can be empowering or disempowering, oftentimes both (for a discussion of racialised hashtags see Sharma, 2013). In the end, hashtags have two main pragmatic functions:

tagging (used to connect, organise, and circulate memes) and commentary (used to evaluate, express emotion, etc.), a division that is oftentimes blurry in practice (Shapp, 2014). As we have seen in the study presented here, it is precisely the interplay between these basic functions that gives hashtags their creative edge and considerable power to influence.

Overall, we can conclude that users tweeting anti-immigration content actively create echo chambers, and their online activity seems to be an end in itself. The "ambient affiliation" of these users is made obvious by the seemingly endless and arguably mindless repetition of slogans such as "build the wall", "make America great again", or "lock her up". And yet, there is something even more intriguing at play when considering the use of creativity in this context. In order to gain visibility and popularity on Twitter and other social media platforms, the same hashtags need to be used consistently. And yet, the creative uses we evidenced (at least for part of the broader online community discussing immigration) are prefaced on generating variations rather than sticking to the original formula. These variations might not bring the user popularity, but they are likely to attract attention and, through following and retweets, to build community. The final, surprising conclusion coming out of studying malevolent creativity on social media might be exactly this: that creative expression can sacrifice individuality, in the context of Twitter, on the altar of achieving togetherness. If this medium is to be pursued by pro-immigration users, this might be a lesson to reflect on.

Notes

1. A positive delta means that anti-immigration accounts tend to score higher, while a negative delta means that pro-refugee accounts have higher values. The evaluations of the magnitude are based on Cohen (1992) for his measure and Romano, Kromrey, Coraggio, and Skowronek (2006) for Cliff's delta. Although the deltas are often close, Cliff's delta are smaller and always between −1 and +1, which is reflected in the evaluation of the magnitude.
2. Friendships on Twitter are not reciprocal: a friend is someone you follow, and a follower is someone who follows you.
3. The variables do not follow a normal distribution, thus a non-parametric test such as Mann-Whitney rank test had to be used.
4. Given the size of the samples, we opted for a very low p-value of 0.0001.
5. Equivalent of Cohen's delta for non-normally distributed variables. The values are always between −1 and 1, thus it is usually lower than Cohen's delta. The opposite directions sometimes observed between the means differences and the Cliff's delta come from very skewed distributions. In these cases, Cliff's delta can be considered to reflect better the distribution of the data than the mean.
6. Cliff's delta can also be used as a non-parametric test (Cliff, 1993), more robust than a Mann-Whitney rank test in cases when the groups do not have equal variance (Kitchenham, et al., 2016), which is the case here for most variables. We have thus included here the confidence interval as an additional validation (Cliff, 1996), for a 0.9999 level of confidence.

7. This would perhaps explain the fact that creative tweets are more often bots than creative tweets in the data (although $p = 0.789$), as they may imitate more established accounts who have been present for a longer time.
8. The tweets have been modified in order not to be easily searchable in a search engine and to preserve anonymity, but without altering the content.

References

Awan, I. (2014). Islamophobia and Twitter: A typology of online hate against Muslims on social media. *Policy & Internet, 6*(2), 133–150.

Bonilla, Y., & Rosa, J. (2015). # Ferguson: Digital protest, hashtag ethnography, and the racial politics of social media in the United States. *American Ethnologist, 42*(1), 4–17.

Bruns, A., & Burgess, J. E. (2011, August). The use of Twitter hashtags in the formation of ad hoc publics. In *Proceedings of the 6th European Consortium for Political Research (ECPR) general conference 2011*, University of Iceland, Reykjavik.

Chaudhry, I. (2015). # Hashtagging hate: Using Twitter to track racism online. *First Monday, 20*(2). Retrieved from http://uncommonculture.org/ojs/index.php/fm/article/view/5450/4207

Clapp, E. P. (2016). *Participatory creativity: Introducing access and equity to the creative classroom*. New York: Routledge.

Cliff, N. (1993). Dominance statistics: Ordinal analyses to answer ordinal questions. *Psychological Bulletin, 114*(3), 494–509. http://doi.org/10.1037/0033-2909.114.3.494

Cliff, N. (1996). *Ordinal methods for behavioral data analysis*. London: Routledge.

Cohen, J. (1992). A power primer. *Psychological Bulletin, 112*, 155–159.

Cropley, D. H., Cropley, A. J., Kaufman, J. C., & Runco, M. A. (Eds.). (2010). *The dark side of creativity*. New York: Cambridge University Press.

Ehrenberg, R. (2012). Social media sway: Worries over political misinformation on Twitter attract scientists' attention. *Science News, 182*(8), 22–25.

Ferra, I., & Nguyen, D. (2017). #Migrantcrisis: "Tagging" the European migration crisis on Twitter. *Journal of Communication Management, 21*(4), 411–426.

Gerbaudo, P. (2018). *Tweets and the streets: Social media and contemporary activism*. London: Pluto Press.

Giglietto, F., & Lee, Y. (2016). To be or not to be Charlie: Twitter hashtags as a discourse and counter-discourse in the aftermath of the 2015 Charlie Hebdo shooting in France. *AoIR Selected Papers of Internet Research, 5*.

Gillen, J. (2018). Cricket bats,# riotcleanup, and rhubarb: Everyday creativity in Twitter interactions around Test Match special. *Language Sciences, 65*, 37–47.

Glăveanu, V. P. (2014). *Distributed creativity: Thinking outside the box of the creative individual*. Cham: Springer.

Glăveanu, V. P. (2015). Creativity as a sociocultural act. *Journal of Creative Behavior, 49*(3), 165–180.

Glăveanu, V. P., & Gillespie, A. (2015). Creativity out of difference: Theorising the semiotic, social and temporal origin of creative acts. In V. P. Glăveanu, A. Gillespie, & J. Valsiner (Eds.), *Rethinking creativity: Contributions from social and cultural psychology* (pp. 1–15). Hove: Routledge.

Grosswiler, P. (1998). Historical hopes, media fears, and the electronic town meeting concept: Where technology meets democracy or demagogy? *Journal of Communication Inquiry, 22*(2), 133–151.

Gualda, E., & Rebollo Díaz, C. (2016). The refugee crisis on Twitter: A diversity of discourses at a European crossroads. *Journal of Spatial and Organizational Dynamics, IV*(3), 199–212.

Highfield, T., Harrington, S., & Bruns, A. (2013). Twitter as a technology for audiencing and fandom: The# Eurovision phenomenon. *Information, Communication & Society, 16*(3), 315–339.

Janis, I. L. (1982). *Groupthink: Psychological studies of policy decisions and fiascoes* (2nd ed.). Boston, MA: Houghton Mifflin.

Kaufman, J. C., & Beghetto, R. A. (2009). Beyond big and little: The four C model of creativity. *Review of General Psychology, 13*(1), 1–12.

Keen, A. (2015). *The Internet is not the answer.* New York: Atlantic Monthly Press.

Kitchenham, B., Madeyski, L., Budgen, D., Keung, J., Brereton, P., Charters, S., . . . Pohthong, A. (2016). Robust statistical methods for empirical software engineering. *Empirical Software Engineering, 22*, 579–630.

Konnelly, A. (2015). #Activism: Identity, affiliation, and political discourse-making on Twitter. *The Arbutus Review, 6*(1), 1–16.

Kreis, R. (2017). #Refugeesnotwelcome: Anti-refugee discourse on Twitter. *Discourse & Communication, 11*(5), 498–514.

Literat, I., & Glăveanu, V. P. (2016). Same but different? Distributed creativity in the Internet age. *Creativity: Theories – Research – Applications, 3*(2), 330–342.

Literat, I., & Glăveanu, V. P. (2018). Distributed creativity on the Internet: A theoretical foundation for online creative participation. *International Journal of Communication, 12*, 893–908.

Maas, M. K., McCauley, H. L., Bonomi, A. E., & Leija, S. G. (2018). "I was grabbed by my pussy and its# NotOkay": A Twitter backlash against Donald Trump's degrading commentary. *Violence Against Women, 24*(14), 1739–1750. http://doi.org/10.1177/1077801217743340

Meraz, S., & Papacharissi, Z. (2016). Networked framing and gatekeeping. In T. Witschge, W. Anderson, D. Domingo, & A. Hermida (Eds.), *The SAGE handbook of digital journalism* (pp. 95–112). London: Sage.

Murthy, D. (2013). *Twitter: Social communication in the Twitter age.* Cambridge: Polity Press.

Öztürk, N., & Ayvaz, S. (2018). Sentiment analysis on Twitter: A text mining approach to the Syrian refugee crisis. *Telematics and Informatics, 35*(1), 136–147.

Page, R. (2012). The linguistics of self-branding and micro-celebrity in Twitter: The role of hashtags. *Discourse & Communication, 6*(2), 181–201.

Peppler, K. A., & Solomou, M. (2011). Building creativity: Collaborative learning and creativity in social media environments. *On the Horizon, 19*(1), 13–23.

Pope, D., & Griffith, J. (2016). An analysis of online Twitter sentiment surrounding the European refugee crisis. In *Proceedings of the 8th international joint conference on knowledge discovery, knowledge engineering and knowledge management*, Volume 1: KDIR (IC3K 2016), pp. 299–306.

Ratten, V. (2017). Social media innovations and creativity. In A. Brem & E. Viardot (Eds.), *Revolution of innovation management* (pp. 199–220). London: Palgrave.

Rheingold, H. (1993). *The virtual community.* Cambridge, MA: MIT Press.

Romano, J., Kromrey, J., Coraggio, J., & Skowronek, J. (2006). Appropriate statistics for ordinal level data: Should we really be using t-test and Cohen's d for evaluating group differences on the NSSE and other surveys? In *Annual meeting of the Florida association of institutional research* (pp. 1–3). Cocoa Beach, FL: Association of Institutional Research.

Shapp, A. (2014). *Variation in the use of Twitter hashtags*. Qualifying paper in sociolinguistics. New York: New York University Press.

Sharma, S. (2013). Black Twitter? Racial hashtags, networks and contagion. *New Formations*, *78*(78), 46–64.

Siapera, E., Boudourides, M., Lenis, S., & Suiter, J. (2018). Refugees and network publics on Twitter: Networked framing, affect, and capture. *Social Media + Society*, *4*(1), 1–21.

Stathopoulou, A., Borel, L., Christodoulides, G., & West, D. (2017). Consumer branded# hashtag engagement: Can creativity in TV advertising influence hashtag engagement? *Psychology & Marketing*, *34*(4), 448–462.

Stein, M. I. (1953). Creativity and culture. *The Journal of Psychology*, *36*(2), 311–322.

Vaidhyanathan, S. (2018). *Antisocial media: How Facebook disconnects us and undermines democracy*. New York: Oxford University Press.

Wagner, C., & Jiang, L. (2012). Harnessing the power of social media for creativity support: A three-pronged approach. *Knowledge Management & E-Learning*, *4*(2), 174–194.

Wang, A. H. (2010, July). Don't follow me: Spam detection in twitter. In *2010 international conference on security and cryptography* (SECRYPT) (pp. 1–10). IEEE.

Zappavigna, M. (2011). Ambient affiliation: A linguistic perspective on Twitter. *New Media & Society*, *13*(5), 788–806.

Zollo, F., & Quattrociocchi, W. (2018). Misinformation spreading on Facebook. In S. Lehmann & Y. Y. Ahn (Eds.), *Complex spreading phenomena in social systems: Computational social sciences* (pp 177–196). Cham: Springer.

7 Potential in Creativity

Individual, Social, Material Perspectives, and a Dynamic Integrative Framework

Giovanni Emanuele Corazza and Vlad P. Glăveanu

Introduction: Re-examining Potential

The notion of potential plays an important role in creativity studies, but its meaning is not devoid of diverse interpretations which depend on the specific epistemological commitments taken by the observer. Misunderstandings and contrapositions can follow when we fail to clarify the terms and notice the limitations in one's own discourse on creative potential. Considering the etymology of this word, potential comes from the Latin adjective *potis*, which has two different meanings: capable or possible. While the first refers to an individual entity, the second meaning can imply much wider associations, from socio-cultural to cosmological. A first dichotomy can thus be traced to the origin of this word. Interestingly, the noun form of potential came into life only in the 18th century, likely in association with the scientific study of electricity. Today, in the Merriam-Webster dictionary, potential is defined both as an adjective, meaning "existing in possibility: capable of development into actuality", and as a noun, meaning "something that can develop or become actual". In general, the use of this term induces a mental projection of a present reality onto a possible future, hence a form of forecast, foresight, or anticipation, as defined in future studies (Corazza, 2017a; Poli, 2011).

When the concept of potential is specifically mapped onto the creativity realm, the discussion can develop along quite different trajectories depending on a number of assumptions and decisions: the posited definition for creativity and its way of accounting for the dynamic development of the entities involved in the process; the fact that an individual perspective or a sociocultural perspective is being adopted; the consideration of the fact that the sociocultural perspective can be further defined by a focus on social relations and material affordances; the possible adoption of a 4P's (Rhodes, 1961), 4C's (Kaufman & Beghetto, 2009), or 5A's (Glăveanu, 2013); conceptual classification of perspectives on creativity; the ambition to measure the potential quantitatively or document it from a qualitative perspective; the adoption of a positivistic versus constructivist epistemological position; and so on.

The aim of this chapter is to address the concept of potential through four main lenses – individual, social, material, and dynamic – and discuss the possibility of reaching an integrated view based on the latter that can serve as a general theoretical framework or, at least, as the beginning of one. As we will see, in the course of this development we will encounter fifteen different variations of *potential* associated to creativity, some of which can be considered "classical", while others are introduced here for the first time. The notions of potential depend on the focus being placed on the Individual/ Person/Actor (mini-c potential, little-c potential, Pro-c potential, Big-C potential, embedded individual potential), the Process/Action (systemic process potential, embedded process potential, universal process potential), the Product/Artefact (instantaneous potential, experiential potential, condensation potential, cultural evolution potential), or the Press/Audience/ Affordance (sociocultural context potential, action potential, virtual world potential) elements of the creativity eco-system. Given this perhaps surprising conceptual complexity, the need for systematisation should become apparent to the reader.

Individual and Sociocultural Approaches: Opposite or Complementary?

While the history of creativity studies goes much further back in time (Glăveanu, 2019), there is general agreement that Guilford's presidential address to the American Psychological Association (APA) in 1950 drew a significant starting line for modern approaches to this construct. In that address, Guilford (1950, p. 446) observes that employers "are asking how to recognize the individuals who have inventive potentialities". This is a clear indication of the pragmatic value of the objective of measuring creative potential under an individual perspective, a value that led, in time, to the development of several psychometric test batteries (Agnoli, Corazza, & Runco, 2016; Lubart, Zenasni, & Barbot, 2013; Torrance, 1988). Specific forms of these batteries can be used with students, e.g., as a tool supporting the introduction of creativity in education, others with adults in organisations, to support personnel selection, training, or management. Whenever possible, longitudinal studies and meta-analyses should be carried out to interconnect the outcomes of these test batteries on large populations and subsequent creative achievements in real life (e.g., Gajda, Karwowski, & Beghetto, 2017). We observe that the underlying rationale of this approach draws on three *positivistic* assumptions: (1) creative potential exists within the individual, (2) the measurement process is able to determine its magnitude with sufficient precision, and (3) the ensuing results hold predictive validity for the individual's future creative achievement, albeit in statistical terms. Of course, these predictions cannot be taken as a guarantee, since creative potential is typically latent: it may be awakened through favourable experiences, training, environments, or stifled by negative versions of these same elements. It should be noted that, in this case, favourable does not necessarily mean pleasant, because creativity may actually be stirred by negative life experiences or heavy constraints.

On the other hand, a sociocultural perspective on creativity would follow a different approach, one based on *constructionist* premises. Within it, one's potential for creativity is fundamentally related to the social and material elements that constitute the environment in which individuals are necessarily embedded; indeed, no individual can exist in isolation. In other words, potential is a *relational* construct that should not be measured only by focusing on a single person. Potential is closely related to human action and what can effectively be "done", and this is why it fundamentally depends on both social and material entities and, most of all, on the way they relate to each other (i.e., a person's capabilities at any moment "connect" with environmental affordances). It requires an appreciation of the evolving interconnection between person and world. This also means that potential is *relative* to the "match" between person and situation and cannot be judged in absolute or abstract terms (or, at least, that absolute or universal assessments of potential need to be treated with caution). Moreover, if we consider that the person–environment system is always changing, then potential is also *dynamic* within the sociocultural approach. In other words, dynamic measures of potential need to take into account both the nature of the sociomaterial system the person is immersed in, and the evolution of this system over time.

While it might be impossible to fully reconcile these dual approaches (as, indeed, they are grounded in very different epistemologies), both have a clear contribution to make towards our understanding of the creativity construct, as well as carry distinct practical applications. In order to illustrate this, let's consider for a moment two thought experiments: (1) same person in different environments, and (2) different persons in the same environment. Let us assume (in contradiction to the sociocultural view of person–context interdependence) that we could ever separate the individual with his/her abilities and psychological makeup on the one hand, and the environment with its affordances and constraints on the other. Would the creative potential of this "self-contained" individual be different if placed in different – including radically different – situations? It is not hard to assume that, indeed, this would be the case. The person's knowledge and abilities will most probably serve him or her better in one context rather than another. As such, his or her embedded potential to act creatively will be greater or lower, depending on the situation. This calls for the development of the socio-cultural approach. Let's now consider the reverse thought experiment. What if two people with very different psychological attributes would be placed in one and the same situation, with identical social and material affordances? We would expect, once more, to have a clear variation in those people's potential to act creatively, depending on their individual characteristics. This calls for a thorough characterisation of the individual's creative potential. What these simple thought experiments help us show is the fact that both person and context have something fundamental to offer to our understanding of potential, and no treatise on this subject can be considered complete if it only considers one of the two in isolation.

Our hope in this chapter to place the concepts of "person" and "context" into an integrative theoretical framework rests upon the dynamic definition of creativity (Corazza, 2016), according to which the concept of potential is an intrinsic element of the creativity phenomenon. More specifically, we will consider how the dynamic approach to potential reinterprets existing frameworks of analysis such as the 4P's (Rhodes, 1961), the 4C's (Kaufman & Beghetto, 2009), as well as the 5A's (Glăveanu, 2013). Before discussing the dynamic approach, however, we start by outlining the specific contributions to this discussion made by individual, social, and material perspectives on potential. In this way, we can notice the multiple points of connection and continuity between these perspectives and the dynamic approach and, in the conclusion, draw indications from this first systematisation effort: it is possible to identify 15 types of creative potential, and their multi-dimensional organisation is a fundamental topic for creativity studies.

Individual Perspective: Measuring Potential

Under the individual perspective, prominently in line with the aforementioned Guilford's APA presidential address (1950), the goal in the study of creative potential is *to identify and measure the evident or latent factors and characteristics of a person that may predict future creative behaviour when the person will be faced by a real challenge in a real environment with sufficient resources, possibly leading to a creative achievement.* Clearly, this goal is quite ambitious and largely dependent on age, i.e., the definition of creative potential, and the relative methods of measurement should be quite different between children and adults, also, because the forms of possible achievement will differ considerably.

There are at least two realms whereby a *methodological approach* to the definition and measurement of individual characteristics are well justified and of interest for society: creative potential for children in educational contexts and creative potential for adults in professional environments. Interestingly, this is perfectly in line with the approach proposed by Lubart, et al. (2013), who discuss a tool identified as EPoC (Evaluation of Potential Creativity) targeting the assessment of creative potential for children and adolescents, together with a "creative profiler", which is intended for the assessment of domain specific creative potential for adults, taking as references the so-called optimal creative profiles, obtained by averaging the profiles of creative champions for the domains of interest. While EPoC is designed according to a production-based philosophy (with tasks including divergent-exploratory and convergent-integrative exercises, in both visual and verbal domains), the creative profiler follows a complementary resource-based strategy, aiming at measuring five cognitive (divergent thinking, analytic thinking, mental flexibility, associative thinking, selective combination) and five conative (tolerance of ambiguity, risk taking, openness, intuitive thinking, motivation to create) resources. The environment is considered as an additional context-centred factor, but clearly there is no attempt to insert that dimension into the profile. These tools are certainly well-designed, and the database of administrations is large, providing a good normative reference.

Recent research efforts are trying to insert neural correlates to creative behaviour inside this picture. Beaty, et al. (2018) identify brain connectivity networks of highly creative individuals (default mode, executive control, and salience networks) and argue that cognitive creative potential can be reliably predicted from these networks. Jauk (2019) adds to this picture the dopaminergic system, which would modulate individual differences in creative performance, as well as openness to experience and intelligence. Lin and Vartanian (2018) introduce neuroeconomic mechanisms that determine subjective preferences and choices, which play a significant role in the creative process. These and other lines of research are very promising, yet not mature enough for application over large populations as the test batteries previously described.

Having established the general value of this work on the individual, one can ask whether the environment is simply an external variable in this discourse, or if rather it is an element of a complex systemic experience that can dynamically impact on the persons involved in an interaction, significantly affecting their profile. Indeed, as Johnson discusses (2000), functional brain development in infants can be explained through a probabilistic epigenesist framework, according to which interactions between genes, structural brain changes, and psychological experiences are bidirectional. In other words, our brains undergo bio-cultural development, and therefore even neural correlates of creative behaviour have a bio-socio-cultural basis.

In the next sub-section we discuss potential under the social perspective.

Social Perspective: Potential in Dialogue

The social approach to creativity emphasises the role of social interaction and communication within creative action (Lebuda & Glăveanu, 2019). More than this, it postulates that creativity is, at all times, *collaboration* (Barron, 1999), given the fact that we don't only collaborate with others while creating something with them, but also when building on the ideas and perspectives of other people as part of our own creative processes (including when alone). To study creativity according to this approach, therefore, requires an in-depth analysis of the visible and invisible networks of collaboration that foster creative ideas, products, and practices. As a consequence, the outcomes of creative work are considered, in fact, as *co-creations* (Ind & Coates, 2013), as they emerge out of exchanges between people rather than the activity of isolated minds.

There are a few social models of creativity available in the literature. The "classic" one was proposed by Csikszentmihalyi (1988) as a systemic model that considers, at once, the individual, the field, and the domain. The field in particular is made up of people who have the power to validate (or not) a certain product as creative. Gatekeepers are, thus, one of the first actors that come to mind when considering the social nature of creativity. There is also a growing literature on how groups create (see Reiter-Palmon, 2018), with a particular focus on the cognitive and social processes that impact creativity in a group context. While these studies add to our knowledge of the facilitators and obstacles faced by those engaged in collaborative creativity, they tend to operate a sharp distinction between what happens inside the mind of each collaborator and what happens between collaborators in interaction. Sociocultural models of creativity challenge this distinction by postulating the individual mind as essentially dialogical, relational, and distributed within the world (Glăveanu, 2014; Hutchins, 1995). One of the latest additions to this line of scholarship is represented by the perspectival model, which postulates that creativity involves acts of repositioning, perspective-taking, and placing perspectives in dialogue with each other.

The perspectival model of creative action (Glăveanu, 2015a) starts from the premise that we all occupy different physical, social, and symbolic position in a shared socio-material world. These positions afford us the development of different perspectives or action orientations within this world (Gillespie, 2006; Martin, 2005). For example, having the perspective that a cup is meant to contain liquid facilitates our actions of drinking from it. The interesting thing when it comes to creativity and creative potential is that the cup can have many other uses, including as paperweight, weapon, or art object. Exploring these requires us to develop new perspectives and, thus, take new positions in relation to what a cup is (e.g., if we look at it from the standpoint of an artist, we might paint on it or add new, unique features). Creativity is thus the process of *putting different perspectives on any given issue in dialogue with each other, a dialogue that is reflective and emergent at the same time* (Ness & Glăveanu, 2019).

Where does this leave the notion of potential? From a social/perspectival approach, potential is not embedded either in the person or in the object but in the dialogue of perspectives. It is relating two or more perspectives that we get to discover the world anew and act on it in a much more flexible manner. To return to the example of the cup, the social approach doesn't consider our creative potential as confined to the individual mind's possibility to engage in divergent thinking or other ideational processes. What substantiates our potential to act creatively in relation to the cup is the number of perspectives we can bring to it and the way we relate them to each other. In turn, these perspectives depend on our social and material experience of the world: on how many interactions we have with cups and how many interactions we have with other people and cultural content about cups. Potential is thus placed within a relational space of social and cultural experience and depends on how our capacity to have this experience informs what we do in the present. Given that experience is not easily quantifiable, our evaluation of potential depends on understanding the context of the person (both immediate and life context) and in particular the kinds of positions and perspectives adopted by him or her in the past and in the present. We must also pay attention to broader cultural norms that invite the person to take certain positions instead of others, that facilitate certain perspectives while obscuring others (Glăveanu & Clapp, 2018).

In terms of the thought experiments we started with, the social approach encourages us to consider the person not as a contained mind that travels from one context to the next, but as a dynamic accumulation of social experience that is constantly transformed in ongoing actions and interactions. Equally, the new environment the person is "transported" to is made up of a series of physical, social, and symbolic positions that the newcomer would have to adapt to, and change based on his/her previous positionings. Potential will be thus defined by how much and how quickly the person's social and cultural experience can be brought to bear within a new life context.

Material Perspective: Affording Potential

The material approach is a relative newcomer within creativity research, traditionally focused on individual minds and, more and more, on social interactions. And yet, it is undeniable that we create within a material world and as embodied beings. We also have a clear sense, when being creative, of what is possible and impossible for our actions from a material perspective. Our imagination might be able to change something into anything, but even imagination is constrained by how objects are and what we know they are for (Vygotsky, 2004). A material focus in creativity studies means recognising the fact that ideas are *co-constituted* in interaction with the physical environment. This is not a reductionist, materialistic point, however. Materiality, at least in the sociocultural tradition, is considered as deeply connected to sociality in the sense that the material world is introduced to us by others, interacted with in relation to others, and changed with the help of others (Glăveanu, 2014).

There aren't many theories developed yet to account for the material dimension of creativity. The ones that do exist typically come from outside psychology, such as actor–network theory (Latour, 2005) and material engagement theory (Malafouris, 2013). In each case, they tend to make problematic claims regarding "object agency" which lead to accusations of anthropomorphism. In fact, according to the socio-material standpoint, we should be talking about co-agency (Glăveanu, 2015b) or the bi-directional relation between people and their environment. This idea is well captured by the notion of *affordance*, initially used by Gibson (1986) to designate what material objects afford (or not) our action. In essence, affordances denote action potential when it comes to interacting with our physical environment. A chair affords sitting but also standing on it and being moved around. But a regular chair, in and of itself, doesn't afford swimming on it or flying into space. If we are to build a material theory of creativity starting from the concept of affordance, we can define the creative process as that of *perceiving new affordances in our environment, inventing objects that have desired affordances, and exploiting those affordances that might go against existing cultural norms* (Glăveanu, 2012, 2016). This formulation underlines the fact that affordances don't simply exist in the object or in the mind of the person. They are actively discovered within the situation by the "meeting" between certain action potentials and action orientations (see the previous section on perspectives and the social approach). Creativity involves finding new matches between affordances and perspectives that lead to novel, surprising, and useful actions and outcomes.

What does a material approach tell us about creative potential? As briefly described earlier, the notion of affordance speaks directly to that of potential as it illustrates what can and/or could be done within a given situation. To perceive an affordance, whether it is used or not, is to discover what is *possible*. Importantly, though, affordances and, thus, potential, equally depend on the person's capabilities and the properties of the socio-material world. Chairs are for sitting, but they don't afford this to babies who are too small to climb on them on their own. Equally, young children will probably perceive other affordances in a chair – for example, the possibility of turning it into a small house or a shelter within episodes of play – that escape most adults in their daily interactions. Creative potential, in this approach, is relational and evolving together with the moment to moment changes in the interplay between perspectives and affordances (Glăveanu, 2018). When an artist discovers, all of the sudden, a new affordance of the material and acts on it, a series of new possibilities are opened to him or her; at the same time, certain other action possibilities are closed due to the route that was chosen.

In terms of our two thought experiments, it is interesting to notice that some basic physical properties of the person and the environment will remain constant even when "transported" within new contexts (presuming that these belong to the world as we know it). As such, there are some aspects of potential that can be more easily predicted or at least predicated. However, the person's history of using objects in a certain manner will certainly play a role in shaping creative potential, and so will the sociocultural norms specific to the old and new contexts when it comes to object use. Potential becomes, thus, the *dynamic space* created between old action orientations and new material arrangements, in which changes in either one redefine the entire space. This emphasis on the dynamic aspect is fully elaborated in one of the newest approaches to the definition of creativity.

Potential in the Dynamic Definition of Creativity

The dynamic definition of creativity (Corazza, 2016) posits that creativity requires a *potential* for originality and effectiveness. The distinction between this definition and others that can be found in the literature, among them the so-called standard definition of creativity (Runco & Jaeger, 2012), is prominently the introduction of the concept of potential *inside* the definition itself. This is a critical theoretical change, because it introduces dynamics into the framework by recognising that the potential might be realised, yielding a *creative achievement* (i.e., an outcome which is recognised by a group of people, at a certain time, within a certain cultural milieu, as both original and effective), but also that, due to various circumstances, the process might not be met with any form of success, leading to a state of *creative inconclusiveness*. The latter, far from being a mere failure, turns out to be a crucial part of the process (Corazza, 2016; Beghetto & Corazza, 2019): high potential in a creative inconclusiveness state entails for example resistance to frustration, strong determination, self-belief. In addition, the extraction of value from the process outcomes, which determines dynamically whether one is met with achievement or inconclusiveness, should be thought of as the activity not of a judge but rather of an *estimator*, because no one has the ability and the possibility to measure the entire potential of an original idea. If we understand that creative achievement is a possible result of an act of estimation (and not of judgement), it follows immediately that this is the result of a dynamic interaction between all the entities involved in the process.

Now, if creativity requires the existence of a potential, the question is where this potential is actually found, in what form, and how this relates to the previous discussions on individual, social, and material perspectives. The answer is that, under the dynamic framework, potential is pervasive, or more precisely it resides in different form in *all* of the elements that exist and interact within the creativity phenomenon. In order to clarify this point, it is useful to take as a reference the classic 4P's classification (Rhodes, 1961): Person, Process, Product, and Press, and then extend it through the more recent 5A's classification (Glăveanu, 2013): Actor, Action, Artefact, Audience, Affordance. Each of these strands, which also correspond to distinguishable research areas in creativity studies, can be shown to be the home of a different form of potential, as we will discuss in the following.

Starting from the consideration of the Person, we are led immediately to the concept of *creative potential of an individual*, i.e., the classic individual perspective on potential, as we have discussed in the previous section. From a dynamic perspective, the individual creative potential can also be seen under the 4C's model by Kaufman and Beghetto (2009), encompassing mini-c, little-c, Pro-c, and Big-C levels, and it includes both production-based and resource-based approaches and corresponding measurement methodologies (Lubart, et al., 2013). This form of potential can be latent, not necessarily activated, and can grow or be stifled through the education system, everyday experiences and work duties, and, in general, by the environments in which the person lives. Neuroscientific aspects, cognition, emotional intelligence, and personality all contribute to the determination of this form of potential

(Mastria, Agnoli, Zanon, Lubart, & Corazza, 2018). The expression in actuality of this latent individual potential requires the initiation of a Process.

When attention is turned to the Process, a new form of potential emerges, which we identify as *systemic potential* as it attains to the overall complex system of resources (time, information, expertise, materials, etc.) available to carry out the process itself, the adopted strategies, the thinking and acting style of those involved in the process, their background knowledge and experiences, the specific domain of application, and the challenges to be faced (Corazza & Agnoli, 2015). Considering as an example the last element, it should be evident that the potential for originality and effectiveness is totally different if the challenge is finding a focused solution for a (possibly ill-defined) problem, as opposed to exploring a vast area of possible advancements beyond the state-of-the-art in a specific domain of human activity. In other words, systemic potential is heavily impacted by intrinsic and extrinsic constraints. Other important distinctions could be made regarding the relationship between potential in a creative process and the resources available in the environment, which justify, for example, why we expect the next innovations to come from certain parts of the world and not others. Finally, if the Process does not relate to a single creativity episode, but is extended to the notion of the Dynamic Universal Creativity Process (Corazza, 2019a), encompassing material, biological, socio-cultural, and artificial layers, and justifying the evolution of our cosmos in all of its complexity, one can introduce the notion of *universal process potential*, indicating that our world is far from static but continues to evolve along trajectories that are intrinsically unpredictable. This view is in line with Whitehead's philosophical cosmology, whereby creativity is considered to be the ultimate metaphysical principle (Whitehead, 1978/1929). Overall, the potential of a creative process is a topic which deserves a significantly larger space than what we will devote here; the full development of this part is left for future work.

Considering the Product, the outcome of a creative process, the discussion of its potential can start by making a fundamental discrimination between those outcomes which are consumed in real-time, such as, for example, a ballet, a live music improvisation, or a theatre performance, and those whose impact will be mainly observed in the future as, for example, could be the case for a disruptive innovation in an industrial product line, but also a work of art such as the frescos in the Sistine Chapel, the value of which has been and continues to be re-interpreted for centuries. The potential for originality and effectiveness of a product with real-time fruition appears to be consumed in the moment, and yet the experience might remain in the episodic memory of those who were present and influence their future actions. Therefore, for real-time Products, there exists both an *instantaneous-potential* in the experience of the originality and effectiveness of a Product, as well as an *experiential-potential*, a sort of long-tail effect. Regarding Products with non-instantaneous fruition, it may be useful to retrieve an element from past literature that appears to have almost been forgotten today. Jackson and

Messick (1964) introduced the concept of *condensation* for those Products that show an endurance, that we seek to re-examine and re-experience, that do not reveal their meaning completely on first viewing. Following these lines of thought, we introduce here the notion of *condensation potential*, which expresses the fact that for future-oriented and time-enduring Products, the real potential is related to experiences that will occur in the future, that will presumably transcend the Person and specific creativity episodes, and that will entail repeated estimation cycles, possibly across different cultures. It is certainly possible that a Product that is not considered creative in a time epoch, through its condensation potential can be estimated as a very important achievement at a subsequent time.

Considering the discussion of potential in the Press, the environment within which the Process is carried out by the Persons involved, and the Products are estimated, this is clearly a notion that is much more precisely described by the 5A's framework, so we now turn our attention to the latter. As discussed in (Glăveanu, 2013), the 4P's framework has served its classification purposes very well, but, as with all categorisations the danger is that of creating barriers, separations between topics which initially create order but when internalised can become forms of intellectual segregation. The 5A's framework has been purposely conceived to give the proper evidence to the irreducible relationships between the elements in the phenomenon. Let's begin again from the start of the classification.

According to Glăveanu (2013), the Actor is a Person embedded in a field of social relations, a socialised self, shaped by a sociocultural context in coordination with others. As a consequence, the potential for originality and effectiveness of the Actor is also embedded within the same sociocultural context, and as such it can and should be observed. We identify this as *embedded individual potential*. This argument does not deny the value of controlled experiences in controlled environments, such as a test in a laboratory, but it points to the necessity of qualifying these elements. The importance of this derives from the fact that the creative potential of a person, measured in a controlled environment, will change significantly when that person becomes an Actor embedded in natural, everyday life environments.

As a second element, Action refers to a two-fold analysis of the creative process: an internal, psychological dimension and an external, behavioural one. Therefore, the potential of a creative Action depends on the integration of these elements into an experience, which involves a dialogue between several Actors, each adding richness to the embedding sociocultural framework of the Action itself. We identify this as *embedded process potential*, with a shift of the emphasis on dynamic collaboration and co-creation. Indeed, supposing a collaboration between two persons in a co-creation exercise, the potential of the ensuing Action will be very different from the simple sum of the potential of the two Actors, given the complex interaction between them that can allow the emergence of unforeseeable resources. Clearly, this can work both in a positive and in a negative direction, i.e., the Action potential can be increased, decreased, or even nulled in the interaction.

Third, referring to Products as Artefacts places a focus on their "cultured" nature and the cumulative character of creation in human civilisation. As such, the instantaneous-potential, experience-potential, and condensation-potential of an Artefact should be examined in view of the contribution that this specific Artefact can give to the evolution of culture of the human species, giving life to a fourth form identified as *cultural evolution potential* of an Artefact. Just to give an example, a wonderful invention could lose its potential due to the emergence of a competing, and better, technology. Vice versa, a standard technology for producing glass could become overnight a cutting-edge technology on the day optical fibres are invented (Cattani, 2006). The estimation of the potential for originality and effectiveness of an Artefact must therefore draw elements from the discipline of cultural evolution.

The consideration of the potential for originality and effectiveness which descends from the notions of Audience and Affordances leads to the introduction of three additional forms of potential: *sociocultural context potential*, *action potential*, and *virtual world potential*. In line with the thought experiments that we described in the Introduction, we intend to show how the consideration of situational elements can at times completely change the picture that is obtained in "neutral", or controlled environments. It has been shown repeatedly that, when measuring individual creative potential in males and females, hardly any significant differences are found (Baer & Kaufman, 2008). However, as shown by Kemmelmeier and Walton (2016), the result can change radically when experimental instructions included the notion of creativity for the benefit of others, and the fact that the process could be conducted under threat. In particular, women outperformed men in originality when the effort was said to be beneficial to others, but this effect disappeared under threat. This is a good example of how the sociocultural context potential of a situation interacts with the individual's creative potential, personality, and gender to provide a very different picture. As we discussed previously, action potential is a characteristic of the affordances in the surrounding environment that points to all the possibilities of use and interaction with material entities. Of course, this is an open ended exercise as no one is able to see and foresee all possible functions, uses, or interactions with one or more surrounding objects: again, it is an exercise in estimation.

Last but not least, it is useful to connect this discussion to the 4C's model of creativity by Kaufman and Beghetto (2009), who distinguish between mini-c (personal discovery of new things, ideas, heuristics), little-c (non-professional creative achievements), Pro-c (professional creative achievements and innovations), and Big-C (eminent creativity) levels and achievements. As discussed by Kaufman and Beghetto, it is possible to use these categories to draw hypothetical developmental trajectories in the creative endeavours over a person's life, that might typically start from mini-c, then go on parallel paths to little-c on one side and Pro-c on the other, the latter possibly leading to Big-C, but only in a few rare cases. Since the concept of potential points to future creative achievement, this classification can help to clarify different situations.

Considering the creative potential for mini-c achievements, and disregarding in this discussion any form of psychological pathology, this can be thought of as the most widespread form of potential, in the sense that anyone should be able to engage and find satisfaction at this level, provided that sufficient stimuli are provided by the environment. The design of education systems that stimulate students and increase their *mini-c creative potential* is certainly in order here (Beghetto & Karwowski, 2019), and this points to the relevance of methodologies for the definition and assessment of mini-c creative potential in populations of students. A different perspective is that of *little-c creative potential*, still quite accessible to large numbers of individuals (if not entire populations), but requiring a form of intrinsic motivation to spend one's own resources in a form of everyday/non-professional activity that has a potential for creative achievement. It is interesting to analyse the impact of this kind of creative achievements, both from an individual and a socio-political perspective. In general, it would appear that little-c creative achievements are optional and not really necessary in one's life. On the other hand, this sort of activity may be related to the individual well-being (Corazza, 2017b, 2019b; Csikszentmihalyi, 1997), and this can indirectly provide benefits also beyond the activity itself, including professional aspects. From a socio-political perspective, it is important to reflect on the policies and institutions that a society might adopt and provide in order to allow its members to live a life in which there is room for creative endeavours, at least at the little-c level. This is becoming more and more of an issue in those societies with reduced work-week load and/or aging populations. Therefore, the specific form of individual little-c creative potential might be seen on a scale that runs continuously from ancillary to socially relevant, but the value and necessity of developing measurement methodologies for this kind of potential could be reasonably argued against. Undoubtedly, it was *Pro-c creative potential* that Guilford had in mind in 1950 when speaking of adults in the work environment. In fact, it would be too ambitious and unrealistic to propose any form of prediction tools towards Big-C creativity, so that *Big-C creative potential* is an entity that is typically studied in retrospective (e.g., what conditions led that person and his/her collaborators to be in the right place at the right time? see Albert, 1983; Eysenck, 1995), while it appears to be reasonable to try to devise models, experiments, measurement methods, and training approaches that are oriented towards the identification and development of creative individuals and teams in professional environments.

Before we close this discussion, it is interesting to note that new information and communication technologies (Corazza, Pedone, & Vanelli-Coralli,

2010; Feather, 2013) have relatively recently introduced different ways of producing virtual realities, including visual immersive experiences but also simpler forms such as social networks and even chat applications. The net result of all these transformations of our way of living and interacting with others is that "artificial" controlled conditions can actually become an environment that we live in for several hours a day. In-vitro can become in-vivo. The question, which is still quite open for investigation, is how do these virtual environments affect the creative process? As a minimum, it is possible to introduce the notion of *virtual world potential*, which includes new forms of social interactions and the digital affordances of virtual objects. It is interesting to note that a trend which is emerging today is that many people enter these virtual worlds through a change of their personal characteristics, such as sex, age, looks, dressing style, and so on. How this affects their creative potential requires much more research, but early evidence points to a large impact (Bourgeois-Bougrine, Richard, Lubart, Burkhardt, & Frantz, 2018).

Conclusion: Multi-fold Creative Potential

We hope the reader will by now be convinced of the multi-fold nature of the notion of potential introduced by the dynamic definition of creativity, which posits the requirement for potential originality and effectiveness, a requirement that can then be specified in multiple alternative and complementary ways. This establishes a theoretical framework, within which the individual, sociocultural, and material perspectives find all a useful collocation. Table 7.1 collects the static/dynamic definitions of creativity and the 15 different forms of potential identified in our discussion. Clearly, when one approaches the study, definition, or measurement of creative potential, it is natural that a single perspective is taken, in order to bring the scientific discourse to considerable depth. However, we feel it is very important to be able to place any specialised perspective into a larger theoretical framework, so that all efforts end up contributing to a larger picture. This problem is not new. As Henri Poincaré stated back at turn of the 20th century (Corazza & Lubart, 2019):

> In proportion as the science develops, it becomes more difficult to take it in in its entirety. Then an attempt is made to cut it in pieces and to be satisfied with one of these pieces – in a word, to specialize. Too great a movement in this direction would constitute a serious obstacle to the progress of the science . . . it is by unexpected concurrences between its different parts that it can make progress.

Our hope is that this work can be a contribution towards finding those "unexpected concurrences" that will emerge when the concept of creative potential is considered critically in its various forms and dimensions.

Table 7.1 Creativity definition and forms of potential

	Definition	*Observations*
Creativity Nature		
Static	Creativity requires originality and effectiveness (O&E)	This defines a creative *achievement*
Dynamic	Creativity requires *potential* originality and effectiveness	This definition includes both *achievement* and *inconclusiveness*
Individual/Person/Actor		
mini-c potential	Potential for personal discovery, learning, creative behaviour	Psychometric measurement possible (e.g., EPoC)
little-c potential	Potential for non-professional creative achievement	Psychometric measurement possible; might gain centrality in future societies
Pro-c potential	Potential for professional creative achievement	Psychometric measurement possible (e.g., creative profiler)
Big-C potential	Potential for eminent creativity	Not easily predictable, typically posthumous recognition
Embedded individual potential	Creative potential of an Actor embedded in a cultural milieu	In-vivo observation necessary
Process/Action		
Systemic process potential	Potential for O&E of a creative process	Depends on system of resources, style, constraints, challenge
Embedded process potential	Potential for O&E of a creative process embedded in a cultural milieu	Emphasis on relations and co-creation in a creative process
Universal process potential	Potential for O&E of the Dynamic Universal Creativity Process	Relevant to cosmic evolution, involving material, biological, socio-cultural, artificial layers
Product/Artefact		
Instantaneous potential	Potential for real-time impression of O&E	Most relevant for live performance
Experiential potential	Potential for episodic memory impression of O&E	Impact in memory of experiencing a creative product
Condensation potential	Potential for continuous re-examination of O&E	Time-enduring creative achievement transcending epochs
Cultural evolution potential	Potential for O&E of an Artefact embedded in a cultural milieu	Impact on cultural evolution of the species
Press/Audience/Affordance		
Sociocultural context potential	Potential of the dialogue of perspectives	A strictly relational construct referring to co-creation
Action potential	Potential for O&E in the affordances of a socio-material entity	Emphasis on discovering possibilities afforded by material entities
Virtual world potential	Potential for O&E of a virtual world entity	Emphasis on discovering/inventing possibilities afforded by virtual entities

Acknowledgement

The authors would like to thank Sergio Agnoli for useful discussions on the individual perspectives.

References

Agnoli, S., Corazza, G. E., & Runco, M. A. (2016). Estimating creativity with a multiple-measurement approach within scientific and artistic domains. *Creativity Research Journal, 28*(2), 171–176.

Albert, R. S. (1983). Genius and eminence: The social psychology of creativity and exceptional achievement. In *International series in experimental social psychology: International series in experimental social psychology* (Vol. 5). Oxford and New York: Pergamon Press.

Baer, J., & Kaufman, J. C. (2008). Gender differences in creativity. *The Journal of Creative Behavior, 42*(2), 75–105.

Barron, F. (1999). All creation is a collaboration. In A. Montuori & R. Purser (Eds.), *Social creativity* (Vol. I, pp. 49–59). Cresskill, NJ: Hampton Press.

Beaty, R. E., Kenett, Y. N., Christensen, A. P., Rosenberg, M. D., Benedek, M., Chen, Q., . . . Silvia, P. J. (2018). Robust prediction of individual creative ability from brain functional connectivity. *Proceedings of the National Academy of Sciences, 115*(5), 1087–1092.

Beghetto, R. A., & Corazza, G. E. (2019). *Dynamic perspectives on creativity: New directions for theory, research, and practice in education*. Cham: Springer.

Beghetto, R. A., & Karwowski, M. (2019). Unfreezing creativity: A dynamic microlongitudinal approach. In R. A. Beghetto & G. E. Corazza (Eds.), *Dynamic perspectives on creativity* (pp. 7–25). Cham: Springer.

Bourgeois-Bougrine, S., Richard, P., Lubart, T., Burkhardt, J. M., & Frantz, B. (2018). Do virtual environments unleash everyone's creative potential? In *Congress of the international ergonomics association* (pp. 1328–1339). Cham: Springer.

Cattani, G. (2006). Technological pre-adaptation, speciation, and emergence of new technologies: How Corning invented and developed fiber optics. *Industrial and Corporate Change, 15*(2), 285–318.

Corazza, G. E. (2016). Potential originality and effectiveness: The dynamic definition of creativity. *Creativity Research Journal, 28*(3), 258–267.

Corazza, G. E. (2017a). Creativity and anticipation. In R. Poli (Ed.), *Handbook of anticipation: Theoretical and applied aspects of the use of future in decision making*. Cham: Springer.

Corazza, G. E. (2017b). Organic creativity for well-being in the post-information society. *Europe's Journal of Psychology, 13*(4), 599.

Corazza, G. E. (2019a). The dynamic universal creativity process. In R. A. Beghetto & G. E. Corazza (Eds.), *Dynamic perspectives on creativity: New directions for theory, research, and practice in education*. Cham: Springer.

Corazza, G. E. (2019b). Life in the cyber-physical society: The need for organic creativity. In I. Lebuda & V. P. Glăveanu (Eds.), *The Palgrave handbook of social creativity research* (pp. 463–471). Cham: Palgrave Macmillan.

Corazza, G. E., & Agnoli, S. (2015). On the path towards the science of creative thinking. In G. E. Corazza & S. Agnoli (Eds.), *Multidisciplinary contributions to the science of creative thinking* (pp. 3–20). Singapore: Springer.

Corazza, G. E., & Lubart, T. (2019). Science and method: Henri Poincaré. In V. P. Glăveanu (Ed.), *Creativity reader* (pp. 33–47). Oxford: Oxford University Press.

Corazza, G. E., Pedone, R., & Vanelli-Coralli, A. (2010). Technology as a need: Trends in the evolving information society. *Advances in Electronics and Telecommunications, 1*, 124–132.

Csikszentmihalyi, M. (1988). Society, culture, and person: A systems view of creativity. In R. Sternberg (Ed.), *The nature of creativity: Contemporary psychological perspectives* (pp. 325–339). Cambridge: Cambridge University Press.

Csikszentmihalyi, M. (1997). Happiness and creativity. *The Futurist, 31*(5), S8.

Eysenck, H. J. (1995). *Genius: The natural history of creativity* (Vol. 12). Cambridge: Cambridge University Press.

Feather, J. (2013). *The information society: A study of continuity and change*. London: Facet Publishing.

Gajda, A., Karwowski, M., & Beghetto, R. A. (2017). Creativity and academic achievement: A meta-analysis. *Journal of Educational Psychology, 109*(2), 269.

Gibson, J. J. (1986). *The ecological approach to visual perception*. Hillsdale, NJ: Lawrence Erlbaum Associates.

Gillespie, A. (2006). *Becoming other: From social interaction to self-reflection*. Greenwich, CT: Information Age.

Glăveanu, V. P. (2012). What can be done with an egg? Creativity, material objects and the theory of affordances. *Journal of Creative Behavior, 46*(3), 192–208.

Glăveanu, V. P. (2013). Rewriting the language of creativity: The five A's framework. *Review of General Psychology, 17*(1), 69.

Glăveanu, V. P. (2014). *Distributed creativity: Thinking outside the box of the creative individual*. Cham: Springer.

Glăveanu, V. P. (2015a). Creativity as a sociocultural act. *Journal of Creative Behavior, 49*(3), 165–180.

Glăveanu, V. P. (2015b). From individual to co-agency. In C. W. Gruber, M. G. Clark, S. Hroar Klempe, & J. Valsiner (Eds.), *Constraints of agency: Explorations of theory in everyday life* (pp. 245–266). London: Springer.

Glăveanu, V. P. (2016). Affordance. In V. P. Glăveanu, L. Tanggaard, & C. Wegener (Eds.), *Creativity: A new vocabulary* (pp. 10–17). London: Palgrave.

Glăveanu, V. P. (2018). The sociocultural study of creative action. In A. Rosa & J. Valsiner (Eds.), *The Cambridge handbook of sociocultural psychology* (2nd ed., pp. 163–177). Cambridge: Cambridge University Press.

Glăveanu, V. P. (2019). *Creativity reader*. Oxford: Oxford University Press.

Glăveanu, V. P., & Clapp, E. (2018). Distributed and participatory creativity as a form of cultural empowerment: The role of alterity, difference and collaboration. In A. U. Branco & M. C. Lopes-de-Oliveira (Eds.), *Alterity, values and socialization: Human development within educational contexts* (pp. 51–63). Cham: Springer.

Guilford, J. P. (1950). Creativity. *American Psychologist, 5*(9), 444–454.

Hutchins, E. (1995). *Cognition in the wild*. Cambridge, MA: MIT Press.

Ind, N., & Coates, N. (2013). The meanings of co-creation. *European Business Review, 25*(1), 86–95.

Jackson, P. W., & Messick, S. (1964). The person, the product, and the response: Conceptual problems in the assessment of creativity. 1. *ETS Research Bulletin Series, 1964*(2), i–27.

Jauk, E. (2019). A bio-psycho-behavioral model of creativity. *Current Opinion in Behavioral Sciences, 27*, 1–6. ISSN: 2352-1546.

Johnson, M. H. (2000). Functional brain development in infants: Elements of an interactive specialization framework. *Child Development, 71*(1), 75–81.

Kaufman, J. C., & Beghetto, R. A. (2009). Beyond big and little: The four C model of creativity. *Review of General Psychology, 13*(1), 1.

Kemmelmeier, M., & Walton, A. P. (2016). Creativity in men and women: Threat, other-interest, and self-assessment. *Creativity Research Journal, 28*(1), 78–88.

Latour, B. (2005). *Reassembling the social: An introduction to actor-network-theory*. Oxford: Oxford University Press.

Lebuda, I., & Glăveanu, V. P. (2019). *The Palgrave handbook of social creativity research*. London: Palgrave.

Lin, H., & Vartanian, O. (2018). A neuroeconomic framework for creative cognition. *Perspectives on Psychological Science, 13*(6), 655–677.

Lubart, T. I., Zenasni, F., & Barbot, B. (2013). Creative potential and its measurement. *International Journal of Talent Development and Creativity, 1*(2), 41–51.

Malafouris, L. (2013). *How things shape the mind*. Cambridge, MA: MIT Press.

Martin, J. (2005). Perspectival selves in interaction with others: Re-reading G. H. Mead's social psychology. *The Journal for the Theory of Social Behaviour, 35*, 231–253.

Mastria, S., Agnoli, S., Zanon, M., Lubart, T., & Corazza, G. E. (2018). Creative brain, creative mind, creative person. In *Exploring transdisciplinarity in art and sciences* (pp. 3–29). Cham: Springer.

Ness, I. J., & Glăveanu, V. P. (2019). Polyphonic orchestration: The dialogical nature of creativity. In R. Beghetto & G. Corazza (Eds.), *Dynamic perspectives on creativity: New directions for theory, research, and practice in education*. Cham: Springer.

Poli, R. (2011). Steps toward an explicit ontology of the future. *Journal of Futures Studies, 16*(1), 67–78.

Reiter-Palmon, R. (Ed.). (2018). *Team creativity and innovation*. New York, NY: Oxford University Press.

Rhodes, M. (1961). An analysis of creativity. *Phi Delta Kappan, 42*, 305–310.

Runco, M. A., & Jaeger, G. J. (2012). The standard definition of creativity. *Creativity Research Journal, 24*(1), 92–96.

Torrance, E. P. (1988). The nature of creativity as manifest in its testing. *The Nature of Creativity: Contemporary Psychological Perspectives, 43*.

Vygotsky, L. S. (2004). Imagination and creativity in childhood. *Journal of Russian and East European Psychology, 42*(1), 7–97.

Whitehead, A. N. (1978/1929). *Process and reality: An essay in cosmology* (Corrected ed., D. Ray Griffin & D. W. Sherburne, Eds.). New York: Free Press.

8 Creative Learning in Digital and Virtual Environments During COVID-19 and Beyond

Vlad P. Glăveanu, Ronald A. Beghetto, Martina Benvenuti, Samira Bourgeois-Bougrine, Claude Chaudet, Alice Chirico, Giovanni Emanuele Corazza, Constance de Saint Laurent, Olga Dysthe, Nataly Essonnier, Andrea Gaggioli, Chronis Kynigos, Elvis Mazzoni, Ingunn Johanne Ness, and Jana Trgalová

The importance of digital and virtual environments for both creativity and learning has been recognised for a number of years (e.g., Craft, 2010; Greenhow, Eppler, & Solomou, 2011; Hsiao, Chang, Lin, & Hu, 2014). However, the scale at which teaching and learning have been taking place online or remotely during the current COVID-19 pandemic is unprecedented. From a luxury reserved for the very few or the distant future, digital and virtual environments in education became a necessity and an everyday reality for millions of people around the world. And nobody is expecting for things to go back to "normal" any time soon – the fact that students and teachers alike now see technology-mediated education as real rather than possible will certainly encourage many to continue exploring it long after the pandemic has (hopefully) ended. In this context, it is important to ask ourselves: what are the challenges and the opportunities associated with creative learning in digital and virtual worlds?

The present set of chapters focused on different aspects of creativity and learning, and several of them referred to how these phenomena are mediated by the use of various technologies. In this final chapter, authors engage in a conversation specifically about digital and virtual environments and use some of the findings reported in this book, results from their previous research, as well as their general expertise, to shed a new light on this complex topic. The conversation format, we believe, adds a dialogical and emerging element to what is nowadays a highly debated topic. In this way, we offer in what follows an overview of the main topics covered in this book and add to them, conceptually and practically. The focus is twofold: on the one hand, on theoretical notions that help us understand the current situation and, on the other, on practical advice that can guide those interested in technology-enhanced learning and creativity, now and in the future.

Vlad P. Glăveanu

As a sociocultural psychologist, I am concerned first and foremost with how cultural tools and signs mediate human thinking and action. Technological tools, including those that enable digital and virtual environments, are a fundamental part of today's culture across spheres of activity, from home and school to industry and organisations. Sociocultural theory also has considerable insights to offer creativity and learning scholars (see, for example, Vygotsky, 1967/2004; Lave & Wenger, 1991), in particular concerning the role of other people and social interaction in the way we acquire and create new objects and meanings. Taken together, these points of focus raise the question of how technological means impact processes of creative learning. Do they only shape the kind of contents people learn from and create with? Or, at a more fundamental level, do they change how we create and learn in the 21st century?

These questions don't have a simple answer (for a discussion of how the Internet changes creative expression, see Literat & Glăveanu, 2016), and the chapters included in this book bring evidence of both types of influence. My own sociocultural approach to learning and creativity considers these phenomena in terms of differences of position and dialogues of perspective resulting from these positions (for more details, see Glăveanu, Johanne Ness, Wasson, & Lubart, 2019). What digital and virtual technologies afford, in this context, is adopting completely new positions – in terms of avatars, tasks, situations, and their affordances – and, therefore, developing a set of original perspectives on what we do, including on the way we learn, express our creativity, and envision education. Being a technology user is not an extra role or position for today's teachers and learners, it is a common reality that changes, often radically, what we consider as possible in the classroom, offline and online, with both positive and negative consequences.

Giovanni Emanuele Corazza

I could say that my point of view on the issues raised by Vlad Glăveanu comes from a threefold position: as a telecommunications engineer, I deal with the design of the tools and infrastructure that afford the world of online experiences; as a professor at the University of Bologna, I had to go through the rapid transition from teaching in presence to remote classes; finally, as the founder of the Marconi Institute for Creativity, I am specifically concerned with how this process is affected by and affects creative potential, in the multiple possible nuances of meaning discussed in the chapter by Corazza and Glăveanu (Chapter 7, this volume).

Starting from the first perspective, it is a source of pride to see how the telecommunications infrastructure and the Internet that runs on top of it has today become such an integral part of our lives, and in these times of crisis, most of our social interactions would effectively be halted if these technological means weren't in place. The digital alphabetisation of large sectors of the population underwent a sharp acceleration, so significant that it would have probably taken the span of a generation to obtain the same results in normal circumstances. This form of "learning technology by doing" has also led to a deluge of creative audio-visual expressions over social networks, chats and forums of many kinds. It's a triumph of everyday creativity, clearly with a highly variable quality level. On the other hand, this fast transition has also exacerbated the criticalities of the Internet as we know it today in terms of privacy and security, but also of alienation, and much work needs to be done here not only from a technological point of view, but also psychological, social, normative, and ethical.

This fast transition impacted also large academic institutions, such as for example the University of Bologna with its nearly 90,000 students. In the space of but a week, teaching was transformed from in-class to online, with surprisingly few technical problems notwithstanding the huge load on the network. In general, students' reactions and feedback to this experience were largely positive, so much so that it is already clear that even when the immediate emergency will be over, the world will not return to its former state. We will have to collect and exploit the many lessons learned, also in terms of making our teaching more creative in the way we keep the students' attention and we involve them, irrespective of the virtual experience. One element that has turned out to be extremely effective is the introduction of game-based approaches. Introducing even very simple forms of games has the effect of completely turning around the mood of a class, stirring participation and serious amusement, with arguably very positive effects on long-term retention of the subject material. However, not everything is positive in remote teaching experiences; for example, monitoring of the students' attention level and tiredness might not be immediate, and examinations might not be as effective as they would be in person.

Finally, from the more theoretical standpoint of creativity studies, the question is to establish what the impact of these virtual world experiences on the creative potential of individuals, teams, and society in general is. As Vlad Glăveanu already mentioned, we cannot draw any simple conclusions and hope for any monotonic effect, be it positive or negative. Indeed, living in a situation of social confinement, characterised by online communications and multiple virtual worlds, each one with its own means of communication, should altogether be considered as a wholly new experience in a novel socio-cultural milieu, in which some of the past affordances are missing, while new ones are born. While this topic is definitely worth a much deeper reflection, let's only give two simple examples here. The extension of our minds provided by information technology should enlarge our creative potential by greatly reducing the existing inter-disciplinary subdivisions. Specialisation will give way to flexibility. On the other hand, continuous interruptions and reduced attention spans should reduce our creative potential, mainly due to effects of early closure of our creativity episodes as well as to a feeling of being lost in an ocean of uncontrolled information exchange.

In conclusion, I believe that we are dealing with a profoundly different world, one for which simple extension of past knowledge will not be sufficient. Much work is in front of us!

Ingunn Johanne Ness

This book is reflecting on creative learning in digital and virtual environments and, having a PhD in Education from the Faculty of Psychology and leading the Cluster on "Creativity, Learning, and Technology" at the University of Bergen, I have focused on the subject for a number of years. How can technological tools support creative learning? Due to the COVID-19 pandemic we face an urgent need to include various digital tools in teaching since all teaching activities must happen remotely. From the sociocultural perspective I adopt on knowledge development, similar to the one mentioned by Vlad Glăveanu before, I am interested in how people co-construct meaning and learn together in collaboration. From a sociocultural view, this kind of co-construction is often seen in the context of an active and dynamic relationship between the social and the individual. Humans exist and develop in intellectual interdependence and social interaction, and they co-construct their knowledge through this interaction (Linell, 2009; Valsiner & van der Veer, 2000). This takes place both in workplaces and in educational institutions.

In the chapter on "Polyphonic Imagination" (Ness & Dysthe, Chapter 3, this volume) we see how interdisciplinary team members that engaged with innovative idea generation became more creative when they were introduced to other perspectives and other ways of understanding something. Different technological tools were used to support the creative learning processes and functioned as a mediating tool. Vygotsky states that human action, on both individual and social planes, is mediated by tools and signs (Vygotsky, 1981, p. 137). The group members learned from each other and, together, they could imagine new solutions and innovative ideas.

Such skills, creativity, and the ability to collaborate with others are seen as important skills for the 21st century in order to cope with the changing society and global challenges. Students need to learn the value of bringing together knowledge from different fields and how to co-construct new knowledge in interdisciplinary and creative collaboration, as Giovanni Emanuele Corazza mentioned. They should learn the benefits from meeting other views, to see this as a resource for their own thinking and imagination. Using different digital technological tools can be a good way for teachers to facilitate discussions and collaborative assignments in order to stimulate students' imagination and to open up different perspectives (see also Glăveanu, Ness, Wasson, & Lubart, 2019). This can be done through posing open questions. The benefits of such questions are that they are open to discussion and a variety of perspectives which again will stimulate the Polyphonic Imagination among the students. This is a Vygotskian view on imagination (John-Steiner, 2000; Vygotsky, 1930/2004) describing how many voices co-construct knowledge together in supportive collaboration and goes against the more traditional individual approach.

Chronis Kynigos

As an educational design researcher, I look for ways in which interventions in current educational practice may become a lever for transformation, in this case, enhancement and recognition of little-c (abundant, everyday creativity in all of us, Kaufmann & Beghetto, 2009) in the ways we learn and design for others to learn (Gruber, 1988). In our chapter (Kynigos, Essonnier, & Trgalová, Chapter 2, this volume), we try to shed light on how diverse teams of actors collaboratively design and develop digital resources with which students can creatively engage in learning mathematics. We connected a socio-cultural point of view in the way Vlad Glăveanu has articulated (Glăveanu, 2011) to a socio-constructionist activity where learning and creativity becomes part of collective design and discourse over the design (Kynigos, 2015). To study this, we perceived teachers as designers (Laurillard, 2012) and creativity within socio-technical environments (Fischer, 2001) involving complex interactions shaping both knowledge and digital objects under co-construction (Nardi, 1996). We looked for creativity emerging from diversity and the need for each individual to cross boundaries and understand the others' point of view about the building of a digital learning object. These objects thus became cultural artefacts and signs around the design of which many unexpected creative ideas emerged (Akkerman & Bakker, 2011). These kinds of processes are likely to be very common in education as we move beyond the pandemic, and they should be studied further, across domains, disciplines, and levels of study.

Nataly Essonnier and Jana Trgalová

As mathematics education researchers interested in the use of technologies for teaching and learning mathematics (Aldon & Trgalová, 2019), we see teachers mostly as users and sometimes co-designers of digital tools, but also as designers of (digital and non-digital) resources they use in their classes with their students, as noted by Chronis Kynigos.

Referring to Rabardel's (2002) instrumental approach, we consider a digital tool as an artefact that needs to be transformed into an instrument. This approach enriches the Vygotskian one evoked by Vlad Glăveanu and Ingunn Johanne Ness in this chapter, by stressing not only the mediation function of tools, called instrumentation by Rabardel, but also the transformation of tools by the user in the process of instrumentalisation. Instrumental genesis, that involves these two interrelated processes and that results in an instrument likely to foster creative processes, is a long-term process. During the design process of digital resources, tensions occurring between the intended and the effective design choices may be interpreted as consequences of instrumentation. For example, during the collaborative design of one of the c-books within the MC Squared project, we observed designers struggling with creating activities in the socio-constructivist perspective because of technical limitations of the digital tools; instead, the designed activities were very much guided, thus relating to behaviourism. Indeed, it appeared difficult to create a rich digital environment enabling personalised feedback depending on students' actions, allowing them to build knowledge themselves (Essonnier & Trgalová, 2018) or to foster some dimensions of creative mathematical thinking such as fluency, flexibility, or originality. On the other hand, instrumentalisation of the digital authoring environment manifested itself by integrating external widgets created by designers with advanced technological knowledge. Therefore, diversity in terms of complementary professional knowledge intertwining mathematics, pedagogy, and technology turned out to be a lever of the collective instrumental genesis and allowed to enhance social creativity, viewed as the generation of new, appropriate, and usable ideas among the designers (Essonnier, 2018).

Looking at the pandemic situation from an educational point of view, the spread and acceleration of the use of digital technology among teachers, allowing them to keep teaching mathematics and doing so without any anticipation or preparation, has revealed a disparity of situations among teachers. They had to adapt their teaching very quickly to remote lessons, turning them more than ever into creative designers. Many teachers were not prepared to use technology for online teaching and lacked time for the instrumentation of the digital tools. Collaboration has been a key element for the instrumental genesis of technology. For instance, during their first online classes, some of the teachers were concentrated on the technicalities of using a new web-conference tool and did not anticipate the lack of interactions and feedback from the students. Hence, being able to talk about it in group discussion or with colleagues helped them feel less isolated, and gave them a reflective position from which to think on how to create conditions for explicit student feedback during lessons. At times, team collaboration made it possible to test a tool with other colleagues before using it with students, or to build on the experience and practice of other teachers, which generated a kind of collective instrumentation. We also noticed that organising massive online examinations in a very short amount of time proved impossible. Some examinations, such as the final secondary evaluation in France, have been cancelled, some others postponed, yet some others were simply sent via a platform to students who were expected to send back their paper-pencil productions. Assessment thus appears as the most difficult teaching component to be creatively transformed through technological means, and very often is approached from a migratory rather than transformative perspective (Ripley, 2009). These observations and remarks are complementary with the perspectives proposed in this chapter and the experience of other colleagues.

Samira Bourgeois-Bougrine

As an ergonomist, university teacher, and facilitator of human centred design (HCD) workshops, I consider that we face at least two challenges when it comes to the issue raised by Vlad Glăveanu, as well as by Nataly Essonnier and Jana Trgalová, about the teacher being a technology user: the usability of online teaching platforms and their affordances to promote a safe virtual environment for creative interaction with and between students. Similar to Giovanni Emanuele Corazza and many other teachers, I had to go through a rapid transition from teaching in situ to online classes during the coronavirus pandemic. This transition involved reviewing the pedagogical content to adapt it to the new media and learning how to use the software of distant learning provided by my university. Measuring the difficulty of learning how to use a system is a key indicator of a system's usability (Chorfi & Al-hudhud, 2019). From the perspective of the user of any educational interactive software, usability is one of the most important aspects of the system as it determines the success of teaching and learning. Usability, which is defined in ISO[1] as the extent to which a product can be used by specified users to achieve specified goals with effectiveness, efficiency and satisfaction in a specified context of use, is related to the clarity of the functions provided by the system, the expressiveness of the icons' roles, the easiness to perceive the interface components and to remember the hierarchy while navigating the deep menus in order to discover, to select, and use the right option, etc. (Ardito, et al., 2006; Chorfi & Al-hudhud, 2019). If the interface is too rigid, slow, and unpleasant, the teachers spend more time learning how to use the software rather than focusing on the didactic effectiveness, leading to an increase of both frustration and the probability of abandonment.

Beyond functional usability, as a facilitator of creativity workshops in HCD context, I consider that a major challenge would be to provide teachers with the ability to switch, in one click within the same platform interface, from passive distant delivery method (e.g., lecture-based instruction) to a Multi-User Virtual Environment (MUVE) such as Second Life or Unity. This would provide students with the opportunity to interact via their avatars and to express their creative potential (see Bourgeois-Bougrine, et al., Chapter 5, this volume) and help creativity teachers extend their pedagogical repertoire beyond "Sage-on-the-Stage" or "Guide-on-the-Side" to include a role of "Meddler-in-the-Middle" (McWilliam, 2009; Bourgeois-Bougrine, Buisine, Vandendriessche, Glăveanu, & Lubart, 2017). Blending my university distant teaching platform with Zoom, Jitsimeet, or Discord during this transition period allowed me to experience first-hand the several socio-cognitive mechanisms (Diehl & Stroebe, 1987), like the apprehension of evaluation (social inhibition) in face-to-face interactions with students whom I met for the first time this semester. By enabling the sharing of ideas simultaneously amongst the participants while preserving anonymity, MUVEs offer a "liberating" atmosphere that would cognitively disinhibit participants and favour the expression of their creative potential (see Bourgeois-Bougrine, et al., Chapter 5, this volume).

Elvis Mazzoni and Martina Benvenuti

Traditionally, scholars have analysed creative processes by focusing primarily on individual characteristics or attributes to explain the observed process (Eysenck, 1993; Williams, 1980; Reilly, 2008; Kaufman & Baer, 2005). However, as underlined in the previous interventions of Glăveanu and Ness, a sociocultural perspective on knowledge development gives considerable insights on creativity processes, particularly on the mediation of tools (e.g., Internet applications) and signs (e.g., language). Based on this perspective, our contribution refers to two models of knowledge development: the zone of proximal development (Vygotskij, 1978) and the socio-cognitive conflict (Doise & Mugny, 1984; Butera & Darnon, 2010).

From a Vygotskian point of view, each person is characterised by a potential of the development determined by the difference between what he/she can do and what he/she might do if supported by an expert person. In online contexts, we may suppose the existence of a sort of mutual zone of proximal development that pushes persons toward objectives and goals otherwise impossible to obtain. However, interacting in online contexts means also considering many points of views and coping with possible conflicts, not only receiving or giving support and collaborating. From this point of view, divergent thinking represents one of the key factors that can activate creative processes in a group or in a network of persons (Gaggioli, Riva, Milani, & Mazzoni, 2013) because it requires one to consider many alternatives before making a decision on how to proceed. About that, studies on socio-cognitive conflict (Butera & Darnon, 2010; Mazzoni & Benvenuti, 2015), in which participants with divergent points of view must negotiate a collective decision or a collective solution to a problem, show that the final result is more creative than any solution generated by an individual, and is not simply a sum of the different expressed contributions but a new result coming from their progressive integration and accommodation.

Starting from the cultural-historical perspective of Vygotskij (1978) and Leont'ev (1978), Activity Theory (Greeno, 2006; Engeström, 2015) suggests that creative processes emerge not only from small groups (like those analysed in Chapter 4), but also from complex systems of people attempting to achieve specific results (e.g., a company or an association). Each activity system is characterised by a dynamic equilibrium (Gaggioli, et al., 2013; Mazzoni & Gaffuri, 2009), i.e., it is constantly evolving, but always finding a balance to ensure a good adaptation to achieve the result.

New needs arise in individuals (determined by trends, changes in society, career demands in those who work within a company, etc.), and new artefacts are produced to improve productivity. This creates what in Activity Theory is called a contradiction between elements of the system (Engeström & Sannino, 2011; Foot & Groleau, 2011). When contradictions require solutions that can easily be integrated within the existing system, the system recovers balance (Piaget could call it accommodation). However, when they cannot be solved using solutions previously adopted, the activity system should expand the vision beyond the limits of what has been done up to that point and find alternative solutions that have not yet been thought of or imagined. This is called "expansive learning" (Engeström & Sannino, 2011), which results from the need to resolve a contradiction never faced previously, and which requires a creative process that involves the entire system.

Considering this point of view, Internet applications during the COVID-19 pandemic can be seen as tools allowing an activity system (in education, in industry, in business, etc.) to go over the current cultural limits (previous practices, behaviours, tools, ideas, solutions, etc.) and achieve innovative, creative, and more advanced solutions.

Andrea Gaggioli and Alice Chirico

Digital tools hold a significant potential to support creative learning. We agree with Samira Bourgeois-Bougrine that ensuring usability is a crucial requirement. However, we also contend that for this potential to be realised, the focus of analysis should be extended from the functional aspects of technology to the overall experience that results from interacting with it, which encompasses perceptual, cognitive, emotional, and motivational dimensions. According to Hassenzahl (2010), when a user interacts with a product, two broad categories of attributes are at stake: pragmatic and hedonic. Pragmatic quality refers to characteristics such as "easy", "predictable", or "clear": these features indicate the potential achievement of particular "do-goals" that an actor wants to complete, such as "watching a video lesson" or "doing an exercise online". In contrast, hedonic quality refers to the perceived ability of a product to support the fulfilment of "be-goals", such as "being autonomous", "being competent", "being admired", "being stimulated", "being related to others", etc. Pragmatic quality supports the achievement of "be-goals", but only indirectly; as such, the usability of a product is valuable insofar as it contributes to pursue more basic human needs. In this perspective, to design a good creative learning experience – be it virtual or conventional – involves fulfilling the be-goals that are implicated.

The theory of flow provides a meaningful framework to identify the positive experiential features that are relevant for designing virtual educational environments. According to Csikszentmihalyi (1975, 1990), flow is an optimal experience characterised by a perceived balance between high opportunities for action and skills/abilities to face these challenges.

Further characteristics of this state include high concentration and involvement in the task at hand, a feeling of mastery, and a loss of reflective self-consciousness (Nakamura & Csikszentmihalyi, 2002). If this has been real for conventional educational practices based on positive psychology (Seligman, Ernst, Gillham, Reivich, & Linkins, 2009; Kristjánsson, 2012), why should it not be so also for advanced digital ones?

The implications of flow for learning are manifold. This experience is associated with positive emotions and deep engagement with the learning task. Furthermore, since the experience of flow is intrinsically rewarding, learners are motivated to further their efforts, which leads to increasing skills and leveraging their individual potential. Indeed, previous research has shown a positive relationship between flow and students' academic performance in both conventional and e-learning settings (Engeser & Rheinberg, 2008; Rodríguez-Ardura & Meseguer-Artola, 2017). Flow is also closely linked to creativity: not only do people commonly associate flow with a highly creative state (Csikszentmihalyi, 1996), but also it has been suggested that flow could lead to enhanced creative performance (MacDonald, Byrne, & Carlton, 2006; Landhäußer & Keller, 2012), although empirical evidence of a direct causal relationship is still limited. Whilst the original flow framework developed by Csikszentmihalyi focused on individual flow, more recent theorisations have proposed the existence of a shared optimal experience, termed "group flow" (Sawyer, 2007) or "networked flow" (Gaggioli, et al., 2013). The study of how flow emerges in both real and digital social networks could help defining novel principles to design distributed creative learning environments that support this optimal experience across different collaboration platforms (Koffka, 1935).

Claude Chaudet

As a professor of computer science, I have witnessed the rise of digital culture. Today, instructors and learners are, on average, more technology savvy and more eager to use virtual meeting rooms, pre-recorded videos, online exercises, and virtualised labs. This has been a life saver for online learning in these times of social isolation. Remote knowledge transmission had taken off with the rise of Massively Open Online Courses (MOOCs), which were envisioned to replace BOOKs. Artificial intelligence starts to be used to help detect missing knowledge and personalise the learning process. Gamification, as Corazza mentions, also brings a whole new perspective to learning without pain. Creative uses of technology have emerged from the opportunities offered and from new constraints, driven by the motivation of people willing to achieve the same result, as Mazzoni and Benvenuti explain, and catalysing the motivation of enthusiastic, self-learning, and inherently motivated students. Technology lets them choose the modality and the pace of their learning process, but they would find a way to achieve their goals under any circumstances.

Education is not only about these learners, though, but also about students who struggle to understand or to keep their motivation on the long run. For that population, the isolation period we are undergoing turns technology into a constraint, a requirement. Even if usability, as Bourgeois-Bougrine mentions, has improved, online sessions limit subtle interactions and implicit communication that even the most creative usages fail to replace. Such students will often behave like good soldiers, attending the sessions, turning in assignments in time, but will remain in a place where they feel safe or slowly vanish over time.

Education is also about certification through diploma, and this is why the number of integrity issues has exploded since the beginning of social isolation. Students have been suspected or reported to get help or fully outsource work to a friend, or in exchange for payment, but also to have other people impersonate them for oral exams, or to let other people control their screen through remote desktop utilities, while they act. We witness, in that domain, a certain malevolent creativity that is driven by pure interest.

Engaged students will benefit from the creative use of technology and often perform better than in class, as the social pressure vanishes. Malevolent students will initiate a cat-and-mouse game in which each player has to be more creative than its opponent, at the image of cybersecurity. In the middle lie the uncertain students, who lack confidence but have good intentions. Uncertainty creates fear to fail, which drives students to seek safety by avoiding risk, and therefore limits their creativity. Just like in the business world, processes, procedures, and fear of punishment lead employees in doing exactly what they are told to, no more, no less, so that nobody can tell them they did something wrong.

Olga Dysthe

I would like to ground my reflections in three examples from my long career as a teacher and researcher. The first one is from the early days of teaching with computers. I was a high school teacher in Tromsø, and my Norwegian class had just read a novel for young people on the tragic conflict in Northern Ireland between Catholics and Protestants, when I managed to establish contact with a high school class in Northern Ireland. At that historic time in the evolution of online teaching, I had to book the computer room as well as a data specialist to ensure the class was able to connect online. Thus, my students got first-hand accounts of the lives of the Irish youth and how this related to the characters in the book. It was obvious that for the participating students this was an "opening, widening and deepening of dialogic space" as Wegerif (2013, 2020) expressed it. I witnessed how the ongoing conversation between the two classes, online and by emails, supported their participation in a global dialogue of culture and widened their perspectives, not only of the conflict in general, but first and foremost of the daily dilemmas students of their own age had to endure. This became manifest in the student book essays, which mirrored their deeper understanding of the conflict, but also of their own place in the world.

The second example is from UCSD where for half a year I observed two "Fifth Dimension" sites, where 6–12 year olds were voluntarily engaged in computer-mediated activities focusing on games and telecommunication. This project, which lasted for more than ten years and was exported to many countries, among them Sweden, was initiated by Michael Cole and other researchers. Undergraduates from UCSD worked as organisers, facilitators, dialogue partners, and as "the Wizard's assistants", helping the children develop their capacities for problem solving (Cole, 1996, pp. 289–326). While the boys preferred games, the girls favoured telecommunication with children in Mexico. I observed a two-faceted dialogic interaction, on the one hand the important role of the undergraduates in their involved dialogues with the children, and on the other hand the increasingly intense online conversations and discussions between the American and Mexican children.

My third example is from a study I made with Sølvi Lillejord of a part time distant education Master Programme, organised by the University of Bergen, where digital, peer feedback was one of the cornerstones (Dysthe & Lillejord, 2012). Crucial factors in the building of a productive writing community were the intersections between academic leadership, study design, and students' participation in online writing communities. Interestingly, the concept of "community" has a historical grounding in the European Humboldtian university tradition that goes to the core of how academic knowledge is produced and developed. It is therefore equally relevant in all disciplines. Basic to modern universities is the assumption that because nobody owns the "truth", academics have to discuss and test various knowledge claims in scientific communities. A major trait of this tradition is that writing is not a decontextualised learnable skill, but training in learning to think through being confronted by other voices. The German writing researcher Otto Kruse has documented how students at the time of Humboldt got feedback on their writing and their presentation of content, both orally through discussions at the seminar and in writing from two peer opponents (Kruse, 2006, p. 342). Our study shows a modern version of this in a digital networked design, which resulted in students' creative thinking around their own texts. In the web-based master, peer feedback was a key to establish the collaborative dependencies referred to by Dirckinck-Holmfeldt, Jones, and Lindstrøm (2009, p. 7).

What do these examples have in common, and how do they relate to the chapter on Polyphonic Imagination and the theme of this book? The obvious answer is the third dimension in our findings earlier: the Bakhtinian concept of dialogue and creative potential of divergent voices. The students in my three examples vary greatly in age, from basic school in the US to Norwegian high school students and adults in mid-career seeking to widen their professional basis. All three show, however, how technology expands the dialogic space of the students involved by exposing them to divergent and foreign voices, and thus trigger new ways of thinking. In the first two cases, students confronted cultural differences between their home country and Northern Ireland and Mexico, respectively, while the adults' understanding of their master thesis topic was confronted by readers with different professional and intellectual experiences. Bakhtin has underlined that our encounter with a foreign culture is a two-way affair, as we seek answers to what seem strange to us: "We raise new questions for a foreign culture, ones that it did not raise itself; we seek answers to our own questions in it; and the foreign culture responds to us by revealing to us its new aspects and new semantic depths" (Bakhtin, 1986, p. 7). This is equally relevant whether the "foreign culture" is real or metaphorically interpreted.

Ronald A. Beghetto

As an educational psychologist, my work has increasingly focused on the role uncertainty plays in creative thought and action in educational settings. This includes considering how uncertainty serves as a catalyst and condition for creative learning. More specifically, I'm interested in situations whereby uncertainty not only serves as a signifier that new thought and action is needed, but also under what conditions people view uncertainty as actionable. Indeed, as has been discussed elsewhere (Beghetto, in press, 2018), not all encounters with uncertainty prompt a creative response or result in creative learning outcomes that contribute to new ways of understanding and behaviour for oneself and others.

It is not difficult to understate the levels of profound uncertainty the COVID-19 pandemic prompted across the globe and in almost all aspects of life. With respect to teaching and learning, a key uncertainty pertained to whether and how formal schooling could continue in a time where many other aspects of life were put on indefinite hold.

To the extent that digital and virtual platforms were available and accessible, the uncertainty surrounding the continuation of formal educational efforts afforded a creative response in the form of a massive and rapid change in how people thought about and engaged in teaching and learning. This has also resulted in almost incalculable amounts of time spent in virtual rather than material learning environments. Indeed, somewhat early on in the COVID-19 response, my university reported that in one month and two days (March through 2 April) members of our university community logged nearly 150,000 Zoom sessions on the university platform, accounting for a staggering "60 million minutes worth of interactions" which they estimated equates to "roughly 115 years of Zoom" (ASU, 2020).

Although the massive migration to digital and virtual schooling has helped resolve some of the uncertainty surrounding the question of how formal education might continue in the midst of a pandemic, it has surfaced new and complex uncertainties. Indeed, as the commentators to this final chapter have noted, the move to digital and virtual schooling has raised numerous questions, uncertainties, and considerations regarding how technology might support or impede creativity and learning. These questions and uncertainties can and likely will prompt new programmes of research and further creative learning and practice.

One area of uncertainty that I have been thinking about is the role of physical spaces and materiality in creativity and learning. This area of uncertainty raises numerous questions for researchers to consider, including what has been gained and lost when a tool, like digital and virtual technologies, serves as the location for creative learning? What might happen to physical spaces that have become abandoned? What inequities and imbalances are caused by such a move? How might physical spaces be repurposed as a kind of third space – a space where people can step away from the first spaces of home and work and second spaces of virtual environments to learn and create? Could these spaces become a creative common where people come together to think and learn in different ways? Can the physical spaces of schools and universities serve as creative pop-up commons for people in the local community to engage in creative learning? The uncertainties surrounding questions like these can serve as a stimulus for new ways of conceptualising and experiencing creative learning.

Constance de Saint Laurent

Reading the contributions made to this chapter, I am struck by the commonalities between our local experiences of the effects of the pandemic on education: everywhere, we had to adapt extremely fast to a complex situation, moving a heavily presence-based education entirely online, learning to use pre-existing tools in new ways. As Giovanni Emanuele Corazza is, I am amazed at how the technological progresses made over the past decades have allowed for a relatively smooth transition, given the conditions. However, as many have mentioned, this did not come without challenges, and although transitioning to online education has been a global effect of the pandemic, it has been declined into an infinity of specific situations. Beyond regional specificities that have affected both the strength of the measures taken and what has been expected of educators during this difficult period, the contributions made by Samira Bourgeois-Bougrine, Nataly Essonnier, and Jana Trgalová in this chapter highlight the importance of the tools made available to teachers and of how well they actually master them: while some universities and schools had already experimented with virtual environments and digital teaching resources, others have been slower to join the movement – either by lack of volition or lack of means – making the current transition only more difficult.

And indeed, as multiple authors in this chapter have discussed, the tools we use mediate how we learn and how we understand the world we live in, which is probably all the more the case when technology comes to mediate even the most basic student–teacher interactions. A smooth working online classroom, allowing participants to appropriate the space – for instance, by using avatars – will necessarily have different effects than a basic conference call style class with a limited Internet connection. That said, I think we can all agree that technology is not everything, even in this context: learning is not only mediated by tools, but also by others. For me, the real question is not so much what tools are available to teachers, but how well they can use them to "connect" with their students. In this regard, teachers around the world have had to adapt extremely fast, with huge disparities in terms of how comfortable they were with technology to begin with and how willing they have been to learn more. Once the emergency of the crisis has passed, it will be important to not assume that because we have all globally adapted quite well and because new technologies have raised to the challenge, it means it is enough: we will need to make sure that teachers are properly trained to use adapted technology in order to teach online, and to take stock of what aspects of learning have been facilitated or hindered by this digital migration.

Finally, I would like to go back to some of the points raised by Claude Chaudet about some students "slipping through the net". Education has always had the potential to both increase and decrease inequalities. Online teaching, however, raises new issues in this regard. On the one hand, students in difficult situations may more easily feel left behind and drop out, and it is harder for teachers to notice them outside of face-to-face interactions. Inequalities can take the form of uneven access to technology, but also of a lack of confidence, making it harder to intervene online, and which can easily be hidden behind a camera that has not been turned on. On the other hand, remote education makes new forms of cheating possible – from having others do assignments to abusing the leniency we have all felt towards our students in these times of crisis. While it is sometimes difficult in the current context to act against students abusing the system, ignoring them is unfair for the vast majority of students who have made the effort to play by the rules. In this area, as in many others, the pandemic has led to a major reorganisation of public life, which will have lasting consequences for our societies, both good and bad. While urgency has been the driving force in this transition, it will be important in the future to properly learn the lessons of this global experiment – with all of its successes and failures – and leverage it to transform education for the better.

Note

1. https://www.iso.org/obp/ui/#iso:std:iso:ts:20282:-2:ed-2:v1:en.

References

Akkerman, S. F., & Bakker, A. (2011). Boundary crossing and boundary objects. *Review of Educational Research, 81*(2), 132–169.

Aldon, G., & Trgalová, J. (Eds.). (2019). *Technology in mathematics teaching: Selected papers of the 13th ICTMT conference.* Cham: Springer.

Ardito, C., Costabile, M. F., De Marsico, M., Lanzilotti, R., Levialdi, S., Roselli, T., & Rossano, V. (2006). An approach to usability evaluation of e-learning applications. *Universal Access in the Information Society, 4*(3), 270–283.

Arizona State University (ASU). (2020). *ASU passes milestone of 100,000 Zoom sessions in March.* Retrieved from https://asunow.asu.edu/20200402-asu-news-march-100k-zoom-sessions

Bakhtin, M. M. (1986). *Speech genres and other late essays.* Austin, TX: University of Texas Press.

Beghetto, R. A. (2018). Structured uncertainty: How creativity thrives under constraints and uncertainty. In C. Mullen (Ed.), *Creativity under duress in education? Resistive theories, practices, and actions.* Switzerland: Springer.

Beghetto, R. A. (in press). Uncertainty. In V. P. Glăveanu (Ed.), *The Palgrave encyclopedia of the possible.* London: Palgrave.

Bourgeois-Bougrine, S., Buisine, S., Vandendriessche, C., Glăveanu, V., & Lubart, T. (2017). Engineering students' use of creativity and development tools in conceptual product design: What, when and how? *Thinking Skills and Creativity, 24,* 104–117.

Butera, F., & Darnon, C. (2010, June). Socio-cognitive conflict and learning: Past and present. In *Proceedings of the 9th international conference of the learning sciences* (Vol. 2, pp. 212–213). International Society of the Learning Sciences.

Chorfi, H. O., & Al-hudhud, G. (2019). Optimizing e-learning cognitive ergonomics based on structural analysis of dynamic responses. *International Journal of Emerging Technologies in Learning (iJET), 14*(10), 150–160.

Cole, M. (1996). *Cultural psychology.* Cambridge, MA: The Belknap Press of Harvard University.

Craft, A. (2010). *Creativity and education futures: Learning in a digital age.* Stoke-on-Trent: Trentham Books.

Csikszentmihalyi, M. (1975). *Beyond boredom and anxiety.* San Francisco, CA: Jossey-Bass.

Csikszentmihalyi, M. (1990). *Flow: The psychology of optimal experience.* New York, NY: Harper and Row.

Csikszentmihalyi, M. (1996). *Creativity: Flow and the psychology of discovery and invention.* New York, NY: Harper Perennial.

Diehl, M., & Stroebe, W. (1987). Productivity loss in brainstorming groups: Toward the solution of a riddle. *Journal of Personality and Social Psychology, 53*(3), 497.

Dirckinck-Holmfeldt, D., Jones, C., & Lindstrøm, B. (Eds.). (2009). *Analysing networked learning practices in higher education and continuing professional development.* Rotterdam: Sense Publications.

Doise, W., & Mugny, G. (1984). *The social development of the intellect.* Oxford: Pergamon Press.

Dysthe, O., & Lillejord, S. (2012). From Humboldt to Bologna: Using peer-feedback to foster productive writing practices among online master students. *International Journal of Web Based Communities, 4*(8), 471–485.

Engeser, S., & Rheinberg, F. (2008). Flow, performance and moderators of challenge-skill balance. *Motivation and Emotion, 32*(3), 158–172.

Engeström, Y. (2015). *Learning by expanding.* Cambridge: Cambridge University Press.

Engeström, Y., & Sannino, A. (2011). Discursive manifestations of contradictions in organizational change efforts: A methodological framework. *Journal of Organizational Change Management, 24*(3), 368–387.

Essonnier, N. (2018). *Étude de la conception collaborative de ressources numériques mathématiques au sein d'une communauté d'intérêt.* Thèse de doctorat, Université Claude Bernard Lyon 1.

Essonnier, N., & Trgalová, J. (2018). Design principles supported by the collaborative design of mathematical digital resources within a CoI. In A. Clark-Wilson, et al. (Eds.), *Proceedings of the fifth ERME topic conference (ETC 5) on mathematics education in the digital age (MEDA)* (pp. 75–82). Copenhagen: University of Copenhagen and ERME.

Eysenck, H. J. (1993). Creativity and personality: Suggestions for a theory. *Psychological Inquiry*, *4*(3), 147–178.

Fischer, G. (2001). *Communities of interest: Learning through the interaction of multiple knowledge systems*. Paper presented at 24th Annual Information Systems Research Seminar in Scandinavia (IRIS 24), Ulvik, Norway.

Foot, K., & Groleau, C. (2011). Contradictions, transitions, and materiality in organizing processes: An activity theory perspective. *First Monday*, *16*(6).

Gaggioli, A., Riva, G., Milani, L., & Mazzoni, E. (2013). *Networked flow: Towards an understanding of creative networks*. Dordrecht, Netherlands: Springer.

Glăveanu, V. P. (2011). How are we creative together? Comparing sociocognitive and sociocultural answers. *Theory & Psychology*, *21*(4), 473–492.

Glăveanu, V. P., Johanne Ness, I., Wasson, B., & Lubart, T. (2019). Sociocultural perspectives on creativity, learning, and technology. In C. A. Mullen (Ed.), *Creativity under duress in education? Resistive theories, practices, and actions* (pp. 63–82). New York, NY: Springer.

Greenhow, C., Peppler, K. A., & Solomou, M. (2011). Building creativity: Collaborative learning and creativity in social media environments. *On the Horizon*, *19*(1), 13–23.

Greeno, J. G. (2006). Learning in activity. In R. K. Sawyer (Ed.), *The Cambridge handbook of the learning sciences* (pp. 79–96). New York, NY: Cambridge University Press.

Gruber, H. E. (1988). The evolving systems approach to creative work. *Creativity Research Journal*, *1*(1), 27–51.

Hassenzahl, M. (2010). Experience design: Technology for all the right reasons. *Synthesis Lectures on Human-centered Informatics*, *3*(1), 1–95.

Hsiao, H. S., Chang, C. S., Lin, C. Y., & Hu, P. M. (2014). Development of children's creativity and manual skills within digital game-based learning environment. *Journal of Computer Assisted Learning*, *30*(4), 377–395.

John-Steiner, V. (2000). *Creative collaboration*. Oxford: Oxford University Press.

Kaufman, J. C., & Baer, J. (Eds.). (2005). *Creativity across domains: Faces of the muse*. Mahwah, NJ: Lawrence Erlbaum Associates.

Kaufman, J. C., & Beghetto, R. A. (2009). Beyond big and little: The four C model of creativity. *Review of General Psychology*, *13*(1), 1–12.

Koffka, K. (1935). *Principles of gestalt psychology*. London: Lund Humphries.

Kristjánsson, K. (2012). Positive psychology and positive education: Old wine in new bottles? *Educational Psychologist*, *47*(2), 86–105.

Kruse, O. (2006). The origins of writing in the discipline: Traditions of seminar writing and the Humboldtian ideal of the research university. *Written Communication*, *23*(3), 331–352.

Kynigos, C. (2015). Constructionism: Theory of learning or theory of design? In *Selected regular lectures from the 12th international congress on mathematical education* (pp. 417–438). Cham: Springer.

Landhäußer, A., & Keller, J. (2012). Flow and its affective, cognitive, and performance-related consequences. In S. Engeser (Ed.), *Advances in flow research* (pp. 65–85). New York: Springer.

Laurillard, D. (2012). *Teaching as a design science: Building pedagogical patterns for learning and technology*. London: Routledge.

Lave, J., & Wenger, E. (1991). *Situated learning: Legitimate peripheral participation*. Cambridge: Cambridge University Press.

Leont'ev, A. N. (1978). *Activity, consciousness and personality*. Englewood Cliffs, NJ: Prentice-Hall.

Linell, P. (2009). *Rethinking language, mind, and world dialogically*. Charlotte, NC: Information Age Publishing.

Literat, I., & Glăveanu, V. P. (2016). Same but different? Distributed creativity in the Internet age. *Creativity: Theories – Research – Applications, 3*(2), 330–342.

MacDonald, R., Byrne, C., & Carlton, L. (2006). Creativity and flow in musical composition: An empirical investigation. *Psychology of Music, 34*(3), 292–306.

Mazzoni, E., & Benvenuti, M. (2015). A robot-partner for preschool children learning English using socio-cognitive conflict. *Educational Technology & Society, 18*(4), 474–485.

Mazzoni, E., & Gaffuri, P. (2009), Personal learning environments for overcoming knowledge boundaries between activity systems in emerging adulthood. *eLearning Papers, 15*(2009), 1–10.

McWilliam, E. (2009). Teaching for creativity: From sage to guide to meddler. *Asia Pacific Journal of Education, 29*(3), 281–293.

Nakamura, J., & Csikszentmihalyi, M. (2002). The concept of flow. In C. R. Snyder & S. J. Lopez (Eds.), *Handbook of positive psychology* (pp. 89–105). Oxford: Oxford University Press.

Nardi, B. A. (Ed.). (1996). *Context and consciousness: Activity theory and human – Computer interaction*. Cambridge, MA: MIT Press.

Rabardel, P. (2002). *People and technology – A cognitive approach to contemporary instruments*. Paris: Université Paris 8.

Reilly, R. C. (2008). Is expertise a necessary precondition for creativity?: A case of four novice learning group facilitators. *Thinking Skills and Creativity, 3*(1), 59–76.

Ripley, M. (2009). Transformational computer-based testing. In F. Scheuermann & J. Björnsson (Eds.), *The transition to computer-based assessment* (pp. 92–98). Luxemburg: Office for Official Publications of the European Communities.

Rodríguez-Ardura, I., & Meseguer-Artola, A. (2017). Flow in e-learning: What drives it and why it matters. *British Journal of Educational Technology, 48*(4), 899–915.

Sawyer, K. (2007). *Group genius: The collective power of collaboration*. New York: Basic Books.

Seligman, M. E., Ernst, R. M., Gillham, J., Reivich, K., & Linkins, M. (2009). Positive education: Positive psychology and classroom interventions. *Oxford Review of Education, 35*(3), 293–311.

Valsiner, J., & van der Veer, R. (2000). *The social mind: Construction of the idea*. New York: Cambridge University Press.

Vygotskij, L. S. (1978). *Mind in society: The development of higher psychological processes* (M. Cole, V. J. Steiner, S. Scribner, & E. Souberman, Eds.). Cambridge, MA: Harvard University Press.

Vygotsky, L. S. (1981). The instrumental method in psychology. In J. V. Wertsch (Ed.), *The concept of activity in soviet psychology* (pp. 134–143). Armonk, NY: M.E. Sharpe.

Vygotsky, L. S. (2004). Imagination and creativity in childhood. *Journal of Russian & East European Psychology, 42*(1), 7–97.

Wegerif, R. (2013). *Dialogic education for the internet age*. New York: Routledge.

Wegerif, R. (2020).

Williams, F. E. (1980). *Creativity assessment packet (CAP)*. East Aurora, NY: DOK Publishers.

Index

Note: Page numbers in *italics* indicate a figure and page numbers in **bold** indicate a table on the corresponding page.